W9-CKR-945

HOW TO TEACH YOUR CHILDREN SHAKESPEARE

To be, or not to be: that is the question: Whether 't
nobler in the mind to suffer The slings and arrows
outrageous fortune, Or to take arms against a sea
troubles, And by opposing end them? To die: to slee
No more; and by a sleep to say we end The heart-ac
and the thousand natural shocks That flesh is heir to, '
a consummation Devoutly to be wish'd. To die, to slee
To sleep: perchance to dream: ay, there's the rub; F
in that sleep of death what dreams may come When v
have shuffled off this mortal coil, Must give us paus
there's the respect That makes calamity of so long lif
For who would bear the whips and scorns of time, T
oppressor's wrong, the proud man's contumely, T
pangs of despised love, the law's delay, The insolence
office and the spurns That patient merit of the unworth
takes, When he himself might his quietus make With
bare bodkin? who would fardels bear, To grunt and swe
under a weary life, But that the dread of something aft
death, The undiscover'd country from whose bourn N
traveller returns, puzzles the will And makes us rath

HOW TO
TEACH YOUR CHILDREN

SHAKESPEARE

Ken Ludwig

CROWN PUBLISHERS
NEW YORK

Library of Congress Cataloging-in-Publication data is available upon request.

ISBN 978-0-307-95149-6
eISBN 978-0-307-95151-9

PRINTED IN THE UNITED STATES OF AMERICA

Photo credits appear on pages 347–348 as an extension of the copyright page.

Book design by Jennifer Daddio/Bookmark Design & Media Inc.
Jacket design by Christopher Brand

1   3   5   7   9   10   8   6   4   2

First Edition

THIS BOOK IS DEDICATED TO MY CHILDREN,

Olivia and Jack Ludwig,

WHO INSPIRED IT.

IT IS ALSO DEDICATED TO

Barbara Mowat,

GREAT SHAKESPEAREAN, FOR HER FRIENDSHIP AND ADVICE.

VIOLA

What country, friends, is this?

CAPTAIN

This is Illyria, lady.

VIOLA

And what should I do in Illyria?
My brother he is in Elysium.
Perchance he is not drowned.—What think you, sailors?

CAPTAIN

It is perchance that you yourself were saved.

Twelfth Night, Act I, Scene 2, lines 1–7

A NOTE ON TEACHING

Please bear in mind that this book is intended for teachers of all kinds, not just parents. I developed the techniques in this book by teaching Shakespeare to my children, hence the title of the book. But as I can attest from the teaching I've done over the years at various schools and universities, these techniques work just as well in the classroom as they do in the living room.

A NOTE ON THE TEXT

The quotations and line numberings in this book are based on the Folger Shakespeare Library edition of Shakespeare's plays, edited by Barbara A. Mowat and Paul Werstine. Editions of Shakespeare differ from each other in a number of respects. First, editors must choose which underlying printings of the plays to use as their source material. Second, editors edit their source material for punctuation, spelling, missing words, etc., bringing to bear their wealth of scholarship, endeavoring to present the most accurate text possible to the reader. Finally, editors provide secondary materials to enhance the text, such as definitions of words, explanatory notes, and accompanying essays. There are many fine editions of Shakespeare's plays on the market, each with its own advantages and level of detail, but I personally prefer the Folger Shakespeare Library edition for scholarship, ease of use, clarity, and price. Also, I urge readers of this book, when they want to consult one of the plays, to use individual copies—one play per book—and not a *Complete Works* as are often used in colleges. Those can be difficult to read and difficult to handle physically, which can be off-putting, especially for children.

Contents

PART TWO

Introduction

By John Lithgow

When it came to Shakespeare, I was a lucky boy. My childhood was full of Shakespeare. My father, you see, was an itinerant regional theater producer. He ran four outdoor summer Shakespeare festivals out in Ohio when I was a kid. In the decade of the 1950s alone, he presented every single one of the Bard's plays, many of them more than once. I knew Shakespearean characters the way my schoolmates knew big league ballplayers: Trinculo, Charmian, Hotspur, Osric, Celia, Benvolio, Froth.

My three siblings and I spent our summers hanging around rehearsals and precociously befriending the actors. When we reached our teens, we provided my father with cheap labor. We built props, stitched costumes, operated light boards, ran concession stands, and mopped the stage. And the background music of our lives in those days was the sound of Shakespearean verse, spoken out loud.

Best of all, we got to play the parts of various children in the plays. My brother was a servant in *Julius Caesar*. My sister was a murdered prince in *Richard III*. And in one of the happiest moments of my boyhood, I was cast as Mustardseed, one of the fairies waiting on Titania, in *A Midsummer Night's Dream*. This meant that I got to prance around onstage night after night, a seven-year-old in a leotard, fairy wings, and pointy yellow fake fur hat, lit up by silvery stage lights and bathed in Shakespeare's gorgeous language.

For me the highlight of every performance was the first encounter between Oberon and Titania, the estranged king and queen of the Fairies. In this scene, the two carry on an angry marital squabble, all of it expressed in exquisitely poetic phrases and images. It is as if, when he wrote their dialogue, Shakespeare had been intoxicated by the heady pleasure of writing for fairy royalty. To be honest, at seven years old I had no idea what the couple was fighting about—who knew that the argument was an ugly Elizabethan custody dispute? But every night I was dizzy with the beauty of their glorious speeches.

My favorite involved a young woman who had served Titania, a mortal who had died in childbirth, whose child the Fairy Queen had raised as her own son. The speech begins:

> *His mother was a vot'ress of my order*
> *And in the spiced Indian air by night,*
> *Full often hath she gossiped by my side . . .*

Each night I sat onstage in the spiced air of Yellow Springs, Ohio, and memorized a few more words.

So imagine my delight when, halfway through this marvelous book, I came upon a page that was entirely devoted to this very passage and read Ken Ludwig's description of it as "one of the most beautiful speeches in all of Shakespeare." That was the moment when I knew that Ludwig and I, to an uncanny degree, had Shakespeare in common.

Ken Ludwig is not a scholar by profession. He is a playwright and a man of the theater. To him, Shakespeare is primarily a storyteller, an entertainer, and the ultimate authority on the craft of playwriting. Hence, Ludwig's approach to the plays is more passionate than academic. His enthusiasm bubbles over on every page of his book and makes you want to track down whatever Shakespeare play is being performed nearby and rush off to see it.

Ludwig is also a father. He discovered early on that his love of Shakespeare was something that he could share with his children. In hours of reading and reciting with them, he learned a surprising truth: that children are ready, willing, and able to master these four-hundred-year-old plays. Give them the opportunity and they will hungrily devour them.

Children, after all, are like sponges. Their young minds are in a constant state of verbal absorption. They are far better students of language than we adults are. Every day they are digesting scores of new words and phrases. What better time to feed them a rich diet of Shakespeare's poetry and prose?

This book is a teaching primer for parents and a manual for making Shakespeare manageable and fun for kids. On these terms alone, it succeeds splendidly. But it has an extraordinary hidden virtue. It is equally informative, readable, and fun for *adults*. It is essential reading for anyone who has grown to adulthood with the misfortune of missing out on Shakespeare. And it is just as rich for those of us with a long history with the Bard. Shakespeare's mind is so limitless and Ludwig is so knowledgeable that we discover little gems on every page. And for parents, making such discoveries in the company of their children is especially precious.

Not every child gets to play Mustardseed. Few sit onstage nightly and hear Oberon quarrel with Titania. But *How to Teach Your Children Shakespeare* is a pretty good substitute. In many ways it's even better. You will recall that, at seven years old, I didn't understand a word that Titania was saying. Ludwig explains *everything*. So by way of introduction, let me invite you to dive into his book. Read it with your child at your side or in the privacy of your own receptive thoughts. Through Ken Ludwig's good offices, William Shakespeare will speak "with most miraculous organ," to you and to your children, from across the ages.

Part One

To be, or not to be: that is the question: Whether 'tis nobler in the mind to suffer The slings and arrows of outrageous fortune, Or to take arms against a sea of troubles, And by opposing end them? To die: to sleep; No more; and by a sleep to say we end The heart-ache and th... o, 'tis cons... sleep; to sle... ; For tha... en we we s... pause: ere'... g life; or who would bear the whips and scorns of time, The oppressor's wrong, the proud man's contumely, The pangs of despised love, the law's delay, The insolence of office and the spurns That patient merit of the unworthy takes, When he himself might his quietus make With a bare bodkin? who would fardels bear, To grunt and sweat under a weary life, But that the dread of something after death, The undiscover'd country from whose bourn No traveller returns, puzzles the will And makes us rather

CHAPTER 1

Passage 1
Learning the First Line

I know a bank where the wild thyme blows

Nine words. Each word has one syllable. Nine syllables.

That's all it is.

It isn't hard to learn this line of poetry. It's from the play *A Midsummer Night's Dream* by William Shakespeare, and I'll bet your son or daughter can memorize it in less than a minute.

There are two keys to memorizing it:

First, say it aloud.

Second, repeat it.

So let's do it together: Say this aloud:

I know a bank

Now say it again:

I know a bank

Now say it four times in a row. No kidding. Just do it—and promise me that you'll do it aloud:

I know a bank
I know a bank
I know a bank
I know a bank

Did you say it aloud? Because if you didn't, this won't work, I assure you. In order to do it properly, you have to go to a place where you won't be embarrassed. Just pick a room and close the door. Then sit down with your son or daughter and do it together. Say it aloud four times. If you've done this honestly, as I've described, you've now got it in your brain, and you'll never forget it.

I know a bank

Now do the same thing with the second half of the line. The words are more complex but not difficult at all. Have your child say them aloud:

where the wild thyme blows

Now say them again:

where the wild thyme blows

It's important when you learn Shakespeare that you understand every word you're reading or memorizing. Your children should understand that a *bank* is a mound of grass on the side of a stream or river, and that *thyme* is a flowering plant with a strong smell. It is less commonly known that *blow* in Shakespeare's day meant "burst into flower." So what the speaker is describing is a mound of grass, probably near a stream, where the wild thyme is blowing in the breeze and bursting into flower.

Now let's go back to the words. Say the second half of the line again, four times, out loud:

where the wild thyme blows
where the wild thyme blows
where the wild thyme blows
where the wild thyme blows

If you've said these words aloud, you and your child can now put the whole line together without difficulty. Do it. Say it aloud:

I know a bank where the wild thyme blows

Say it again, and really enjoy saying it, because it's good for the soul:

I know a bank where the wild thyme blows

One last time, and this time say it in a hushed tone, painting a picture with the words, describing a place of great beauty and depth:

I know a bank where the wild thyme blows

And now you and your child have memorized some Shakespeare. Believe me, it will stay with both of you for the rest of your lives. And it will change your lives.

CHAPTER 2

The Reason for the Book

Let's pause for a moment so I can give you some background. When I'm finished, we'll dig right back into the first passage.

I've been teaching Shakespeare to my children since they were six years old. I'm a bit of a Shakespeare fanatic, and it occurred to me when my daughter was in first grade that if there was any skill—any single area of learning and culture—that I could impart to her while we were both healthy and happy and able to share things together in a calm, focused, pre-teen way, then Shakespeare was it.

I began the process by teaching her lines from my favorite Shakespeare comedies; and as I continued with this method and expanded it to include my son, I became convinced that the way into the subject—the way to introduce someone to Shakespeare for the first time so that it doesn't feel daunting and yet has real integrity—is to memorize it. First a few lines, then whole speeches.

With Shakespeare, memorizing is the key to everything.

A great deal of this book will involve memorizing speeches from Shakespeare's plays. Along the way we'll discuss other important aspects of Shakespeare—the stories, the verse, the imagery, the characters—everything that you and your children should know in order to understand how Shakespeare changed the world.

Two good questions arise right away: Why Shakespeare? And why memorize it?

Why Shakespeare?

The answer to the first question is that Shakespeare isn't just one of the many great authors in the English language; Shakespeare is, indisputably, one of the two great bedrocks of Western civilization in English. (The other is the King James translation of the Bible.) Not only do Shakespeare's plays themselves contain the finest writing of the past 450 years, but most of the best novels, plays, poetry, and films in the English language produced since Shakespeare's death in 1616—from Jane Austen to Charles Dickens, from *Ulysses* to *The Godfather*—are heavily influenced by Shakespeare's stories, characters, language, and themes. As Falstaff says in *Henry IV, Part 2*:

> *I am not only witty in myself, but the cause that wit is in other men.*

Shakespeare is not only creative in himself—he is the cause of creation in other writers.

For many of us, Shakespeare has become a kind of Bible for the modern world, bringing us together intellectually the way religious services have traditionally done. For more than five thousand years, Moses, Jesus, and the other towering figures of the Old and New Testaments were the archetypes of our consciousness. In modern society, Hamlet and Macbeth, Juliet and Ophelia, have been added to their number. To know some Shakespeare gives you a head start in life.

Also, Shakespeare's powers as a writer simply exceed those of every other writer in the history of the English language. Here is an excerpt from the diary of the distinguished English novelist and essayist Virginia Woolf, who speaks here for every writer I know:

> I read Shakespeare *directly* after I have finished writing, when my mind is agape and red and hot. Then it is astonishing. I never yet knew how amazing his stretch and speed and word-coining power is, until I felt it

utterly outpace and outrace my own, seeming to start equal and then I see him draw ahead and do things I could not in my wildest tumult and utmost press of mind imagine. [T]he words drop so fast one can't pick them up. . . . Why then should anyone else attempt to write. This is not "writing" at all. Indeed, I could say that Shakespeare surpasses literature altogether, if I knew what I meant.

Why Memorize It?

As for memorization, I'm convinced that it unlocks the whole world of Shakespeare in a unique way. In order to memorize something, you have to be very specific and very honest with yourself. You have to work slowly, and you have to understand every word of what you're memorizing. There was a time not long ago when memorization was considered to be one of the basic tools of an academic education. Students were expected to learn hundreds of lines from the Greek and Roman classics, then, later, from poetry in their native tongues. This tradition has faded from our lives, and something powerful has been lost.

That said, Shakespeare can be difficult to read, let alone memorize, without some help. Most people who pick up one of Shakespeare's plays and try to read it for pleasure end up putting it down after the first few pages because they find it confusing. And this is true for adults, let alone children.

There are several reasons for this. First, many of Shakespeare's words are unfamiliar to us. When Hamlet, in the most famous speech in the English language (*To be or not to be*), refers to something called a *bodkin*, most of us just scratch our heads and want to give up. (A bodkin is a dagger.)

Second, Shakespeare's sentence structure often sounds odd to our ears. This is partly because Shakespeare wrote his plays more than four hundred years ago and partly because a substantial portion of his plays are in poetry. Thus he's frequently saying things like *Conceal me what I am* instead of "Disguise me."

Hamlet at the Royal Shakespeare Company, with Toby Stephens as Hamlet, holding a bodkin

Third, Shakespeare frequently writes in metaphors. His mind was so lively and cunning, so profound and imaginative, that he was always telling us how something was like something else, and it often takes some effort to puzzle out his meaning. For example, in one of Shakespeare's most famous speeches from *Romeo and Juliet,* he has Romeo compare Juliet's eyes to stars in the night sky. He has Romeo say that the real stars have to hurry away, and they (the stars) have asked Juliet's eyes to take their place. Then Romeo adds that Juliet's eyes would—in place of the stars—shine *so* brightly that birds would start singing because they'd think it was daytime, not nighttime. Here's what he actually says:

> *Two of the fairest stars in all the heaven,*
> *Having some business, do entreat her eyes*
> *To twinkle in their spheres till they return. . . .*
> > *Her eye in heaven*
> *Would through the airy regions stream so bright*
> *That birds would sing and think it were not night.*

The movie *Romeo + Juliet*, with Leonardo DiCaprio and Claire Danes

This is obviously a complex piece of writing, yet my son won a recitation contest with this speech when he was eleven years old.

The point is that Shakespeare is like a foreign language. In order to learn it, we need to understand every word, then practice until we feel comfortable. If your children memorize one line at a time, then a short speech, then a longer speech, they'll become self-assured and then fluent. At that point, Shakespeare will become part of their literary vocabulary.

The Value of Knowing Shakespeare

Knowing Shakespeare in depth has profound implications for your children. It means that they can begin to view life through a Shakespearean lens, using the questions that Shakespeare raises in his plays as a point of reference as they learn to form their own opinions. What does *Twelfth Night* tell us about the relationship between brothers and sisters? What does *Hamlet* tell us about the anxiety we feel when a parent dies?

In addition, Shakespeare articulates emotions that help children understand the stresses of their daily lives. When children hear Juliet say:

> *Give me my Romeo; and when I shall die*
> *Take him and cut him out in little stars,*
> *And he will make the face of heaven so fine*
> *That all the world will be in love with night*

or they hear Macbeth utter:

> *Life's but a walking shadow, . . . It is a tale*
> *Told by an idiot, full of sound and fury,*
> *Signifying nothing.*

they are likely to feel that thoughts of longing, death, and hopelessness are less alien to them.

From the beginning, I had a number of additional goals in mind in teaching my children Shakespeare. One was to give them the tools to read Shakespeare's works with intelligence for the rest of their lives. On the simplest level, this will enrich their lives and give them a lifetime of pleasure.

Another goal was to expose them to literature of such universal depth and worth that it would inspire them to want to achieve great things as they marched forward into maturity. I have staked my life as a writer on the proposition that the arts make a difference in how we see the world and how we conduct our lives—how we view charity to our neighbors and justice to our communities—and Shakespeare, as the greatest artist in the history of our civilization, has worlds to teach us as long as we have the tools we need to understand him.

From a very personal standpoint, the course of Shakespeare studies outlined in this book also provided me and my children with hundreds of hours of one-on-one time together that we never would have shared otherwise. These hours spent together have made our family stronger and more tolerant of one another.

On a practical note, I had another, very specific goal in mind: to teach my children at least twenty-five passages from Shakespeare's plays so that they could have the lines at their fingertips and spout them whenever the occasion presented itself. The occasion might be citing a literary reference in an English essay, or it might include making an intelligent point in conversation. These uses, frankly, open doors for our children, which is what we as parents are always trying to do.

Being fluent in Shakespeare from an early age imparts one last advantage that has a significance all its own: It gives my children self-confidence. It gives them the tools, as Falstaff might say, to be witty in themselves and be proud of it. As a father, this is one of the best parts of the whole exercise.

CHAPTER 3

The Plan of the Book

L et me outline the plan of this book so you know what's coming. Then we'll get right back to *I know a bank*.

The Twenty-five Passages

Together you and I will teach your children twenty-five passages of Shakespeare by heart. We'll start with short, accessible passages; then gradually we'll increase the length and complexity of the passages until, toward the end, we'll go for a few entire soliloquies.

I have strong views about which plays—and which passages from these plays—your children will find it easiest to start with, and I have put them in a very specific order. If you follow this order, I can just about guarantee that your kids won't get bogged down and frustrated.

I think that children do best by starting with the comedies. Specifically, I find that *A Midsummer Night's Dream* and *Twelfth Night* are the most child-friendly of all the plays, and we'll spend a good deal of time on them. We'll then move more quickly through the canon in order to expose your children to some of Shakespeare's most famous works. *Hamlet*, *Macbeth*, and *Romeo and Juliet*, for example, are simply part of our cultural DNA and cannot be missed.

Shakespeare's Language

In every chapter, I'll be quoting a great deal of Shakespeare's poetry and prose in addition to the passages being memorized. I'm doing this to expose your children to as much of Shakespeare's language as possible. I've chosen these additional passages carefully, as I want your children to come away from this book with a level of familiarity with Shakespeare that they can't get elsewhere. In every case, you and your children should read the additional passages aloud.

The Stories and Characters

Along with the passages themselves, we'll teach your children the plots and characters to go with them. This is not only valuable in itself but will help them memorize the passages more quickly, and they'll remember them longer. If you learn the line *Lord what fools these mortals be!* and associate it with a hilarious little sprite named Robin Goodfellow in *A Midsummer Night's Dream*, you'll never forget either the character or the line.

Additional Materials

At the end of the book, I've added some materials that I think you'll find useful, including a chronology of Shakespeare's plays, two lists of additional passages in case your children want to push their Shakespeare studies further, a list of my favorite Shakespeare epigrams, and a bibliography of some of my favorite Shakespeare books, movies, and audio recordings.

The Quotation Pages

Soon after I realized that memorization was the key to teaching my kids to love Shakespeare, I stumbled onto a trick that made the whole thing easier. The trick is to present each quotation in an attractive, easy-to-read format, using one page for every few lines. To this end, I broke every passage up into short, logical chunks based on rhythm and meaning, and I printed them on typing paper, using large, attractive fonts. Thus, the first page of *I know a bank* ended up looking like the sample below.

I know a bank
　　　　　　where the wild thyme blows,

Where oxlips
　　　　　　and the nodding violet grows,

For any child from six to sixteen, looking at a page like this is simply less daunting than looking at a page full of small type. For my own children it made all the difference, especially for the first five or six years. (Frankly, they still like to learn new passages this way, and they're now sixteen and twenty.)

In the early parts of this book, I'll print the Quotation Pages right in the text so you and your children can get familiar with using them. After that I'll ask you to go to howtoteachyourchildrenshakespeare.com, where you'll be able to download and print all the Quotation Pages at your convenience. Just go to your browser—Safari or Explorer or whatever you like to use—and type this address into your search engine: howtoteach yourchildrenshakespeare.com. The Quotation Pages will appear on your screen, and you can immediately print them and start using them.

I strongly urge you to use the Quotation Pages as part of the memorization process. We may be in the computer age, but by using the Quotation Pages, you'll have much more success than trying to learn the passages from a computer screen or a page with small type.

Listening

The other technique that turned out to be crucial for my children was to have them listen to the passages aloud so that they could imitate what they heard. Since I was so familiar with Shakespeare, I was able to recite the passages myself and have my children repeat what I said. For some parents and teachers, this may not be an option; therefore you can find recordings of all the major passages in this book, recited by two great Shakespearean actors, Derek Jacobi and Richard Clifford, at howtoteach yourchildrenshakespeare.com.

Now let's return to *I know a bank*.

CHAPTER 4

Passage 1, Continued Imagery and Rhythm

I know a bank where the wild thyme blows,
Where oxlips and the nodding violet grows,
Quite overcanopied with luscious woodbine,
With sweet muskroses, and with eglantine.

(A Midsummer Night's Dream,
Act II, Scene 1, lines 257–60)

In chapter 1, your children learned the first line of *I know a bank.*

I know a bank where the wild thyme blows

Now let's look at the next three lines. We're going to

1. define the difficult words and talk about imagery, and
2. learn how the rhythm of the words makes them easier to memorize (remember: Shakespeare wrote with memorization in mind).

Learning these lines will take your children less than half an hour. Don't forget to use the Quotation Page, which looks like this:

I know a bank

         where the wild thyme blows,

Where oxlips
        and the nodding violet grows,

Quite overcanopied
        with luscious woodbine,

With sweet muskroses,
        and with eglantine.

Here is the second line of the speech:

Where oxlips and the nodding violet grows,

Say it aloud with your child. You know the drill: Quiet room. Four times. Break it in half. No embarrassment.

Where oxlips
Where oxlips
Where oxlips
Where oxlips

An *oxlip* is another kind of flower (a hybrid between a cowslip and a primrose).

Also notice that the two words *where* and *oxlips*, taken together, create a tongue twister: You have to pause after *where* in order to pronounce *oxlips*. The thing to be aware of is that Shakespeare has done this deliberately to slow down the reader. He pulls linguistic tricks like this all the time to give the actor a sort of playbook on how to say his poetry aloud. He uses his vowels and consonants with enormous care, creating sounds that can slow you down, speed you up, make you pause at the right place, or add an emotion that you didn't see coming. (This aspect of Shakespeare's poetry is the subject of an entire book by Sir Peter Hall, one of the founders of the Royal Shakespeare Company. I've listed it in the Bibliography.)

Turn this tongue twister into a game. Tell your daughter to say the phrase *where oxlips* six times in a row as fast as she can.

where oxlips where oxlips where oxlips where oxlips where oxlips where oxlips

It's tough, isn't it? Well, that's what Shakespeare intended. He doesn't want you to rush through this description of a bank of flowers. He wants you to take your time to paint the word picture and make it sound beautiful. He's teaching you how to recite his speech.

Where oxlips and the nodding violet grows,

Here the interesting choice is the word *nodding*, which creates a visual image of violets bending sleepily in the breeze as though they're humans, nodding their heads. By giving the flowers this human quality (a poetic device called personification), Shakespeare makes the bank of flowers come alive. This is particularly clever because this bank of flowers is going to be an important setting in the play.

Imagery

Imagery like this is a powerful tool in all poetry but particularly in Shakespeare. He uses images like this every few lines to deepen his text and make it feel more universal. (The great book on this subject is *Shakespeare's Imagery and What It Tells Us* by Caroline Spurgeon. In it she lists hundreds of Shakespeare's favorite images, showing us how Shakespeare felt about everything from dogs to cats, from ambition to jealousy.)

The word *nodding* actually creates two images. It suggests that the flowers have a sleepy human quality; it also suggests that they are bowing their heads in respect—which in turn suggests that the bank is a place where someone important, like a queen, might come to sleep. As we'll see in a moment, that is exactly what the bank is for, and the queen's name is Titania.

A nodding violet

I know a bank where the wild thyme blows,
Where oxlips and the nodding violet grows,

Quite overcanopied with luscious woodbine,
With sweet muskroses, and with eglantine,

Woodbine, muskroses, and *eglantine* are three more types of flowers. (I guess we know that we're on a bank of flowers by this time.) *Overcanopied* is a word that Shakespeare invented, and we can guess that it means just what it sounds like: that the flowers form a canopy over the ground, or perhaps even over the head of the person lying on the ground.

> *Quite overcanopied*
> *Quite overcanopied*
>> *with luscious woodbine,*
>> *with luscious woodbine,*

The word *luscious* is a pretty wonderful choice, isn't it? Not just *delicious*. Not just *mouthwatering*. But *luscious*: something so delicious that you lust after it.

Memorization Tips

Line-into-Line Tip

Here's a good trick that my children and I use all the time: Because it's easy to get stuck at the end of a line where there's a natural pause, have your kids learn the beginning of a new line by making it sound like part of the line before it. So in this case you would say:

> *violet grows quite overcanopied*
> *violet grows quite overcanopied*

Now watch how much easier it is to recite the passage:

> *I know a bank where the wild thyme blows,*
> *Where oxlips and the nodding violet grows,*
> *Quite overcanopied with luscious woodbine*

And now let's add the fourth line of the passage.

> *With sweet muskroses, and with eglantine.*

This time have your children say the whole line without breaking the line in half. I'll bet they're ready for it:

> *With sweet muskroses, and with eglantine.*

Best Tip Ever

We're now ready for the best tip in this book. You'll use it again and again during your study of Shakespeare.

USE THE NATURAL RHYTHM OF THE LINES TO HELP
MEMORIZE THEM.

The natural rhythm of the last two lines is as follows:

> ⌃ ⌃ ⌃ ⌃ ⌃
> **QUITE** *over***CAN***opied with* **LUSC***ious* **WOOD-BINE**,

> ⌃ ⌃ ⌃ ⌃ ⌃
> *With* **SWEET** *musk***ROSE***s, and with* **EG-LAN-TINE**.

The way to teach these lines to your children so that they'll never forget them is to set up a kind of marching rhythm, then chant the lines to the rhythm.

> *BOM! (rest) BOM! (rest) BOM BOM BOM!*

> ⌃ ⌃ ⌃ ⌃ ⌃
> **QUITE** *over***CAN***opied with* **LUSC***ious* **WOOD-BINE**,

    ^   ^   ^   ^   ^

*With **SWEET** muskROSEs, and with **EG-LAN-TINE**.*
BOM! (rest) BOM! (rest) BOM BOM BOM!

Professional actors use techniques like this all the time. The important thing is to say the words out loud and let the natural rhythm of the line take over. In our family, we played a form of patty-cake with lines like these, clapping out the rhythms on the palms of each other's hands and on our knees. We started doing it when the kids were six years old, but to be honest, we continued it for the next four or five years. It sounds silly, but we enjoyed it and it worked wonders.

CHAPTER 5

The Final Six Lines

There sleeps Titania sometime of the night,
Lulled in these flowers with dances and delight.
And there the snake throws her enameled skin,
Weed wide enough to wrap a fairy in.
And with the juice of this I'll streak her eyes
And make her full of hateful fantasies.

(A Midsummer Night's Dream,
Act II, Scene 1, lines 61–66)

Your children have learned the first four lines of the passage. Now let's teach them the last six lines. We'll do it much more quickly. (It takes a lot less time to use these techniques than it does to read about them.)

There sleeps Titania sometime of the night,
Lulled in these flowers with dances and delight.
And there the snake throws her enameled skin,
Weed wide enough to wrap a fairy in.
And with the juice of this I'll streak her eyes
And make her full of hateful fantasies.

I'm not going to insult your intelligence by describing all the repetition you'll want to use with your children to teach them this passage. I'll only insult your intelligence a little bit with a few reminders along the way. For now, please remember the three cardinal rules:

There Sleeps Titania by Frederick Howard Michael

1. Use the Quotation Pages, with their easy print and spacing,
2. Say the lines aloud, and
3. Repeat them again and again. The repetition will pay off.

Here is part of one of the Quotation Pages you'll need:

Lulled in these flowers

> *with dances and delight.*

And there the snake

> *throws her enameled skin,*

Weed wide enough

> *to wrap a fairy in.*

And with the juice of this

> *I'll streak her eyes*

And make her full of

hateful fantasies.

The Main Characters

Titania is one of the main characters in the play. She's Queen of the Fairies, and her husband, who is King of the Fairies, is named Oberon. Oberon has a helper who is a type of fairy called a puck, and his name is Robin Goodfellow. Sometimes he's referred to as Puck, as if Puck were his name.

Oberon, Titania, and Robin Goodfellow form the nucleus of one of the four plots in *A Midsummer Night's Dream.* Basically, Shakespeare dreamed up the idea of setting a comedy partly in the real world of thwarted lovers and an angry father, and partly in the world of a fairy kingdom. During the course of the play, a young couple who want to get married flee the girl's overly strict father and run into a nearby forest—which happens to be the forest where the fairies live.

Titania (Vivien Leigh)

As the Fairies' Plot begins, Oberon and Titania are having a fight over the custody of a young Indian boy. Titania wants to raise the boy herself and make him her page, while Oberon wants the boy to be his servant. When Titania refuses to give the boy up, she and Oberon have an earth-shattering argument. (It is literally earth-shattering, because when these two otherworldly creatures argue, it causes floods and earthquakes.)

The speech that we're learning occurs at the very moment when Puck has brought Oberon a magic flower. The flower (which has the beautiful but rather odd name *love-in-idleness*) has the power to make someone who is sleeping fall instantly in love with the next live creature that he sees when he wakes up.

> *There sleeps Titania sometime of the night,*
> *Lulled in these flowers with dances and delight.*
> *And there the snake throws her enameled skin,*
> *Weed wide enough to wrap a fairy in.*
> *And with the juice of this I'll streak her eyes*
> *And make her full of hateful fantasies.*

This speech could be called Oberon's Revenge. Basically, what he's saying is, "I know where Titania sleeps. It's at that bank of flowers with the thyme and the woodbine. I'll go find her, and while she's asleep, I'll streak her eyes with the juice of this magic flower. That way, when she wakes up, she'll fall in love with the first horrible creature that she sees. What a great way to revenge myself. Titania will fall in love with a monster!"

One of the reasons we know exactly what Oberon is thinking is that he has told us about his scheme a few minutes earlier in the same scene. Read this speech aloud with your children.

OBERON
> *Having once this juice,*
> *I'll watch Titania when she is asleep*
> *And drop the liquor of it in her eyes.*
> *The next thing then she, waking, looks upon*
> *(Be it on lion, bear, or wolf, or bull,*

On meddling monkey, or on busy ape)
She shall pursue it with the soul of love.
And ere [before] I take this charm from off her sight
(As I can take it with another herb),
I'll make her render up her page [the Indian boy] to me.

Thus, there is no doubt whatsoever what Oberon is thinking. This is typical of Shakespeare. When you read him carefully, he is always as clear as a bell.

There sleeps Titania sometime of the night,

Sometime of the night means "sometimes during the night" or "for some part of the night." So the sentence in a more modern rendering would be, "Sometimes at night Titania sleeps there."

Lulled in these flowers with dances and delight.

We are now told that Titania is lulled in these flowers with dances and delight. What does that mean? What an odd thing to say. My own guess is that it's meant to suggest that Titania, while she's asleep, is dreaming about delightful things like dancing. After all, the play is called A Midsummer Night's Dream, and the theme of dreaming recurs throughout the play. Oberon is probably thinking that his revenge will be all the sweeter if Titania is dreaming about something happy—and what a clue this gives us to Oberon's character: He's not nice in any conventional sense. He may be romantic, clever, attractive, cunning, temperamental, and mystical—but he's not nice.

And there the snake throws her enameled skin,
Weed wide enough to wrap a fairy in.

Here Oberon is telling us something new about Titania and the rest of the fairies. Use this as a game with your children. Ask them "What do you think Oberon is telling us about the fairies in those two lines?"

And there the snake throws her enameled skin,
Weed wide enough to wrap a fairy in.

The answer: He's telling us that, physically, the fairies are *tiny*.

We know how big a normal snake is: anywhere from, say, six inches to three feet long. And we know that snakes shed their skin every so often. We should also note that the word *weeds* in Shakespeare's time meant garments in addition to unwanted plants.

So: Oberon is saying that there, on the bank, snakes throw off their skins every now and then, and the skin of a snake is just the right size to wrap a fairy in. Therefore Titania (and the rest of the fairies, including Oberon) are smaller than snakes. And in another part of the play we're told that fairies can hide in acorn cups. So while fairies vary in size in Shakespeare's fairy world, they're all very small. Titania may be a queen, but she's probably about the size of your son's finger.

And with the juice of this I'll streak her eyes
And make her full of hateful fantasies.

This part of the speech reminds us that we're in the middle of an exciting story. Oberon says that he is going to streak Titania's eyes with magic fairy juice so that she has hateful dreams.

*And with the juice of **this** I'll streak her eyes*

And make her full of what? *Hateful fantasies!* He wants revenge. And what is it that she'll wake up and see? We don't know yet. We're on tenterhooks, which is exactly what Shakespeare intends. He is toying with us so that we can't wait to see the next scene.

Have your children say the passage aloud one more time for good measure. Then, after a few days' rest, we'll move on.

I know a bank where the wild thyme blows,
Where oxlips and the nodding violet grows,
Quite overcanopied with luscious woodbine,
With sweet muskroses, and with eglantine.

My play *Shakespeare in Hollywood* at Arena Stage, with
Emily Donahoe as Puck and Casey Biggs as Oberon.

There sleeps Titania sometime of the night,
Lulled in these flowers with dances and delight.
And there the snake throws her enameled skin,
Weed wide enough to wrap a fairy in.
And with the juice of this I'll streak her eyes
And make her full of hateful fantasies.

Ten lines. Seventy-five words. Verse. Meter. Imagery. Fairyland. Three
famous characters. Quality time. Self-confidence. Time well spent.

CHAPTER 6

Passage 2
Puck's Announcement and the Story of *A Midsummer Night's Dream*

Captain of our fairy band,
Helena is here at hand,
And the youth, mistook by me,
Pleading for a lover's fee.
Shall we their fond pageant see?
Lord, what fools these mortals be!

(A Midsummer Night's Dream,
Act III, Scene 2, lines 112–17)

The second passage that we'll learn together is short, but it tells us a great deal about *A Midsummer Night's Dream* and a great deal about Shakespeare. It is easier to learn than the first passage, and it should take you and your children about fifteen minutes. It is a particularly good passage for younger children because the speaker is Puck, everyone's favorite mischief maker, and it ends with one of the great one-liners of all time:

Lord, what fools these mortals be!

As before, you should start by sitting next to your child and looking at the Quotation Page together. Note: The word *fee* in this passage means "reward." And a *fond pageant* is a "foolish spectacle."

Captain of our fairy band,
Helena is here at hand,

And the youth, mistook by me,
Pleading for a lover's fee.

Shall we their fond pageant see?
Lord, what fools these mortals be!

Begin by tackling the first two lines, using, as always, the techniques we discussed above: Use the Quotation Page, say the lines aloud, and repeat them.

> *Captain of our fairy band,*
> *Captain of our fairy band,*

> *Helena is here at hand,*

(*Helena* is pronounced "HEL-eh-na.")

> *Helena is here at hand,*

> *Captain of our fairy band,*
> *Helena is here at hand,*

Unlike the first passage, which had five beats per line,

    ^   ^   ^   ^   ^
I *know a* **BANK** *where the* **WILD THYME BLOWS**.

the lines of this passage have four beats each, and the rhythm is the same from line to line.

```
    ^   (^)      ^     ^
```
CAPtain **OF** our **FAIR**y **BAND**,

```
    ^   (^)    ^        ^
```
HELen**A** is **HERE** at **HAND**,

Four beats per line is a simpler tempo. It resembles a nursery rhyme, and it is easier to memorize. Shakespeare uses this meter only occasionally in his plays, for the lyrics of most of his songs and, more rarely, when he wants to say something in a ritualistic manner. For example, he uses this meter at the end of *A Midsummer Night's Dream*, when Oberon and Robin say goodnight to the audience.

> **If** we shadows **have** offended,
> **Think** but **this** and **all** is **mend**ed:
> That you have but slumbered here
> While these visions did appear. . . .
> Give me your hands [clap for us], if we be friends,
> And Robin shall restore amends.

Use the fact that there are only four beats in each line to make the passage into a game for your children, the way you would a nursery rhyme.

```
    ^   (^)      ^     ^
```
CAPtain **OF** our **FAIR**y **BAND**,

```
    ^   (^)    ^        ^
```
HELen**A** is **HERE** at **HAND**,

You should point out to your children that all three couplets are rhymed, which makes them easy to memorize.

Captain of our fairy **BAND**,
Helena is here at **HAND**,
And the youth, mistook by **ME**,
Pleading for a lover's **FEE**.
Shall we their fond pageant **SEE**?
Lord, what fools these mortals **BE**!

The Story of A Midsummer Night's Dream

A *Midsummer Night's Dream* has four plots, all spinning along at the same time. The play is a miracle of dramatic architecture: Despite the constant crisscrossing of the plots, we're never confused for an instant about what's going on in the story.

One of the plots (the Lovers' Plot) revolves around two young women, Hermia and Helena, and the two young men with whom they're in love,

A *Midsummer Night's Dream* at the Rose Theatre, Kingston, with Tam Williams as Lysander, Ben Mansfield as Demetrius, Annabel Scholey as Hermia, and Rachael Stirling as Helena

Lysander and Demetrius. In this plot, the lovers keep changing partners, creating one love triangle after another.

The story begins when Hermia's father forbids her to marry the man she loves. To make matters worse, under Athenian law, if she doesn't obey her father, she can be put to death or be confined to a convent for the rest of her life. One of my favorite passages in the play is where the Duke of Athens urges Hermia to reconsider her decision.

DUKE THESEUS

What say you, Hermia? Be advised, fair maid.
To you, your father should be as a god,

Whenever I read this passage to my children, I stop and repeat the phrase *To you, your father should be as a god*. Needless to say, they roll their eyes and say "Oh, sure, Dad."

DUKE THESEUS

What say you, Hermia? Be advised, fair maid.
To you, your father should be as a god, . . .

HERMIA

I do entreat your Grace to pardon me.
I know not by what power I am made bold, . . .
But I beseech [beg] your Grace that I may know
The worst that may befall me [happen to me] in this case
If I refuse to wed Demetrius.

DUKE THESEUS

Either to die the death, or to abjure [give up]
Forever the society of men.
Therefore, fair Hermia, question your desires,
Know of your youth, examine well your blood, . . .
For aye to be in shady cloister mew'd,
[Forever to be caged up in a nunnery,]
To live a barren sister all your life,
Chanting faint hymns to the cold, fruitless moon. . . .

HERMIA

So will I grow, so live, so die, my lord,
Ere I will yield my virgin patent up . . .
[Before I will give up my virginity].

Two things I find especially moving about this passage are that the Duke is so clearly on Hermia's side, and that Hermia simply cannot yield because she is so deeply in love.

When the Duke leaves Hermia alone to reconsider her decision, what does Hermia do? She does what every headstrong teenager in the world dreams of doing: She elopes. That night she and Lysander flee into the woods outside Athens. Then, to make matters more interesting, Demetrius runs after them—and Helena runs after Demetrius.

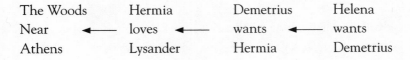

The Woods	Hermia		Demetrius		Helena
Near	loves	←	wants	←	wants
Athens	Lysander		Hermia		Demetrius

And when these four hormonal, mismatched, articulate teenagers arrive in the famous Wood near Athens, what do they find?

Magic!

Point out to your children that the whole story sounds a bit like a Harry Potter novel: Ordinary teenagers encounter a magical world, and it changes their lives forever. (That Shakespeare fellow knew what he was doing.)

It is at this point that Shakespeare decides to mix together the Lovers' Plot and the Fairies' Plot, and he does it in a fiendishly clever way. He has Oberon tell Puck to use the magic flower on Demetrius to try to straighten out Helena's love life. But Puck puts the juice of the flower in the eyes of the wrong lover (Lysander) by mistake, at which point everything goes wrong.

Bonus Passage

When Oberon first realizes Puck's mistake, he orders him to hurry as fast as he can and go find Helena. To which Puck replies:

> *I go, I go, look how I go,*
> *Swifter than arrow from the Tartar's bow.*

In our family, this is one of our favorite speeches, and we use it whenever we're in a hurry.

> *I go, I go, look how I go,*
> *Swifter than arrow from the Tartar's bow.*

See if your children can learn these two lines right now, on the spot. Note: A *Tartar* is an ancient Oriental fighter with a strong bow.

> *I go, I go, look how I go,*
> *Swifter than arrow from the Tartar's bow.*

Make a point of using this speech with your children the next time you're in a hurry. Chances are, they'll repeat it back to you.

CHAPTER 7

Digging Deeper into
A Midsummer Night's Dream

Hermia. Helena. Lysander. Demetrius. Is it hard to keep these lovers straight when we read the play? Absolutely. Should we care? Absolutely not. When *A Midsummer Night's Dream* is played onstage, the Lovers' Plot is crystal clear. However, we should bear in mind that Shakespeare is up to something with all these teenage lovers who keep falling in and out of love with each other, and it has to do with the nature of love itself.

It could be argued that all the round-robin shenanigans in the play about who loves whom are caused by the magic flower and not by the actual desires of the lovers. And yet isn't falling in love a bit like magic? A gift, a song, a look—all these can alter our hearts in an instant. Shakespeare seems to be acknowledging this and using the flower as a colorful, theatrical literary device. Indeed, the magic flower is a metaphor for the central theme of the play, which, it seems to me, is the power of love in its many guises.

Love is the theme of most of Shakespeare's comedies, but in each one he treats the theme in a different way. Sometimes he emphasizes the melancholy, more philosophical side of love (*Twelfth Night*); sometimes the irrepressible, youthful side (*Love's Labour's Lost*); sometimes it's farcical (*The Merry Wives of Windsor*); sometimes sardonic (*Troilus and Cressida*);

sometimes wise (*As You Like It*); sometimes clear-sighted and earthy (*Much Ado About Nothing*); and sometimes ironic (*The Taming of the Shrew*). In *A Midsummer Night's Dream*, Shakespeare is focusing on the intellectual side of love, turning love over and over, analyzing its odd behaviors and unique powers.

Shakespeare, as usual, tells us clearly, right up front, what he's up to:

> *Love looks not with the eyes but with the mind;*
> *And therefore is winged Cupid painted blind.*

(Cupid was the Roman god of erotic love and was frequently depicted with wings and a blindfold.) These two lines occur in the middle of a soliloquy by Helena when she is railing against her fate: Why should Demetrius love Hermia and not me?! I'm as pretty as she is! Everyone in Athens thinks so!

> *How happy some o'er other some can be!*
> *Through Athens I am thought as fair as she.*
> *But what of that? Demetrius thinks not so.*
> *He will not know what all but he do know.*

Shakespeare makes it clear that Helena and Hermia are equally beautiful by objective standards. And yet Demetrius thinks Hermia is more beautiful because he sees her that way. Then when the juice of the magic flower is squeezed into his eyes, he falls in love with Helena and thinks that she's more beautiful. Love is fickle, says Shakespeare. We see what we want to see. We don't fall in love because of what our eyes tell us, but what our minds tell us.

> *Love looks not with the eyes but with the mind;*
> *And therefore is winged Cupid painted blind.*

Throughout this play, Shakespeare appears to be suggesting that the experience of love is like the experience of a dream—they are both irrational and changeable. The change can be caused by the juice of a magic flower. Or when we're not in a magic forest, love can change for any number of reasons. In one of the most beautiful exchanges in the play, just after

Hermia's father has forbidden her to marry Lysander, the two lovers bewail their fate. *Ay me,* cries Lysander,

> *For aught* [all] *that I could ever read,*
> *Could ever hear by tale or history,*
> *The course of true love never did run smooth.*

The lovers then remind each other of the many ways that love can be thwarted: Lovers can be from different social classes (*O cross! Too high to be enthralled to low.*); they can be from different age groups (*O spite! Too old to be engaged to young.*); their relatives might not like each other (*O hell, to choose love by another's eyes!*); or—more profoundly—their love can be beset by *war, death, or sickness,*

> *Making it momentary as a sound,*
> *Swift as a shadow, short as any dream,*
> *Brief as the lightning in the collied* [coal-black] *night, . . .*
> *And, ere* [before] *a man hath power to say "Behold!"*
> *The jaws of darkness do devour it up.*
> *So quick bright things come to confusion.*

Short as any dream. Shakespeare does not mince words. For the lovers in this play, love is a dream, a midsummer night's dream, a dream that can change as quickly as lightning in the coal-black night.

CHAPTER 8

Passage 3
Bottom's Dream

*I have had a most rare vision. I have had a dream past the
wit of man to say what dream it was. Man is but an ass if
he go about to expound this dream. . . . The eye of man
hath not heard, the ear of man hath not seen, man's hand
is not able to taste, his tongue to conceive, nor his heart to
report what my dream was. I will get Peter Quince to write
a ballad of this dream. It shall be called "Bottom's Dream"
because it hath no bottom.*

(A Midsummer Night's Dream,
Act IV, Scene 1, lines 214–26)

Our third passage from *A Midsummer Night's Dream* is spoken by a
tradesman, an ordinary man of Athens named Nick Bottom who
has just awakened from a dream. In his dream, two strange things
happened: He had the head of a donkey, and a beautiful fairy queen fell
in love with him.

In fact, these two things were not just a dream; they really did happen to Bottom, and we see them happen earlier in the play. We'll discuss
Bottom's part in the plot in more detail in a moment, but here's what you
need to know right now: First, Puck comes across Bottom and his friends
in the woods (they are there to rehearse a play); and then Puck, to be mischievous, puts a donkey's head on Bottom's shoulders. A few minutes later,
Titania wakes up with the juice of the magic flower in her eyes (remember:

Oberon put it there to get his revenge); and Titania falls in love with this monster who is a man from the neck down and a donkey from the neck up. So when Bottom wakes up later with the ass-head removed, he thinks he had a dream: a "most rare vision."

Quotation Pages

At this point, for ease of reading, I'll stop printing the Quotation Pages as part of the text. However, you and your children should have the proper Quotation Pages next to you as you memorize this and the other passages in this book, and you should download them from howtoteachyourchildren shakespeare.com.

Bottom's Dream

I have had a most rare vision.

I am always struck by the beauty of the phrase *a most rare vision*. Repeat it to your children and tell them to think about the words. If your children like to act, this is an ideal passage to practice their skills. Remind them that Bottom is just waking up from a deep sleep and has just had a pleasant but confusing dream.

You will also notice from the way the speech is printed at the beginning of the chapter that it is not poetry, but rather prose. We'll talk about what that means in the next chapter.

> *I have had a dream*
> > *past the wit of man*
> > > *to say what dream it was.*

In this sentence, I'm especially fond of the word *wit*. *The wit of man*. As used in this sentence, the word *wit* means not only "understanding" or "knowledge"; it also has the connotation of "cleverness." The phrase *the wit of man* seems to me the perfect choice of words from the perspective of a tradesman who would like to appear wise.

I have had a dream past the wit of man to say what dream it was.
Man is but an ass
>   *if he go about to expound [explain] this dream.*

Man is but an ass. Shakespeare constantly uses puns throughout his plays. In this case, *ass* means both (1) a donkey and (2) a foolish person. (In

James Cagney and Anita Louise in the 1935 film directed by Max Reinhardt

Shakespeare's day, it did not apparently mean a part of the body. I have checked all the glossaries and spoken to several Shakespeare experts, and they all agree that "ass" did not mean what we today would call a backside. And yet the name Bottom implies otherwise and I'll go to my grave believing that the word had three connotations in Shakespeare's day.)

Now comes the juiciest part of the passage.

> *The eye of man hath not heard,*
> *the ear of man hath not seen,*
> *man's hand is not able to taste,*
> *his tongue to conceive,*
> *nor his heart to report*
> *what my dream was.*

Obviously, Bottom is getting mixed up: An eye cannot hear, and an ear cannot see. A hand cannot taste, a tongue cannot think, and a heart cannot talk. While Bottom is getting the words mixed up in part because he's groggy, he is also trying to be profound. We know this because Bottom's words echo a passage in the Bible that he is trying to quote. In 1 Corinthians (2:9–10), Saint Paul says:

> The eye hath not seen, & the ear hath not heard, neither have entered
> into the heart of man, the things which God hath prepared for them

that love Him. . . . For the spirit searcheth all things, yea, the deep things of God.

My children have always loved Bottom's speech, and we came up with an easy way to learn it—by using hand gestures. If you do this with your children, no matter what age they are, it will help them enormously in learning the passage.

Say	Touch
The EYE of man hath not	eye
HEARD,	ear
the EAR of man hath not	ear
SEEN,	eye
man's HAND is not able to	(gesture forward with hand)
TASTE,	lips
his TONGUE	lips
to conceive,	temple
nor his heart	heart
to report	(gesture forward with hand)
what my dream was.	

In our house, the hand gestures became a game, with all of us competing to see who could say the passage fastest. The kids won, of course, and after ten minutes we all knew the passage cold.

The final two sentences of the passage are straightforward and declarative.

I will get Peter Quince to write a ballad of this dream.

Peter Quince is one of Bottom's friends. (A quince is also a pear-shaped fruit.)

It shall be called "Bottom's Dream" because it hath no bottom.

Here Shakespeare is punning again. Bottom is the character's name; and the dream is bottomless, which suggests that it is deep and profound. Bottom is once again echoing 1 Corinthians: "For the spirit searcheth all things, yea, the deep things of God."

For Shakespeare, Bottom's dream is deep. It is a dream about imagination and the possibilities of mankind. In this dream, a simple tradesman is the object of a queen's adoration. He accepts the role and becomes her consort for a night. And remember, Bottom is the only mortal in the entire play who ever sees any of the fairies. He gets to see worlds that no other mortal in the play gets to see. His dream has no bottom indeed.

Review the speech one last time with your children, and then we can put it into context.

> *I have had a most rare vision. I have had a dream past the wit of man to*
> *say what dream it was. Man is but an ass if he go about to expound this*
> *dream. . . . The eye of man hath not heard, the ear of man hath not*
> *seen, man's hand is not able to taste, his tongue to conceive, nor his heart*
> *to report what my dream was. I will get Peter Quince to write a ballad*
> *of this dream. It shall be called "Bottom's Dream" because it hath no*
> *bottom.*

Bottom's Story

Bottom is at the center of the third plotline of *A Midsummer Night's Dream*, and his story is simple. He and his friends, with the colorful names Peter Quince, Francis Flute, Tom Snout, Snug, and Robin Starveling, decide to put on a play called *Pyramus and Thisbe* during the wedding celebrations of the Duke of Athens. The six friends are Athenian craftsmen (a carpenter, a weaver, a bellows mender, etc.) and are known in the world of Shakespeare as the "rude Mechanicals" (or humble workmen), a name that Puck gives them. We meet them in the second scene of *A Midsummer Night's Dream* when their leader, Peter Quince, is passing out the parts for the play. They will need to rehearse, of course, and they decide to meet the following night in the Wood near Athens—yes, that's right, the same woods to which the lovers are fleeing, which is also the woods where the fairies live.

One of the great charms of A Midsummer Night's Dream is watching these honest, unaffected men trying to put on a play. Pyramus and Thisbe is a melodrama that involves a knight, the knight's lady who is played by a man, a talking wall that separates the two lovers, and a death scene that almost never ends. The plot of this play-within-a-play closely resembles that of Romeo and Juliet, and Shakespeare takes enormous joy in poking gentle fun at amateur actors putting on a play.

FLUTE
(as Thisbe, discovering Pyramus dead on the ground)
Asleep, my love?
  What, dead, my dove?
O Pyramus, arise!
  Speak, speak. Quite dumb?
  Dead? Dead? A tomb
Must cover thy sweet eyes.
  These lily lips,
  This cherry nose,
These yellow cowslip cheeks
  Are gone, are gone!
  Lovers, make moan;
His eyes were green as leeks.

Have your children enact this speech aloud. You lie down and play dead and have one of them play poor grieving Thisbe, bemoaning the loss of her beloved Pyramus. It's guaranteed to make them laugh.

Bottom's story begins taking off about halfway through the play. In Act IV, Scene 1, we come upon Bottom and his friends rehearsing their play in a clearing in the woods. Amid mangled words and missed cues, Puck wanders onto the scene and transforms Bottom by putting an ass head on his shoulders. His fellow actors are frightened and run off, at which point, Titania—who is asleep nearby under the spell of Oberon's magic flower—wakes up. As you'll remember, the power of the magic flower is that anyone who has been anointed by its juice will fall in love with the next live creature that he sees; and the first live creature that Titania sees on waking up is Bottom. So she falls instantly in love with this monster—half man, half donkey—and leads him away to her bed of flowers (*where the wild thyme blows*).

Two scenes later we see Titania and her fairies pampering Bottom with every donkey luxury imaginable. Here is what Titania says to Bottom when we come upon them among the flowers—and if you have a daughter, here's her chance to play a fairy queen:

> *Come sit thee down upon this flowery bed,*
> > *While I thy amiable cheeks do coy* [caress]
> *And stick muskroses in thy sleek smooth head,*
> > *And kiss thy fair large ears, my gentle joy.*

A *Midsummer Night's Dream* at the Rose Theatre, Kingston, with Judi Dench as Titania and Oliver Chris as Bottom

As you can imagine, Bottom is lapping up all this attention.

BOTTOM

Where's Peaseblossom?

PEASEBLOSSOM

Ready.

BOTTOM

Scratch my head, Peaseblossom. Where's Monsieur Cobweb?

COBWEB

Ready.

BOTTOM

*Monsieur Cobweb, good monsieur, get you your weapons in your hand and
kill me a red-hipped humble-bee and . . . bring me the honey-bag. . . .
I must to the barber's, monsieur, for methinks I am marvels [marvelous]
hairy about the face. And I am such a tender ass, if my hair do but tickle
me, I must scratch.*

The end of the Mechanicals' Plot is a happy one. Titania and Oberon
are reunited, and as they dance together, Puck removes the ass head from
Bottom's shoulders. When Bottom awakes, whole again, he remembers the
luscious experience with Titania as though it were a dream. He rubs his
eyes and shakes himself and says with wonder:

> *I have had a most rare vision. I have had a dream past the wit of man
> to say what dream it was. Man is but an ass if he go about to expound
> this dream. . . . The eye of man hath not heard, the ear of man hath
> not seen, man's hand is not able to taste, his tongue to conceive, nor
> his heart to report what my dream was. I will get Peter Quince to write
> a ballad of this dream. It shall be called "Bottom's Dream" because it
> hath no bottom.*

CHAPTER 9

Passage 4
Theseus and Hippolyta

THESEUS

Now, fair Hippolyta, our nuptial hour
Draws on apace. Four happy days bring in
Another moon. But, O, methinks how slow
This old moon wanes! . . .

HIPPOLYTA

Four days will quickly steep themselves in night;
Four nights will quickly dream away the time;
And then the moon, like to a silver bow
New bent in heaven, shall behold the night
Of our solemnities.

(A Midsummer Night's Dream,
Act I, Scene 1, lines 1ff.)

The fourth plot of *A Midsummer Night's Dream* is simplicity itself. At the beginning of the play, Duke Theseus, the ruler of Athens, is about to marry Hippolyta, the Queen of the Amazons, and at the end of the play he marries her. That's all that really happens in their story, which functions as a sort of frame around the other three plots. However, Theseus has a civilizing effect on the whole play: He cautions Hermia about the force of Athenian law, and he later overrules Hermia's father and allows her to marry Lysander without punishment.

Also, when Philostrate, Theseus's Master of the Revels, tries to dissuade his master from choosing the Mechanicals' play for the wedding entertainment because it is so poorly written and performed, Theseus insists on having it, and he tells Philostrate why in one of my favorite couplets in the play:

> For never anything can be amiss
> When simpleness and duty tender it.

Theseus has a compassionate heart, and we see it everywhere in the play.

The passage that you are about to teach your children consists of the two opening speeches of the play. Tell your children to imagine sitting in a darkened theater . . . the lights come up . . . and there onstage are two beautiful, exotic adults, the Duke of Athens and an Amazon Queen, discussing their wedding, which is only four days away.

> Now, fair Hippolyta, our nuptial hour
> Draws on apace.

Nuptial means "relating to a wedding." Apace means "quickly."

>   our nuptial hour
> Draws on apace.
>   Four happy days bring in
> Another moon.

In other words, "We'll be married in just four happy days, at the time of the new moon."

> Now, fair Hippolyta, our nuptial hour
> Draws on apace. Four happy days bring in
> Another moon.

And now comes the best part of the speech:

> But, O, methinks how slow
> This old moon wanes!

Theseus is so eager for his wedding day (and night) that time seems to be standing still.

Question: Ask your children how they think Shakespeare is conveying the Duke's sense of longing.

Answer: Through the sounds of the words. He's using a literary device called assonance, which means the repetition of internal vowel sounds in nearby words to create a specific effect. In this case he uses the repeated *o* to make it sound as if time is dragging along slowly. Have your children exaggerate the sounds.

> But, Oooo, methinks hoooow slooooow
> This oooold mooooon wanes!

Make it a contest to see which of you can exaggerate the sound more.

> But, Ooooooooooooooooooooooo, methinks hoooooooooooooooooooow
> slooooooooooooooooooow
> This oooooooooooooooooooooold
> moooooooooooooooooooooooooooooon wanes!

Silly, yes. But I doubt that they'll ever forget the line after this.

Hippolyta answers Theseus by saying:

> Four days will quickly steep themselves in night;
> Four nights will quickly dream away the time;
> And then the moon, like to a silver bow
> New bent in heaven, shall behold the night
> Of our solemnities.

In essence she is saying:

Don't worry. The time will pass quickly. The days will become nights and during the nights we'll dream, and before you know it the new moon will rise, and, like all new moons, it will have the curved shape of a bow, in this case a silver bow that has just been bent, ready for the first arrow. And incidentally, the new moon will look down and watch over us on our wedding night.

Hippolyta says it rather better than I just did:

> *Four days will quickly steep themselves in night;*
> *Four nights will quickly dream away the time;*
> *And then the moon, like to a silver bow*
> *New bent in heaven, shall behold the night*
> *Of our solemnities.*

Notice the use of the word *dream*. This will be a recurring image throughout the play.

> *Four days will quickly steep themselves in night;*
> *Four nights will quickly **dream** away the time;*
> *And then the **moon**,*

The moon is the other central image of the play. The moon waxes and wanes—it grows large, then recedes. It glows in the night sky. There is something mysterious and sexually romantic about it.

> *And then the moon, like to a silver bow*
> *New bent in heaven,*

Ask your children why they think Hippolyta is comparing the moon to a bow that has just been bent. The answer is that Hippolyta is an Amazon. Amazons were the fierce women warriors of Greek mythology who fought with bows and arrows. Indeed, according to myth, every Amazon had one of her breasts removed so that it would not interfere physically as she drew back the bowstring.

>   *shall behold the night*
> *Of our solemnities.*

In other words, "The moon will look down from the heavens and bless our marriage."

Now try the whole speech. When there are slip-ups, just repeat the relevant section again and again. My children and I love the repetition. It has a calming effect on us. For our "Shakespeare time" together, there is nothing else in the world but us and the passage. It simplifies life for those two special hours on the weekend, and by the end of each session, we can—as Bottom might say—recite the lines at our fingertips.

Bonus Passage

When the lovers reach their highest state of confusion, Oberon declares to Puck that it is time to straighten things out. He instructs Puck to use fog to create confusion, then use a magic antidote to sort out the couples. In a hilarious scene of mistaken identities, Puck does just what he's told, and by the end of the scene, the four lovers are asleep on the ground. Puck's final "blessing" on the couples is one that you and your children should memorize right now.

> *Jack shall have Jill;*
> *Naught shall go ill;*
> *The man shall have his mare again, and all shall be well.*

For me, this epigram stands for the endings of all the romantic comedies ever written. On the surface it means "they all lived happily ever after," but the subtext is more complex and has a slightly darker cast. *The man shall have his mare again.* Not his woman, but his mare. Bottom became a donkey and then a fairy queen fell in love with him. There are things going on in our lives that are hard to fathom. They are beyond our reach. They live in our dreams.

> *Jack shall have Jill;*
> *Naught shall go ill;*
> *The man shall have his mare again, and all shall be well.*

It is especially interesting that Shakespeare has Puck comment on this moment from a distance, as though he is the creator of this "play" that the lovers are enacting in front of him. It's as though he's acknowledging that the lovers are operating in a fiction, just the way Jack and Jill are part of a nursery rhyme. Also, Puck is "breaking the fourth wall" of the stage: He is bringing the audience into his conspiracy and acknowledging that he's in a play that we are watching. Again and again throughout Shakespeare's plays, we'll see Shakespeare use the image of a playwright creating a play-within-a-play, making theater versus "real life" a central metaphor of his vision of how we live our lives. At this moment, Puck is the playwright commenting on his "actors":

> *Jack shall have Jill;*
> *Naught shall go ill;*
> *The man shall have his mare again, and all shall be well.*

There is a similar moment in Mozart's opera *The Marriage of Figaro* when the lovers are in jeopardy despite ruse after ruse to put things right. The crafty servant Figaro has confidence, however, that everything will turn out well, and he likens the situation to watching a comedy onstage, thereby distancing himself for a moment from his fellow actors. He sings:

> The theater prescribes
> It all ends with a smile.
> I only hope that wedding bells
> Might keep the peace awhile.

> (*The Marriage of Figaro*,
> Act II, Scene 10, trans. McClatchy)

I'd be willing to bet that the librettist of *The Marriage of Figaro* (Lorenzo da Ponti) was inspired by Puck's similar blessing in *A Midsummer Night's*

Dream. As a writer of stage comedies, I find these lines iconic—they remind me of the whole history of stage comedy—and I have them pinned on the wall just above my desk:

> *Jack shall have Jill;*
> *Naught shall go ill;*
> *The man shall have his mare again, and all shall be well.*

CHAPTER 10

Poetry Versus Prose:
How Does Poetry Work?

Three of the four passages that you have memorized so far with your children are in the form of poetry, and the fourth is in prose. How can your children tell the difference?

As a practical matter, it couldn't be easier. Point out that with most poetry, and certainly Shakespeare's poetry, each line begins with a capital letter and each line has a defined length.

> **I** know a bank where the wild thyme blows,
> **W**here oxlips and the nodding violet grows,

With prose, the lines on the page don't stop at the end of a rhythmic unit; they just keep snaking along continuously.

> I have had a most rare vision. I have had a dream past the wit of man to say what dream it was. Man is but an ass if he go about to expound this dream.

Explain to your children that as a literary matter, the difference between poetry and prose is more complex. In general, prose is the way we speak to each other in everyday language. Poetry, on the other hand, is heightened language that takes us on an emotional, visceral, intellectual journey every time we say it out loud. The poet Samuel Taylor Coleridge said that "prose equals words in their best order; poetry equals the *best* words in the best order." William Wordsworth called poetry "the spontaneous overflow of powerful feelings." And Emily Dickinson said,

> If I read a book and it makes my whole body so cold no fire can ever warm me, I know that is poetry. If I feel physically as if the top of my head were taken off, I know that is poetry.

Shakespeare himself defined a poet, right in *A Midsummer Night's Dream*. Toward the end of the play, Duke Theseus comments on the lovers, who have told him about their strange adventures in the woods. He observes that lovers and poets require the same kinds of seething imaginations in order to turn their dreams into reality:

> *The poet's eye, in a fine frenzy rolling,*
> *Doth glance from heaven to earth, from earth to heaven,*
> *And as imagination bodies forth*
> *The forms of things unknown, the poet's pen*
> *Turns them to shapes and gives to airy nothing*
> *A local habitation and a name.*

This very passage is a good example of poetry at its best. By creating eight uninterrupted beats in lines three and four,

> *And as imagination bodies forth / The forms of things unknown,*

Shakespeare makes the poet's thoughts sound like a long ribbon flowing from his brain.

Poetry, by definition, has two levels of meaning. There is the meaning on the surface, what the characters or narrator literally say and do and think; and there is the meaning underlying the verse, the meaning that is implied by what is on the surface. This is created through the intellectual content of the words themselves, as well as the sounds of the words and the rhythms of the lines. Prose, with its practical purposes, is often (though not always) operating on the surface only.

Poetry is not only the best words in the best order; it is also the best rhythms in the best order. Poetry is meant to sound beautiful (or exciting or touching or frightening) when read aloud, while prose is more mundane-sounding and less rhythmic. As my children put it, Shakespeare's poetry has a heartbeat running through it that they can feel when they read it aloud. Also, in poetry the language tends to be filled with more literary devices, like metaphors and images, with the intention of making the language more rich, complex, and subtle. Prose, on the other hand, feels more like it's meant to convey information.

That said, there are hundreds of prose passages in Shakespeare that are every bit as rich and complex as poetry. A good example is this passage from *Hamlet*:

> *What a piece of work is a man, how noble in reason, how infinite in faculties, in form and moving how express and admirable; in action how like an angel, in apprehension how like a god: the beauty of the world, the paragon of animals—and yet, to me, what is this quintessence of dust?*

Can one imagine a more beautiful, multileveled use of language? And when this passage is read aloud, no one in the world could say whether it was written down as poetry or prose. It is only the arrangement of the words on the page that tells us the category.

It is commonly said that the highborn characters in Shakespeare always speak in poetry while the lowborn always speak in prose. This is an exaggeration, and we see this "rule" being broken all the time in Shakespeare. The claim, however, does have some rough justice. Thus in *A Midsummer Night's Dream*, the Mechanicals consistently speak in prose (except in their play-within-the-play, *Pyramus and Thisbe*, when they're trying to sound highborn), and the fairies and the lovers speak consistently in poetry. In *Hamlet*, on the other hand, the Prince of Denmark speaks a great deal of prose, and it is virtually all exciting. Other examples of great prose speakers in Shakespeare include Sir John Falstaff in *Henry IV, Parts 1 and 2*, Rosalind in *As You Like It*, and Benedick and Beatrice in *Much Ado About Nothing*.

Shakespeare's Poetry

Shakespeare's poetry can be divided into rhymed and unrhymed. When it is unrhymed, it is called blank verse. In his early plays, Shakespeare tended to write a great deal of rhymed verse—he seemed to like the challenge of it, as though he were flexing his young muscles and even showing off a bit. Here is Helena in *A Midsummer Night's Dream* out of breath after chasing Demetrius. Have your children listen for the naturalness of the rhymes, as though writing them were as easy as breathing.

> *O, I am out of breath in this fond chase.*
> *The more my prayer, the lesser is my grace.*
> *Happy is Hermia, wheresoe'er she lies,*
> *For she hath blessèd and attractive eyes.*

And here is Romeo at the moment he falls in love with Juliet in *Romeo and Juliet*. Again, Shakespeare makes rhyming seem like the easiest thing in the world:

> *O, she doth teach the torches to burn bright!*
> *It seems she hangs upon the cheek of night*
> *As a rich jewel in an Ethiop's ear—*
> *Beauty too rich for use, for earth too dear.*

Considering the difficulty of rhyming lines with naturalness and sophistication, it is almost shocking to realize that 45 percent of *A Midsummer Night's Dream* is rhymed.

As Shakespeare matured, his poetic expression became more complex. One of our family's favorite passages of blank verse from Shakespeare's later years is the description of Cleopatra in *Antony and Cleopatra*. Recite it aloud with your children. It is an example of blank verse at its finest.

> *The barge she sat in, like a burnished throne*
> *Burned on the water. The poop [deck] was beaten gold;*
> *Purple the sails, and so perfumèd that*

The winds were love-sick with them; the oars were silver,
Which to the tune of flutes kept stroke, and made
The water which they beat to follow faster . . .

Age cannot wither her, nor custom stale
Her infinite variety: other women cloy
The appetites they feed, but she makes hungry
Where most she satisfies . . .

Iambic Pentameter

Iambic pentameter is the name of the most widely used verse form in English literature. It was used by Chaucer in *The Canterbury Tales* and by Milton in *Paradise Lost*, and Shakespeare uses it as the staple verse form for all his plays. The first passage of Shakespeare that we looked at together in this book is in iambic pentameter:

I know a bank where the wild thyme blows

So is the last passage we just quoted:

The barge she sat in, like a burnished throne

and so are most of the passages that we'll be learning together in this book.

Iambic pentameter is simply a verse form where each line has five beats (hence the word *pentameter*, since *penta* is the Greek root for "five") and each beat is an *iamb* (the Greek root for "foot"). An iamb sounds like this:

da DUM

So a perfectly regular line of iambic pentameter—which is made up of five iambs—sounds like this:

da DUM　da DUM　da DUM　da DUM　da DUM

Here is the first line of *Twelfth Night*. It's an example of perfectly regular iambic pentameter.

>*If music be the food of love play on.*

Say it aloud to your children and ask them if they can hear the five beats.

>*If* **MU** sic **BE** *the* **FOOD** *of* **LOVE** *play* **ON**.
>One   Two   Three   Four   Five
>da DUM   da DUM   da DUM   da DUM   da DUM

Many of the most famous lines in Shakespeare are in regular iambic pentameter.

>*The quality of mercy is not strained.*
>The **QUA** li **TY** *of* **MER** cy **IS** not **STRAINED**

Notice, though, that actors don't speak iambic pentameter with five equal stresses. Instead, they say their lines in the way that sense demands. Thus an actor would speak the first line above with four stresses:

>*If* **MUS**ic *be the* **FOOD** *of* **LOVE**, *play* **ON**.

Have your children say the line this way and listen to how natural it sounds:

>*If* **MUS**ic *be the* **FOOD** *of* **LOVE**, *play* **ON**.

Similarly, an actor would speak the second example with three strong beats:

>*The* **QUA**lity *of* **MER**cy *is not* **STRAINED**.

Some iambic pentameter lines, however, do have five strong beats when spoken properly:

But **SOFT**, *what* **LIGHT** *through* **YON***der* **WIN***dow* **BREAKS**.

One of the most wonderful things about iambic pentameter is how closely it imitates normal English speech. It is just the length we speak before needing a new breath, and it has the bounce and flexibility of a typical English sentence. This is why so many of the great English writers adopted this form as the basis for their dramatic poetry. (French dramatic poetry, by contrast, is based on a six-beat line called an alexandrine, which, I have been told by native French speakers, mirrors natural French speech.)

Bear in mind that when Shakespeare uses iambic pentameter, he isn't trying to be fancy or "poetic." He is simply telling his story as clearly and accurately as possible. The fact that it often sounds "poetic" in the high-flown sense is because he has so much to say, and because what he has to say is so complex.

The Lone Ranger

Not all Shakespeare's lines of poetry, however, are in regular iambic pentameter. In fact, most of his lines are irregular. This means that they still have five beats and they still approximate an English speaker's phrasing, but they don't gallop along only in iambs. A regular line goes:

> da DUM   da DUM   da DUM   da DUM   da DUM

But an irregular line might go:

> da   DUM DUM   da da   DUM da DUM da DUM
> *Where ox lips and the nod ding vio let grows,*

Or it might go:

> DUM da da DUM da da DUM DUM DUM
> *I   know   a   bank   where   the   wild   thyme   blows,*

Point out to your children that the line

I know a bank where the wild thyme blows

is in irregular iambic pentameter and has the same rhythm as the famous Lone Ranger Theme (which is based on the final section of the *William Tell Overture* by Rossini). Have your kids try it out.

> DUM   da da   DUM   da da   DUM   DUM   DUM
> (da da) DUM   da da   DUM   da da   DUM   DUM   DUM
> (da da) DUM   da da   DUM   da da   DUM   DUM   DUM
> (da da) DAAAAAAH! da da da DUM DUM DUM

>   **I**   *know a*   **bank**   *where the*   **wild**   **thyme**   **blows,**
> (oh)   **I**   *know a*   **bank**   *where the*   **wild**   **thyme**   **blows,**
> (oh)   **I**   *know a*   **bank**   *where the*   **wild**   **thyme**   **blows,**
> (I know a)   **baaaaaaank**   *where the*   **wild**   **thyme**   **blows!**

Remind them that they just sang a line of irregular iambic pentameter. Then ask your children why they think Shakespeare doesn't write all his iambic pentameter in regular form. Why does he vary it? There are three reasons, and I'll bet your children will get at least one of them right before you tell them.

First, if you had to hear one regular iambic pentameter line after another for an entire play, it would put you to sleep. It is the variation in the lines that keeps the experience alive and interesting.

> *The barge she sat in, like a burnished throne*
> *Burned on the water. The poop was beaten gold;*
> *Purple the sails, and so perfumèd that*
> *The winds were love-sick with them . . .*

Each line in this passage has a different rhythm, and so it feels vital and exciting.

Second, Shakespeare uses the variations in the rhythm to create the tensions and the releases, the smoothness and staccatos, the bombast and sweetness that tell his story. The great Shakespearean director I mentioned in chapter 4, Sir Peter Hall, likens Shakespeare's manipulation of iambic pentameter to the way a great musician plays jazz. First the musician creates a recurring rhythm to set up the beat. Then he starts riffing, and he brings his art to bear through all the variations that make his interpretation so interesting.

Shakespeare's Best Trick

As we discussed earlier, Shakespeare writes his verse in such a way that he often tells us how to speak his lines. As another great director, John Barton, has said, Shakespeare's verse is "stage-direction in shorthand." Our goal is to teach your children to read carefully and look for the clues that show us when Shakespeare wants us to pause, or speed up, or shout, or interrupt. One of my own favorite examples is in *A Midsummer Night's Dream,* when Titania tells Oberon why she insists on keeping the little Indian boy for herself. She explains with passion that the boy is the son of one of her devoted followers who died giving birth to the child.

Let's look at the whole passage. It's a difficult speech, and it may take a few minutes to read it with understanding; but what we really care about at the moment are the last two lines. Oberon starts the exchange by saying simply:

> *I do but beg a little changeling boy*
> *To be my henchman.*

Titania answers him:

> *Set your heart at rest:*
> *The Fairyland buys not the child of me.*

And now she launches into her speech about the boy's origins—for me, one of the most beautiful speeches in all of Shakespeare. And remember, we're looking for the trick that Shakespeare is going to play in the last two lines, a trick that will tell us exactly how to say them:

TITANIA

His mother was a vot'ress [follower] *of my order,*
And in the spiced Indian air, by night
Full often hath she gossiped by my side,
And sat with me on Neptune's yellow sands [the beach],
Marking th'embarked traders on the flood
[Watching the sailing merchant ships on the tide],

When [at which time] *we have laughed to see the sails conceive*
And grow big-bellied with the wanton wind;
[image: the wind makes the sails puff out the way a
woman's belly puffs out because she's pregnant]

Which she, with pretty and with swimming gait [walk],
Following (her womb then rich with my young squire),
Would imitate, and sail upon the land
To fetch me trifles, and return again,
As from [as though from] *a voyage, rich with merchandise.*
But she, being mortal, of that boy did die,
And for her sake do I rear up her boy;
And for her sake I will not part with him.

Question: What is Shakespeare's trick in the last two lines?

Answer: Every word is a single syllable. It means that the actor playing Titania has to make each word matter—which slows her up and gives the lines a gravity and weight that show us how deeply she cares about what she's saying. It's as if each line has ten strong beats:

And for her sake do I rear up her boy;
And for her sake I will not part with him.

A Note on Simplicity

Shakespeare often gets very straightforward and monosyllabic in his most moving lines. He'll refer to something commonplace to bring us down to earth, and he'll abruptly change from complex poetic lines to simple, monosyllabic statements so that the speech slows down and resounds with a kind of heavy fate. Here is an example from *King Lear*. At the very end of the play, after five acts of rich, complex poetry, when Lear's daughter has been hanged and he has nothing left to live for, he touchingly reverts to monosyllables and asks to have his tunic unbuttoned so he can breathe more easily:

> *Why should a dog, a horse, a rat have life,*
> *And thou no breath at all? . . .*
> *Pray you undo this button. Thank you, sir.*

As one of the greatest Shakespeareans of our time, Stanley Wells, puts it:

> That kind of sudden simplicity is among the things that one con-
> stantly marvels at in Shakespeare: the way that a plain phrase, the sort
> of language that out of context would seem entirely unpoetical . . . ,
> can have a devastating effect because of their placing.

The passage that we're about to tackle in the next chapter is going to tell us worlds about the uses of poetry. It is from *Twelfth Night*, which happens to be my own favorite play in the Shakespeare canon. It always sounds hollow to praise a work of art in general terms, but I hope to show your children why *Twelfth Night* is a masterpiece that ranks along with Michelangelo's statue of David and Mozart's opera *The Marriage of Figaro* as one of the greatest works of the human spirit.

CHAPTER 11

Passage 5
Cesario's Willow Cabin

CESARIO

If I did love you in my master's flame,
With such a suff'ring, such a deadly life,
In your denial I would find no sense.
I would not understand it.

OLIVIA

Why, what would you?

CESARIO

Make me a willow cabin at your gate
And call upon my soul within the house,
Write loyal cantons of contemnèd love
And sing them loud even in the dead of night,
Hallow your name to the reverberate hills
And make the babbling gossip of the air
Cry out "Olivia!" O, you should not rest
Between the elements of air and earth
But you should pity me.

OLIVIA

You might do much.

(*Twelfth Night*, Act I, Scene 5, lines 266–80)

In this passage from *Twelfth Night*, a good-looking, fresh-faced servant, a young man named Cesario, is speaking to an unusually beautiful and headstrong countess named Olivia. Cesario's master is in love with Olivia, but Olivia has turned him down repeatedly. In desperation, the master has sent his servant Cesario to visit Olivia and plead his case.

At this moment in the play, Olivia has just told Cesario that she does *not* love Cesario's master. She recognizes that he is handsome, rich, and virtuous,

> *But yet I cannot love him.*
> *He might have took his answer long ago.*

In the face of this rejection, Cesario replies from the heart, with simplicity and passion.

> *If I did love you in my master's flame,*
> *With such a suff'ring, such a deadly life,*
> *In your denial I would find no sense.*
> *I would not understand it.*

In other words, "If I loved you the way my master does, with all his passionate and deadly suffering, I simply wouldn't understand your rejection of me." Have your children say the lines (out loud, of course, and using the Quotation Pages) with utter simplicity.

> *If I did love you in my master's flame,*

Notice the word *flame*. It means "manner," but it also implies intense emotion, as in someone fanning the flame of someone else's passion.

> *If I did love you in my master's flame,*
> *With such a suff'ring, such a deadly life,*

"With as much deadly suffering as he is going through."

Twelfth Night at the Public Theater, with Audra McDonald as Olivia and Anne Hathaway as Viola.

> *In your denial I would find no sense.*
> *I would not understand it.*

Now have your son or daughter say the whole quatrain:

> *If I did love you in my master's flame,*
> *With such a suff'ring, such a deadly life,*
> *In your denial I would find no sense.*
> *I would not understand it.*

Olivia answers Cesario by saying:

> *Why, what would you?*

Notice that Olivia leaves out the final word "do." Normally one would answer "Why, what would you do?" By leaving out that one little word, Shakespeare makes the line lighter, more bewildered, and less earth-bound.

I would not understand it.

Why, what would you?

Cesario answers:

Make me a willow cabin at your gate
And call upon my soul within the house,
Write loyal cantons of contemnèd love
And sing them loud even in the dead of night,
Hallow your name to the reverberate hills
And make the babbling gossip of the air
Cry out "Olivia!" O, you should not rest
Between the elements of air and earth
But you should pity me.

OLIVIA
You might do much.

Cesario's answer to Olivia is so passionate, so powerful, so poetically breathtaking, that Olivia can only stammer at the end of it:

You might do much.

YOU might do much. You, Cesario, might do much. You, Cesario, might do much with ME. Because of the power of poetry in this one speech, known as the Willow Cabin Speech, Olivia falls in love with the servant instead of the master. Just imagine the whoop of delight from an audience that has never seen the play before.

Now let's look at the Willow Cabin Speech more carefully. Cesario says that he would

Make me a willow cabin at your gate
And call upon my soul within the house,

In other words he would build a small house made of willow branches at Olivia's front gate. (Olivia and Cesario would both know that in Greek and Roman mythology, the willow tree was a symbol of grief for unrequited love.) Have your children say these two lines with simple conviction, as if to say, "What else could I possibly do? Nothing else. I'm in love."

> Make me a willow cabin at your gate
> And call upon my soul within the house,

Call upon my soul. He is referring to Olivia as his soul and says that he would come to her house and call upon her. Another possible meaning is that he would call upon his own soul in his house, the willow cabin he just built, in order to find the strength to approach anyone as tremendous as Olivia. Both meanings are romantic, and perhaps the ambiguity implies that their two souls are one.

What would Cesario do next if he loved her?

> Write loyal cantons of contemnèd love
> And sing them loud even in the dead of night,

A *canton* is a song. *Contemnèd love* is love that is disdained or held in contempt. So Cesario would write songs about his love for Olivia and then he would sing them aloud at night, even when no one was around to hear them.

> Write loyal cantons
>
> > of contemnèd love
>
> And sing them loud
>
> > even in the dead of night,

Next, Cesario would do something even more romantic: He would shout her name at the top of his lungs so loudly that he would make the hills reverberate. Moreover, he would do it with so much passion that it would make a nymph from Greek mythology named Echo—Shakespeare calls her *the babbling gossip of the air*—shout back the very same word:

> Oliviaaaaaaa!

In other words, the air would echo with Olivia's name.

Hallow your name to the reverberate hills
And make the babbling gossip of the air
Cry out "Olivia!"

"Olivia!" Exercise

Need I even suggest the next exercise? See who can cry *"Olivia!"* the loudest. First try just the word itself. Then have your children say the whole speech and end it with the cry

Oliviaaaaaaa!

Also notice that the word *hallow* is an interesting one. In every production of *Twelfth Night* I have ever seen, Cesario has pronounced it "hal-LOO" (with the accent on the second syllable), making it a variant of the word *hello* and therefore synonymous (in this context) with the word *shout*.

Halloo your name to the reverberate hills

It makes my heart skip a beat. But in the only authentic printing of the play (the First Folio of 1623) the word is spelled *hallow*, which suggests not only *halloo* (or *hello*) but also the word *hallow* as in "to make holy."

Hallow your name to the reverberate hills
And make the babbling gossip of the air
Cry out "Olivia!"

I believe that Shakespeare intended this double meaning. As we know, he loved puns, and this is a perfect one, since both words, *halloo* and *hallow*, are equally appropriate. As for pronunciation, I recommend that you use "halloo" since it is an iamb and the rhythm of it makes the line more beautiful.

Finally, Cesario adds a short coda to the speech:

O, you should not rest
Between the elements of air and earth
But you should [unless you] pity me.

After the climax of *"Olivia!"* I always imagine these three lines being spoken deep in the chest, almost in a whisper. Have your children act out these lines with depth and longing.

Remember, always, *always* make the memorization a game for your children. Chest tones, patty-cake, marching, shouting, acting, wearing hats and cloaks, contests, bets, painting on mustaches, bribery by chocolate, whatever it takes. My view was always a ruthless one: Anything I could do to help them memorize the passages was fair game.

Bonus Passage

Soon after giving the Willow Cabin Speech, Cesario leaves Olivia's house. At that point, Olivia has a short dialogue with herself, a sort of soliloquy where she asks herself, in essence, "Where did this wonderful creature come from?" She realizes that she has just fallen in love, and she can hardly believe it. She says to herself:

OLIVIA
Thy tongue, thy face, thy limbs, actions, and spirit
Do give thee fivefold blazon [stature as a gentleman]. *Not too fast! Soft,*
    soft!
Unless the master were the man. How now?

And then she says a line so clever that your children should memorize it right now:

Even so quickly may one catch the plague?

"Even so quickly may one fall in love?"

Olivia is one of the wittiest women in all of Shakespeare, and by likening love to the plague, she deepens the metaphor and makes it more than trivial. Plague was serious business in Shakespeare's time, and it came on quickly. In 1564, the year of Shakespeare's birth, when an outbreak of plague swept England, the death rate in Shakespeare's hometown of Stratford was about ten times higher than normal, with an infant mortality rate of about two-thirds.

> *Even so quickly may one catch the plague?*

The line has a gentle irony and shows Olivia making fun of her own self-imposed gravity, for which we like her the more.

> *Even so quickly may one catch the plague?*

The Final Bribe

Finally, as your children get close to memorizing the whole passage, make them an offer they can't refuse: If they get it down cold, you'll tell them the biggest surprise in the whole play, one so amazing that it will blow back their hair. So here goes. See if they can recite the passage by heart:

CESARIO

If I did love you in my master's flame,
With such a suff'ring, such a deadly life,
In your denial I would find no sense.
I would not understand it.

OLIVIA

Why, what would you?

CESARIO

Make me a willow cabin at your gate
And call upon my soul within the house,
Write loyal cantons of contemnèd love
And sing them loud even in the dead of night,
Hallow your name to the reverberate hills
And make the babbling gossip of the air
Cry out "Olivia!" O, you should not rest

Between the elements of air and earth
But you should pity me.

OLIVIA
You might do much.

If they nailed it, you can now tell them the surprise. Are you ready?

Cesario isn't a boy at all. She is a young woman disguised as a boy. Her real name is Viola. So the Countess Olivia has just fallen deeply in love with a feisty young woman and wants to marry her.

Who wants to hear the rest of the story?

CHAPTER 12

The Viola Plot

With *Twelfth Night* we reach one of the absolute peaks of Shakespeare's career. It was written about 1601, around the time of *Hamlet*, and it runs the gamut of emotions: Some moments in it are genuinely hilarious and others are deeply moving. As usual, I think we'll discover how and why it is such a great work of art by memorizing several passages of it together. Before we continue, however, let's look at the story, which has two almost independent plots, one centering on Viola, the heroine, the other on Malvolio, Olivia's steward, or butler.

The Viola Plot

The Viola Plot opens with a rich bachelor named Orsino who is in love with that beautiful Countess Olivia whom we met in the last chapter. As we saw, Orsino has had no luck wooing Olivia, so he has sent his servant Cesario to give it a try. Unbeknownst to Orsino, his clever new servant is not really a chirpy boy; he is a young woman named Viola who was recently shipwrecked on the shore of Illyria, the country where the play is set.

In many ways, it is Viola's heart that makes the play such a masterpiece. Her curious, spunky, faithful heart is at the play's center. Viola has a sort of yearning in her voice that we'll come to recognize, and the yearning is there because her story begins in heartbreak: When she's washed ashore in Scene 2, she believes that her beloved twin brother, Sebastian, went down with the ship, and she spends the rest of the play searching for the love and security that her brother gave her.

At the end of Act I, as we've seen, Viola (as Cesario) visits Olivia to plead Orsino's case, and she does it so well that Olivia falls head over heels in love with her. Shakespeare resolves this complication with the same elegance with which he got himself into it: Viola's twin brother Sebastian arrives in Illyria, and Olivia marries him, thinking he's Cesario.

The Viola Plot has a couple of more twists and turns in it, and one of them involves Olivia's drunken uncle, Sir Toby Belch, and his cowardly friend, Sir Andrew Aguecheek.

Sir Andrew Aguecheek and Sir Toby Belch

Sir Andrew and Sir Toby enter the play together in the first act and remain throughout as a sort of comic duo. They are profoundly humorous and richly absurd, and in sheer comic genius they stand easily next to Mr. Collins in *Pride and Prejudice,* Lady Bracknell in *The Importance of Being Earnest,* Tony Lumpkin in *She Stoops to Conquer,* and Sam Weller in *The Pickwick Papers.* Sir Toby is the more knowing of the two, rougher and darker, while Sir Andrew is the innocent who thinks well of himself but is in fact clueless.

Sir Toby, who lives at the manor house with his niece Olivia, has invited the rich Sir Andrew to stay with them and woo Olivia. Olivia, of course, has no interest in a fool like Sir Andrew, which leaves him little to do but drink and carouse till all hours with Sir Toby.

A typically rich exchange between the two occurs in their first scene together, just after Maria, the housekeeper, has bested Sir Andrew in a verbal exchange. You and your son or daughter should each take a part and read the following exchange aloud. Comic writing simply does not get any better than this.

TOBY

O knight, thou lack'st a cup of canary [wine]! When did I see thee so put down?

ANDREW

Never in your life, I think, unless you see canary put me down. Methinks sometimes I have no more wit than a Christian or an ordinary man has. But I am a great eater of beef, and I believe that does no harm to my wit. . . . I'll ride home tomorrow, Sir Toby.

TOBY

Pourquoi, my dear knight?

ANDREW

What is "pourquoi"? Do, or not do? I would I had bestowed that time in the tongues [languages] that I have in fencing, dancing, and bearbaiting. O, had I but followed the arts!

TOBY

Then hadst thou had an excellent head of hair.

ANDREW

Why, would that have mended my hair?

Twelfth Night at Westport Country Playhouse with Jordan Coughtry as Andrew Aguecheek and David Schramm as Sir Toby Belch

TOBY

Past question, for thou seest it will not curl by nature. . . . It hangs like flax on a distaff [staff used for spinning thread], *and I hope to see a huswife take thee between her legs and spin it off.*

One of my favorite moments in the play tells us worlds about Sir Andrew in just five words. About midway through the play, Maria the housekeeper has just left the room, and Sir Toby remarks on his affection for her:

She is a beagle true bred, and one that adores me.

To which Sir Andrew replies sadly:

I was adored once, too.

Funny. Touching. It goes right to the heart of Sir Andrew and makes us feel instant sympathy for this foolish, frightened man.

I was adored once, too.

CHAPTER 13

Passage 6
Orsino's Heart

If music be the food of love, play on.
Give me excess of it, that, surfeiting,
The appetite may sicken and so die.
That strain again! It had a dying fall.
O, it came o'er my ear like the sweet sound
That breathes upon a bank of violets,
Stealing and giving odor. Enough; no more.
'Tis not so sweet now as it was before.

(*Twelfth Night*, Act I, Scene 1, lines 1–8)

As *Twelfth Night* opens, Orsino is in his palace listening to music with his friends and servants. As we can hear from this passage, Orsino is Viola's polar opposite: He is moody, subject to excess, and romantic in a saturated, self-reverential sort of way. We will learn in the rest of this scene that Orsino is pining for his beautiful neighbor Olivia and that she refuses to see him.

This is one of the most famous speeches in Shakespeare, and I think this is partly because the language is so beautiful and partly because these eight lines introduce us to virtually all the major themes of the play.

If music be the food of love, play on.

Like all of Shakespeare's comedies, *Twelfth Night* is about love, and it is no coincidence that the word *love* is only the seventh word of the entire play.

*If music be the food of **love**, play on.*

Orsino is using a metaphor that equates love with physical hunger, and the only food that will satisfy that hunger is music.

love = physical hunger
music = food for that hunger

Orsino then says, in essence, that he doesn't want to be in love, so he tells his musicians "please give me *too much* music so that my appetite will be glutted and killed by overeating."

Give me excess of it, that, surfeiting,
The appetite may sicken and so die.

Surfeiting means having too much of something. In other words, it's painful for him to be in love with this beautiful countess, and he wants it to stop. He wants his musicians to overfeed his longing so that he can get sick of it and turn away. Already we have a clue about Orsino's character: He is excessively romantic and on the feverish side.

Give me excess of it, that, surfeiting,
The appetite may sicken and so die.

Another clue to what this play will be about is the word *excess*. All the characters in the play will go to extremes, and it will get them in trouble. Orsino is excessively in love. Olivia is in excessive mourning over the deaths of her father and brother. Malvolio, when it's his turn to woo Olivia, will go to excesses that are against his nature.

The other key word in this couplet is *die*. *Twelfth Night* is filled with issues of dying and death. These allusions create shadows throughout the play, so that as we laugh at the witty lines and revel in the extravagant characters, we are aware that larger issues of life and death are looming just around the corner.

Orsino continues by asking the musicians to repeat a particular passage, or *strain*, of the music that he just heard; and he describes that strain as having a *dying fall*, meaning that the passage is descending. (There's that suggestion of dying again.)

> *That strain again! It had a dying fall.*

And now he describes the music in more detail:

> *O, it came o'er [over] my ear like the sweet sound*
> *That breathes upon a bank of violets,*
> *Stealing and giving odor.*

How interesting that Shakespeare would say that the sound *breathes upon a bank of violets*. Remembering the passage

> *I know a bank where the wild thyme blows*

one might well conclude that Shakespeare was fond of banks of flowers and found them romantic.

> *That breathes upon a bank of violets,*
> *Stealing and giving odor.*

Stealing seems to mean "stealing up on" or "stealing over." And the beautiful sound of the music seems to have an odor, or smell, and it seems to breathe.

But we hear music. We listen to it. How can it *breathe*, then *steal*, then give off *odor*? Point out to your children that Shakespeare is doing something very clever here. He is mingling the senses, as if love knows no bounds and can make us feel and see and smell all at the same time. Thus, in the very first speech of the play, Shakespeare is telling us how multifaceted love can be, and he is hinting that love will be one of the major themes of the play.

> *O, it came o'er my ear like the sweet sound*
> *That breathes upon a bank of violets,*
> *Stealing and giving odor.*

At this point, Orsino stops the musicians from allowing him to indulge in all this richness and says:

> *Enough; no more.*
> *'Tis not so sweet now as it was before.*

Have your children rehearse each phrase as often as possible until the passage is memorized. This passage is no longer than the first passage they learned from *A Midsummer Night's Dream*, but it is considerably more complex. Say it together one final time before taking a well-deserved break.

CHAPTER 14

Passage 7
The Nature of
Shakespearean Comedy

VIOLA

What country, friends, is this?

CAPTAIN

This is Illyria, lady.

VIOLA

And what should I do in Illyria?
My brother he is in Elysium.
Perchance he is not drowned.—What think you, sailors?

CAPTAIN

It is perchance that you yourself were saved. . . .

VIOLA

I prithee—and I'll pay thee bounteously—
Conceal me what I am, and be my aid
For such disguise as haply shall become
The form of my intent. I'll serve this duke.

(*Twelfth Night*, Act I, Scene 2, lines 1ff.)

We are now on a beach on the coast of Illyria right after a shipwreck. (It's the second scene of the play.) A ship was split on a rock, lives were lost, a man tied himself to a mast to save himself, and a few survivors have struggled out of the water onto the beach. It is here that we meet Viola and hear her distinctive, invigorating, yearning voice for the first time.

After hearing Orsino spouting all those hothouse metaphors about love and hunger in the first scene, this simple narrative exchange comes as a breath of fresh air. You play the Captain, and let your child play Viola:

VIOLA

What country, friends, is this?

CAPTAIN

This is Illyria, lady.

VIOLA

And what should I do in Illyria?
My brother he is in Elysium.
Perchance he is not drowned.—What think you, sailors?

CAPTAIN

It is perchance that you yourself were saved.

This scene is characteristic of Shakespeare in the sense that most of his plays open quickly. In general, a play begins when a world in equilibrium is broken into by a significant change. In Shakespeare, the opening disruption usually occurs early in the action. In *Hamlet* we hear about the ghost by line 20 (*What, has this thing appear'd again tonight?*). In *King Lear* we're only up to line 37 when the monarch unwisely divides his kingdom, thereby setting off the entire plot of the play. *The Tempest* opens with an exciting shipwreck that drives the rest of the play's action. And *Romeo and Juliet* opens with a street brawl between warring families that will lead directly to the final tragedy. Similarly, here in *Twelfth Night*, the shipwreck off the coast of Illyria occurs after an opening scene of a mere seven speeches.

Tell your child to imagine a rocky coastline. Waves batter the sand,

and we see a lone ship in the distance, buffeted by a terrible wind. Then suddenly, we're on that ship and people are crying out, fearful for their very lives. *Crack!* The ship hits a rock, and now your daughter tumbles from her bed and across the floor. She's on a beach, and for a moment she's unconscious. Then she wakes up slowly, stunned and aching. A few of her fellow passengers, including the Captain, are sitting nearby, equally stunned from the wreck. She catches her breath and says:

> *What country, friends, is this?*

It sounds so simple, this sentence, yet I find it to be one of the greatest first lines of any character ever written. It reminds me of the opening line of *Hamlet* when, at night, a nervous guard at Elsinore Castle cries *Who's there?!* In both cases, the questioner seems to be asking "Who's out there?" "Why am I here?" "What will become of me?"

> *What country, friends, is this?*

And the Captain replies:

> *This is Illyria, lady.*

Illyria will prove to be a magical place. Not magical like the Wood near Athens—there are no fairies here, no supernatural goings-on. But the world of Illyria will turn out to contain daffy servants and lovelorn travelers, loyal comrades and identical twins, a melancholy jester and a drunken knight. If there is any fictional world I want to live in, it is definitely Illyria.

> *And what shall I do in Illyria?*
> *My brother he is in Elysium.*

In Greek mythology, Elysium was a place at the end of the earth where favored heroes were conveyed by the gods after death. Thus we know immediately that Viola believes that her brother is dead, and we know that she loved him so much that she is certain of his heavenly reward. Also point out to your children that Elysium and Illyria sound somewhat the same. Could Illyria be a kind of Elysium for the blessed who are not yet dead? Also notice that the names Olivia, Viola, and Malvolio are virtual anagrams of one another. Shakespeare is up to something, and it has to do with relationships and the identities of these three main characters.

Next comes an idea and a ray of hope:

Perchance he is not drowned.—What think you, sailors?

To which the Captain replies:

It is perchance that you yourself were saved.

Brothers and chance will play significant roles in this play, and it is not surprising that both are touched upon in these early speeches.

In general, you'll find that passages with two or more characters are especially fun to memorize with your children, as you can each take a different role and turn the passage into a little play.

(Thunder. Lightning. Shipwreck. Children roll off bed.)

VIOLA

What country, friends, is this?

CAPTAIN

This is Illyria, lady.

VIOLA

And what should I do in Illyria?
My brother he is in Elysium.
Perchance he is not drowned.—What think you, sailors?

CAPTAIN

It is perchance that you yourself were saved.

As the scene continues, Viola questions the Captain about Illyria, which is a way for Shakespeare to fill in the backstory. The Captain explains, first, that during the shipwreck, he saw Viola's brother tie himself to a mast. Therefore the young man *might* have saved himself. Next he explains that Illyria is governed by a duke named Orsino, that Orsino is in love with a neighboring countess named Olivia, and that Olivia has turned the Duke away.

> VIOLA
>
> *Who governs here?*

> CAPTAIN
>
> *A noble duke, in nature as in name.*

> VIOLA
>
> *What is his name?*

> CAPTAIN
>
> *Orsino.*

> VIOLA
>
> *Orsino. I have heard my father name him.*
> *He was a bachelor then.*

Isn't it interesting that Viola would remember that he's a bachelor? Already Shakespeare has us thinking romance.

> CAPTAIN
>
> *And is so now, or was so very late* [lately];
> *For but a month ago I went from hence* [here],
> *And then 'twas fresh in murmur (as, you know,*
> *What great ones do the less will prattle of)*
> *That he did seek the love of fair Olivia.*

What a clever epigram Shakespeare throws in like an extra treat: *What great ones do the less will prattle of.* In other words, "What celebrities do, we lesser folks will talk about."

VIOLA

What's she?

CAPTAIN

A virtuous maid, the daughter of a count
That died some twelvemonth since [a year ago]*, then leaving her*
In the protection of his son, her brother,
Who shortly also died, for whose dear love,
They say, she hath abjured [given up, sworn off] *the sight*
And company of men.

And now we know that Olivia is virtuous, that people speak well of her, that her brother died (remember, Viola's brother is also presumed dead), and that she has sworn off men because she is in mourning for her father and her brother. At which point, Viola gets an idea:

O, that I served that lady,

As the greatest literary authority of the eighteenth century, Dr. Samuel Johnson, observed in his *Notes on Shakespeare* in 1765:

[At this point,] Viola seems to have formed a very deep design with very little premeditation: she is thrown by shipwreck on an unknown coast, hears that the prince is a bachelor, and resolves to supplant the lady whom he courts.

The Captain replies that Olivia would never agree to it:

CAPTAIN

That were hard to compass [accomplish]
Because she will admit no kind of suit,
No, not the Duke's.

So the ever-resourceful Viola comes up with *another* idea:

I prithee [pray thee]*—and I'll pay thee bounteously—*
Conceal me what I am, and be my aid

For such disguise as haply shall become
The form of my intent. I'll serve this duke.

Conceal me what I am

This could be the rallying cry for virtually all of Shakespeare's comedies, filled as they are with disguises, ruses, mistaken identities, girls dressed as boys, and identical twins. In this play, everyone is going to conceal himself in one way or another. Malvolio, a pompous servant, is going to conceal his true character to impress his employer. Sir Toby Belch and Sir Andrew Aguecheek are going to conceal themselves behind a bush in order to watch Malvolio make a fool of himself. Sir Andrew is going to try to conceal his cowardice when baited into a duel with Cesario. And Viola, our heroine, is going to conceal her identity—*and* her sex, *and* her feelings—from Orsino, with whom she falls in love.

> *I prithee—and I'll pay thee bounteously—*
> *Conceal me what I am,*
> > *and be my aid*
> *For such disguise as haply shall become*
> *The form of my intent.*

Become in this sentence means "be suitable to." So the sentence means "Please, conceal me, and help me put on the kind of disguise that will be suitable to my intention, which is to serve the duke as his servant." This is a tricky passage to memorize, and the keys are repetition and breaking it into four parts:

> *and be my aid*
> *for such disguise*
> *as haply shall become*
> *the form of my intent.*

> *and be my aid for such disguise*
> *as haply shall become the form of my intent.*

For this kind of rhythmic passage, your child should repeat the phrases until they become second nature, like the sections of a piano piece before a big recital.

> *Conceal me what I am, and be my aid*
> *For such disguise as haply shall become*
> *The form of my intent.*

> *I'll serve this duke.*

The Issue of Realism

At this point in the play, at the end of Scene 2, Shakespeare has set himself up to pull off one of the greatest coups in all of theater: turning Viola into a young man. This brings us to one of the most interesting aspects of Shakespeare's comedies, and as you teach your children about these plays, you'll want to point this out again and again: Shakespeare's comedies are filled with events and characters and plot twists that are *not* realistic. Disguises, mistaken identities, twins, cross-dressing, magic, gods and goddesses, coincidence, fairy sprites, concealments, ruses—all these devices abound in Shakespeare's comedies.

- In no less than five of his fourteen comedies—*The Two Gentlemen of Verona, The Merchant of Venice, As You Like It, Twelfth Night,* and *Cymbeline*—women disguise themselves as men and fool everyone around them, including the men they love.
- Two of his comedies, *Twelfth Night* and *The Comedy of Errors,* contain identical twins who are so much alike that they confuse other characters.
- *A Midsummer Night's Dream* and *The Tempest* contain magic.
- *As You Like It* and *Cymbeline* include visits from gods.
- In two comedies, *All's Well That Ends Well* and *Measure for Measure,* the heroines pull the "bed trick"—that is, they spend a night in bed with the men they love while the men themselves believe that they are sleeping with other women.

- *The Merry Wives of Windsor* involves a fat old knight named Falstaff who dresses up as a woman called the Witch of Brentford in order to fool the neighbors.
- And in *The Winter's Tale,* a wife conceals herself from her husband for sixteen years, then poses as a statue that seemingly comes to life.

Indeed, with only one or two arguable exceptions, all of Shakespeare's comedies contain nonrealistic elements.

Why does Shakespeare do this? There is no simple answer. It is the way Shakespeare saw comedy in his mind and in his heart. It is the way he saw life. Interestingly, this extravagant form of comedy, which Shakespeare effectively invented out of whole cloth, has not been much imitated in the history of stage comedy. Most stage comedies in English since Shakespeare's time have opted instead to try to be more "realistic."

The way I raised this issue with my children was to talk about the sitcoms on television that they love to watch. These shows are generally set in living rooms or kitchens, and they involve people who are essentially like our neighbors next door. Think of the sitcom *Friends,* for example. It is set in apartments and restaurants and is affirmatively literal and nonmagical. In this respect, it resembles most of the stage comedies written since the seventeenth century—everything from Ben Jonson's *Volpone* to Oliver Goldsmith's *She Stoops to Conquer* to Noel Coward's *Private Lives.* And these resemble most of the film and television comedies we've been watching from the early twentieth century to the present day—everything from *I Love Lucy* to *You've Got Mail* to *Seinfeld.* They are all part of a tradition called the "comedy of manners." These plays, movies, and sitcoms rely on witty dialogue, topical references, and moment-to-moment situations for their action and laughs. Shakespeare's comedies don't do that. They are all romance and style. They are filled with fairy queens and shipwrecked twins, disguised tutors and ancient servants pursued by bears. Where the comedy of manners has closets filled with household conveniences, Shakespeare's comedies have leprechauns dancing on the ceiling.

One of my favorite literary critics, Northrop Frye, put it this way in his book *A Natural Perspective*:

In every [Shakespeare] comedy there is some explicitly antirealistic feature introduced: this feature forms a convention that we have to accept. . . . A doctor once remarked to me that he was unable to enjoy a performance of *Twelfth Night* because it was a biological impossibility that boy and girl twins could resemble each other so closely. Shakespeare's answer, apparently, would be for drama what Sir Thomas Browne's is for religion: "Methinks there be not impossibilities enough for an active faith."

Once you have exhausted all the Shakespeare comedies, you'll have to turn to other art forms for the same kind of nonrealistic comic experience. Children's literature sometimes fills the gap (see *Peter Pan* and *Harry Potter*). So do some of the best of the "screwball" film comedies of the 1930s,

The Comedy of Errors at the Royal Shakespeare Company, with Forbes Mason and Jonathan Singer

1940s, and 1950s (e.g., *Bringing Up Baby, To Be or Not to Be, The Major and the Minor,* and *Some Like It Hot*). And so do some of the classic American musical comedies (think of *Guys and Dolls* and *A Funny Thing Happened on the Way to the Forum*).

More profoundly, we find the Shakespearean comic tradition lurking in the best Italian comic operas of the eighteenth and nineteenth centuries, some of which are masterworks. Rossini's *The Barber of Seville* and *La Cenerentola* contain disguised heroes. Donizetti's *The Daughter of the Regiment* involves a heroine raised by a platoon of soldiers; his *Don Pasquale* centers on a false marriage to a disguised heroine; and his *Elixir of Love* involves a supposedly magic potion. And Verdi's *Falstaff* (based on *The Merry Wives of Windsor*) has a wooded grove haunted by a mythic hunter. Best of all is Mozart's *The Marriage of Figaro*, which is the only stage work I can think of that rivals *Twelfth Night* for sheer comic brilliance.

Like Shakespeare, opera can seem a bit frightening if you haven't grown up with it. But if you roll up your sleeves, and your children's sleeves, and take a few minutes to listen to a little Rossini every now and then, your children will soon be humming opera tunes as easily as they're reciting passages from Shakespeare.

The Invention of Modern English Drama

One aspect of Shakespeare's genius that is difficult to see without being a scholar of sixteenth-century drama is the degree to which Shakespeare invented modern English drama, especially comedy. Prior to Shakespeare's comedies, the English had only stage amusements like *Gammer Gurton's Needle* and *Ralph Roister Doister*, perfectly fine little plays that made the audience laugh, but crude in construction and commonplace in language. Shakespeare changed everything, and he did it single-handedly and virtually overnight.

The Taming of the Shrew, Love's Labour's Lost, A Midsummer Night's Dream, The Merry Wives of Windsor, Much Ado About Nothing, As You Like It, and *Twelfth Night* are not only comedies of genius; they are filled with characters and situations that we recognize today and will recognize

The Taming of the Shrew at Shakespeare's Globe, with Samantha Spiro as Kate and Simon Paisley Day as Petruchio

for all time. Shakespeare was able to see our lives and put them onstage, and he was the first English dramatist to do it. Indeed, he did it so profoundly that we soon began to imitate his characters as a way of defining ourselves. It is in this sense that Shakespeare (as the critic Harold Bloom puts it) "invented" us as modern humans.

CHAPTER 15

Passage 8
Cakes and Ale

*Out o' tune, sir? You lie. Art any more than a steward? Dost
thou think, because thou art virtuous, there shall be no more
cakes and ale?*

(*Twelfth Night*, Act II, Scene 3, lines 113–15)

Malvolio, the steward of Olivia's household in *Twelfth Night*, is one
of Shakespeare's most remarkable comic creations. He's a starchy
stick-in-the-mud who has aspirations of "marrying up" but then
gets taken down a peg. Olivia tells him that he is *sick with self-love* and
taste[s] with a distempered appetite. Yet in the end, we identify with his mor-
tification and feel sorry for him.

The passage above is part of an exchange that occurs at a key moment
in the play: We have met Orsino, Viola, and Olivia, and their crisscrossed
love plot is well under way. The scene now shifts to a room in Olivia's house
after midnight, where Sir Toby Belch and Sir Andrew Aguecheek are having a booze-up with Feste the jester and Maria the housekeeper. They are
full of high spirits, drinking, dancing, and singing at the top of their lungs,
when suddenly Malvolio storms in wearing his nightshirt and cries:

*My masters, are you mad? Or what are you? Have you no wit, manners,
nor honesty but to gabble like tinkers at this time of night?* [Tinkers, who
mended pots and pans for a living, were known for their drinking.]

Do you make an ale-house of my lady's house . . . ? Is there no respect of place, persons, nor time in you?

Ask your children: How do you think a hard-drinking, raucous man named Sir Toby Belch is going to respond to a scolding like that from a servant? We all know the answer: He's going to give as good as he gets. He sneers back:

Out o' tune, sir? Ye lie. Art any more than a steward? Dost thou think, because thou art virtuous, there shall be no more cakes and ale?

And here we have the nub of the exchange. "Do you think because *you're* virtuous—because *you're* upright and self-righteous—that the rest of us can't have fun? That the rest of us can't partake of life's joys now and then?"

Out o' tune, sir? Ye lie.

The meaning of the words *Out o' tune, sir?* is not entirely clear. It appears to mean that because Malvolio has belittled Sir Toby's singing ability, Sir Toby is protesting. And now comes the sting:

Art any more than a steward?

Could Sir Toby possibly come up with a more pointed insult? It is clear in the story by this time that Malvolio thinks of himself as more than "just" a servant. He is Olivia's right-hand man; he runs the household and gives advice; and he believes that Olivia values him as such. So for Sir Toby, a knight and a nobleman, to snap back "Do you think you're anything more than a servant?!" is instantly degrading to Malvolio. And then of course, comes the remarkable epigram:

Dost thou think, because thou art virtuous, there shall be no more cakes and ale?

This is one of those moments when Shakespeare manages to crystallize an entire worldview into a few words. In this case, it's the concept of duty versus freedom, rules versus license, virtue versus cakes and ale. It is part of Sir Toby's campaign in favor of the good life against the encroachment of death; the life of the artist versus a life unlived. The phrase *cakes and ale* has entered into our consciousness as if it were part of our vocabulary, and it even became the title of a best-selling novel published in 1930 by Somerset Maugham.

Epigrams

An epigram is a short, witty statement, often satirical, often depending on paradox for its effect. (Another word for it is *aphorism*.) The *cakes and ale* sentence is a perfect example of an epigram.

You should point out to your children that Shakespeare's ability to create epigrams and weave them seamlessly into the dialogue of his plays is a significant, often undervalued aspect of the poet's genius. Often when we

Twelfth Night at the Chichester Festival Theatre, with Paul Shelley as Sir Toby Belch, Patrick Stewart as Malvolio, and Michael Feast as Feste

talk about Shakespeare, we discuss those complex aspects of his art that we study in school: his imagery, his symbolism, his themes, his meaning. But a more down-to-earth aspect of his genius is this extraordinary ability to crystallize thoughts into memorable phrases:

> *All that glitters is not gold.*
>
> *Parting is such sweet sorrow.*
>
> *Speak low if you speak love.*
>
> *Brevity is the soul of wit.*
>
> *Neither a borrower nor a lender be.*
>
> *Screw your courage to the sticking place.*
>
> *Love sought is good, but given unsought is better.*
>
> *The lady doth protest too much.*
>
> *Frailty, thy name is woman.*
>
> *Fair is foul and foul is fair.*
>
> *A rose by any other word would smell as sweet.*
>
> *The better part of valor is discretion.*
>
> *It is a wise father that knows his own child.*

There are hundreds of them. Sometimes Shakespeare borrows the ideas from other writers. Sometimes he repeats ideas. And sometimes Shakespeare's epigrams take the form of longer sentences, no less memorable than the shorter ones:

> *There is a tide in the affairs of men,*
> *Which, taken at the flood, leads on to fortune.*

> *Men are April when they woo, December when they wed: maids are*
> *May when they are maids, but the sky changes when they are wives.*

The point is that Shakespeare is brilliantly quotable in the best sense of the word.

Epigram Exercise

Ask your children to come up with a Shakespeare-like epigram. You could do it around the dinner table, and you could give them various topics to get things started:

- **The young are sometimes wiser than older people.**
- **Love can come upon us quickly.**
- **Love is better when it takes time to happen.**
- **Taking chances is the best way to live your life.**
- **Most people are essentially good.**

These are the kinds of ideas that Shakespeare would turn into memorable sayings in the context of his plays. After your children try it, you should too, and then compare the results. In our household it has given us a greater appreciation of Shakespeare's genius.

CHAPTER 16

The Malvolio Plot

The Malvolio Plot in *Twelfth Night* is a virtually separate story from the Viola Plot, and it begins just after the *cakes and ale* moment. When Malvolio leaves the room after criticizing Sir Toby, the housemaid Maria comes up with a plan to get revenge: She'll write a love letter to Malvolio, sign it "Olivia," and drop it somewhere that Malvolio will find it. She also suggests that Sir Toby and Sir Andrew should watch Malvolio from a hiding place when he finds the letter, and that is exactly what happens two scenes later.

Tip for Budding Dramatists

Shakespeare, particularly in his comedies, uses this dramatic construction all the time. He has a character tell another character about something he's *going* to do, and then he does it just the way he said he would. By setting up major comic scenes this way, Shakespeare accomplishes two things: He keeps the action crystal clear, and he adds a level of comedy that is fueled by our anticipation of what's going to happen.

The Letter Scene

The next morning we see Malvolio walking in the garden, talking to himself about how wonderful it would feel to become "Count Malvolio" by marrying Olivia. Then he spies Maria's letter on the ground and says:

MALVOLIO

What employment have we here? . . . (taking up the letter) By my life, this is my lady's hand! These be her very c's, her u's, and her t's, and thus makes she her great P's.

P for *pee* is a low joke, but a very good one because it's so unexpected, and it never fails to get a big laugh in the theater.

Malvolio proceeds to read the letter aloud, and sure enough, he believes it's from Olivia. In it, to his delight, he discovers (1) that "Olivia" is in love with him, and (2) that she would love him all the more if he did three things: smiled more, wore yellow stockings, and wore his leggings cross-gartered, a fashion whereby your garters were crisscrossed up the leg.

Needless to say, a few scenes later Malvolio appears before Olivia in yellow stockings, cross-gartered, and smiling as widely as his face will allow. Have your children act out the scene:

OLIVIA

How now, Malvolio?

MALVOLIO

Sweet lady, ho, ho!

OLIVIA

Smil'st thou? I sent for thee upon a sad occasion.

MALVOLIO

Sad, lady? I could be sad. This does make some obstruction in the blood, this cross-gartering, but what of that? . . .

OLIVIA

Why, how dost thou, man? What is the matter with thee?

Twelfth Night at the Donmar West End at Wyndham's Theatre, with Derek Jacobi as Malvolio

MALVOLIO

Not black in my mind, though yellow in my legs . . .

OLIVIA

Wilt thou go to bed, Malvolio?

MALVOLIO

To bed? "Ay, sweetheart, and I'll come to thee."

OLIVIA

God comfort thee!

At which point, Olivia is convinced that Malvolio has gone insane and puts him in the care of Sir Toby.

The next twist is a darker one: Sir Toby takes advantage of the situation and has Malvolio bound and put into a dark room. There he is tormented by Feste, the jester, who is dressed as a priest. Finally, at the end

Twelfth Night at the Westport Country Playhouse, with David Adkins as Malvolio crossgartered

of the play, Malvolio complains bitterly to Olivia of his unfair treatment. She realizes that he has been put upon and promises him justice, but the much-abused man storms off bellowing

I'll be revenged on the whole pack of you!

Comedy is balanced by tragedy, and life is balanced by death. To use one of Shakespeare's favorite images, the wheel of fortune is always turning.

CHAPTER 17

Passage 9
Carpe Diem

What is love? 'Tis not hereafter.
Present mirth hath present laughter.
What's to come is still unsure.
In delay there lies no plenty,
Then come kiss me, sweet and twenty.
Youth's a stuff will not endure.

(*Twelfth Night*, Act II, Scene 3, lines 48–53)

Earlier we examined the opening speech of *Twelfth Night* (*If music be the food of love, play on* . . .) and discovered that most of the play's major themes are referred to in those first eight lines: love, appetite, surfeiting, dying. One additional theme is suggested by the opening speech, and it is arguably the most interesting of all:

Enough; no more.
'Tis not so sweet now as it was before.

This theme might be described as "enjoy things while you're young and able to enjoy them, because they won't last forever." "Carpe diem," as the Latin poet Horace put it around 20 B.C. "Seize the day." Shakespeare will emphasize this theme again and again in *Twelfth Night*, most clearly in a song sung by Feste, the wise fool.

In Act II, Scene 3, a moment before Malvolio bursts into the room in his nightshirt (*My masters, are you mad?*), Sir Toby and Sir Andrew ask Feste for a love song, and Feste sings

> *What is love? 'Tis not hereafter.*
> *Present mirth hath present laughter.*
> > *What's to come is still [always] unsure.*
> *In delay there lies no plenty,*
> *Then come kiss me, sweet and twenty.*
> > *Youth's a stuff will not endure.*

Could Shakespeare have made his theme more explicit? *What's to come is still unsure. In delay there lies no plenty, . . . Youth's a stuff will not endure.* This wistful theme will pervade the play and lend the otherwise riotous proceedings an air of ruefulness and weight.

With its strong four-beat rhythm and easy rhymes, your children should try learning this passage a whole line at a time.

> *What is love? 'Tis not hereafter.*
> *Present mirth hath present laughter.*
> *What's to come is still unsure.*

Still in Shakespeare means "always." So the line means "What's to come is always unsure."

> *What's to come is still unsure.*
> *In delay there lies no plenty,*

Plenty in this context means "reward." So the line means "There's no reward for delaying things."

Twelfth Night at the Open Air Theatre, Regent's Park, with Janie Dee as Olivia and Clive Rowe as Feste

> *In delay there lies no plenty,*
> *Then come kiss me, sweet and twenty.*

Here *sweet and twenty* is a metaphor for a sweet young woman. It's as if he's saying:

> Then come kiss me, sweet young woman.

One of Shakespeare's most beautiful verbal ingenuities is to turn adjectives into nouns. *Sweet* and *twenty* are adjectives describing a woman, but Shakespeare turns them into nouns identifying her. (The technical term for a metaphor where something closely associated with a subject is substituted for it is *metonymy*.)

> *Then come kiss me, sweet and twenty.*
> *Youth's a stuff will not endure.*

Meaning "Youth is something that won't last." This line contains two abbreviations that allow the line to scan—that is, to be read with the proper number of rhythmical beats (in this case four). First, he shortens *is* to *'s*. Second, he leaves out the word *that*. If he said,

Youth is a stuff that will not endure,

then the line, in addition to being ungainly, wouldn't be in four beats like the rest of the lyric. Shakespeare turns it into a thing of beauty with a contraction and an omission.

       ∧   ∧   ∧   ∧
YOUTH'S a STUFF will NOT enDURE.

Every writer in the world would give his right arm to write a line like that, indeed, to write any of the lines in this lyric. It's the kind of simple, straightforward, philosophical, and calmly beautiful passage that your children will want to hold on to forever.

CHAPTER 18

Passage 10
Sisters and Brothers

VIOLA / CESARIO

My father had a daughter loved a man
As it might be, perhaps, were I a woman,
I should your Lordship.

ORSINO

And what's her history?

VIOLA / CESARIO

A blank, my lord. She never told her love,
But let concealment like a worm i' th' bud,
Feed on her damask cheek. She pined in thought,
And with a green and yellow melancholy
She sat like Patience on a monument,
Smiling at grief. Was not this love indeed? . . .

ORSINO

But died thy sister of her love, my boy?

VIOLA / CESARIO

I am all the daughters of my father's house,
And all the brothers, too—and yet I know not.

(*Twelfth Night*, Act II, Scene 4, lines 118ff.)

The melancholy tone of the lyric your children memorized in the last chapter is reflected throughout much of *Twelfth Night*, nowhere more touchingly than in a short exchange between Cesario and Orsino in Act II, Scene 4. This is one of the earliest passages that I taught my children, and it has become a family favorite.

The setup is simple: Orsino and Cesario are discussing whether women can ever be as faithful and true as men when it comes to love. Cesario insists that they can and tells the following story to illustrate the point.

> *My father had a daughter loved a man*
> *As it might be, perhaps, were I a woman,*
> *I should your lordship.*

Remember, we in the audience know that Cesario is really Viola and that Viola has fallen in love with Orsino, so when she refers to her "father's daughter," we know that she means herself. Point out to your children the beautiful placement of the word *perhaps*, which gives the actor such a strong hint about how to play the scene:

> *My father had a daughter loved a man*
> *As it might be,*
> > *perhaps,*
> > > *were I a woman,*
> *I should your lordship.*
>
> *And what's her history?*
>
> *A blank, my lord. She never told her love,*
> *But let concealment like a worm i' th' bud,*
> *Feed on her damask [rosy] cheek.*

Her sister's history is a blank because Viola is feeling that her own history is a blank. She has lost a brother, and she is in love with a man who doesn't know it. And like her "sister," she can't tell her beloved what she feels.

A blank, my lord. She never told her love,
But let concealment like a worm i' th' bud,
Feed on her damask cheek.

She pined in thought,
And with a green and yellow melancholy
She sat like Patience on a monument,
Smiling at grief. Was not this love indeed?

Obviously this passage is filled with ambiguities. Why is her melancholy green and yellow? What exactly is Patience on a monument? I find these lines to be hauntingly beautiful, and I think it's because they're so ambiguous.

But died thy sister of her love, my boy?

I am all the daughters of my father's house,
And all the brothers, too—and yet I know not.

Notice how Viola refers to *brothers* at the end of the passage. If she is *all the brothers* of her father's house, then she must believe that her brother died in the shipwreck. But then she adds *and yet I know not*. With that twist of the sentence, she seems to be holding out some hope that perhaps her brother is still alive—and that hope, for me, makes the passage all the more moving. Her brother is still at the forefront of her mind, and as we'll be discussing as we tackle our next passage together, their brother-sister relationship is the very backbone of the play.

Quotation Page Reminder

Please remember that as your children memorize these and the other passages in this book, they should have the Quotation Pages in front of them. While some of these passages (Passage 9, for example) aren't difficult to memorize because of their length and content, the current passage is much more complex, and the Quotation Pages will help your children *enormously* with memorizing it. Let's look at one of the Quotation Pages for the current passage as an example:

VIOLA/CESARIO

My father had a daughter loved a man
As it might be,

       perhaps,

            were I a woman,

I should your lordship.

ORSINO

      And what's her history?

VIOLA/CESARIO

A blank, my lord.
        She never told her love,

But let concealment
        like a worm i' th' bud,

Feed on her damask cheek.

The Quotation Pages simplify the process in a number of ways. First, just by being in large, distinctive print, they make the words less daunting. Second, they separate the sentences and thoughts onto different pages, so that your children memorize the passage in accessible chunks. Third, each page contains formatting that makes each sentence easy and logical. For example, on the first page, by isolating the word *perhaps*, it reminds us to pause, which simplifies what is otherwise a very complex sentence.

So don't forget to go to howtoteachyourchildrenshakespeare.com to print out the Quotation Pages for all the passages in the book. Then— you know the drill: quiet room, no embarrassment, out loud, repetition. I'll remind you only one more time, later in the book, when you're least expecting it.

CHAPTER 19

Passage 11
Do Not Embrace Me

ORSINO

One face, one voice, one habit, and two persons!
A natural perspective, that is and is not!

ANTONIO

An apple cleft in two is not more twin
Than these two creatures. Which is Sebastian?

OLIVIA

Most wonderful!

VIOLA

If nothing lets to make us happy both
But this my masculine usurped attire,
Do not embrace me till each circumstance
Of place, time, fortune, do cohere and jump
That I am Viola.

(*Twelfth Night*, Act V, Scene 1, lines 226 ff.)

This passage never fails to raise a lump in my throat. To understand why it is so touching requires some background. It occurs in the final scene of the play and pulls everything in the Viola Plot together.

Up to this point, a great deal of confusion has been caused by Sebastian's arrival in Illyria. Sebastian, as you know, is Viola's twin brother, and each sibling thinks the other was drowned in a shipwreck. Because Sebastian and Viola look identical, they get taken for each other by all the other characters in the play.

In the final scene, Shakespeare brings all the characters together on-stage, raises the confusion to a dizzying height, then resolves all the plot-lines at the same time. The scene begins with Orsino and Cesario arriving at Olivia's estate. Then, one after another, Antonio, Olivia, Sir Toby, and Sir Andrew arrive, and each has a different story about the treachery of this boy Cesario. Finally, when the confusion has reached a fever pitch, Shakespeare brings Sebastian onto the scene—and suddenly there are two identical human beings on the stage together. Identical. You can't tell them apart.

At which point, everything stops dead.

No one moves.

Then Orsino exclaims:

> *One face, one voice, one habit* [outfit], *and two persons!*
> *A natural perspective, that is and is not!*

In those days, a *perspective* was an optical device made with mirrors that helped artists see visual scenes in proper proportions; and so a *natural perspective* means an optical illusion created naturally without mirrors. And now we have a list:

face,
voice,
habit,
persons.

Repeat it with your children over and over.

face,
voice,
habit,
persons.

One face, one voice, one habit, and two persons!
A natural perspective, that is and is not!

Then Antonio says:

How have you made division of yourself?
An apple cleft in two is not more twin
Than these two creatures. Which is Sebastian?

Antonio is reminding us as clearly as possible that the two creatures in front of him look absolutely identical. Orsino has just said it with his *one face, one voice* speech, and Antonio repeats the idea:

An apple cleft in two is not more twin
Than these two creatures.
  Which is Sebastian?

Shakespeare does not repeat things idly. He is doing it for a reason. In any live production, the two actors in front of us will not actually look identical. They will probably not be related in real life,

An apple cleft in two

and even if they were—even if they were twins—they wouldn't be identical because twins of different sexes are never identical. However, we, the audience, must imagine that they look identical because the other characters onstage are seeing them that way. And in order to make the audience believe that they are identical, Shakespeare has his characters say it twice.

And now comes what is usually the biggest laugh in the whole play. Olivia has just become betrothed to Sebastian, and she's crazy about him. Now, suddenly, from her point of view, there are *two* Sebastians. Her life is about to become doubly happy and pleasurable. So what does she cry?

Most wonderful!

At this point, Viola and Sebastian see each other. In the theater, this moment can, and should, be electrifying. The whole play has been moving toward this moment from the beginning. The first to speak is Sebastian:

SEBASTIAN

Do I stand there? I never had a brother,
Nor can there be that deity in my nature
Of here and everywhere. I had a sister,
Whom the blind waves and surges have devoured.
Of charity, what kin are you to me?
What countryman? What name? What parentage? . . .
Were you a woman, as the rest goes even,
I should my tears let fall upon your cheek
And say "Thrice welcome, drownèd Viola."

This is a tricky passage to understand, so let's parse it out together for your children. I want them to be able to recite it and understand it before we're through. (They needn't memorize it.)

Do I stand there? I never had a brother,
Nor can there be that deity in my nature
Of here and everywhere.

Deity here means "godliness." So Sebastian is saying: "There is nothing in my nature that is like a god, so therefore I can't split myself in two and be both here and over there at the same time!"

I had a sister,
Whom the blind waves and surges have devoured.

The *blind waves and surges* are the watery storm that capsized the ship. Equally, *devoured* is a wonderful word in this context. If Shakespeare had used *drowned* instead, it would not have filled out the metrical line as well and would not have been as powerful.

Sebastian continues:

Of charity [out of charity], *what kin are you to me?*
What countryman? What name? What parentage? . . .
Were you a woman, as the rest goes even,
I should my tears let fall upon your cheek
And say "Thrice welcome, drownèd Viola."

Sebastian is doing a lot of talking here when, logically, he would take one look at his long-lost sister, run to her, and throw his arms around her. But there is something bigger going on. Shakespeare is doing something that all writers try to do effectively: He is pulling the string.

PULLING THE STRING?

What I mean is that Shakespeare is stretching out the conclusion for as long as possible until the final revelation. By this time in the story, Sebastian would realize in any normal sense of reality that this person standing in front of him is his sister. He has adored her since they were children. He knows exactly what she looks like. At most she's wearing trousers and a shirt and has her hair pinned up under a cap. Otherwise it's good old Viola. But Shakespeare doesn't let Sebastian verbalize that realization until lines and lines of poetry have gone by. (I have cut the passage down for purposes of discussion. In fact, there are forty-six lines from the moment Sebastian enters until Viola cries *I am Viola.*)

Shakespeare holds it off because we, as the audience, receive a sort of exquisite pleasure by having to wait for it. We see this phenomenon frequently in the movies. We've known from the beginning that the two gorgeous leads will end up together, but the writer holds off the final explosion of joy until the last possible second because that's what romantic comedy is all about. It's the same with romantic novels. In Jane Austen's *Emma,* will Emma and Mr. Knightley get together at the end? Of course they will, but that's the beauty of a good love story: The author holds off the final partnering until the last possible moment.

That brings us to the other startling feature of *Twelfth Night.* It's a comedy and it's romantic; but it's not about a romantic couple. The central love story is about a brother and sister.

The required "love interest" plot involves Viola and Orsino—but there is virtually no dramatic tension in their story. Viola reveals that she loves Orsino almost as an afterthought, at the end of their first, short, business-like scene together (Act I, Scene 4). Likewise, while Olivia is head over heels in love with "Cesario," we know that Cesario is really a woman and that Olivia has a different kind of romance in mind. However, there is a genuine love story in the middle of *Twelfth Night*, and it's the story of Viola and her brother Sebastian.

> *Were you a woman, as the rest goes even,*
> *I should my tears let fall upon your cheek*
> *And say "Thrice welcome, drownèd Viola."*

As the rest goes even means "since everything else fits together." So Sebastian is saying

> Since everything else fits together, if you were a woman I'd understand
> everything that's going on. I'd embrace you and let my tears fall on
> your cheek and I'd cry "My sister! You're not really drowned!"

Once again, Shakespeare says it a little better than I just did.

> *Were you a woman, as the rest goes even,*
> *I should my tears let fall upon your cheek*
> *And say "Thrice welcome, drownèd Viola."*

And now we come to the best part of the passage: the big revelation.

VIOLA
If nothing lets to make us happy both
But this my masculine usurped attire,
Do not embrace me till each circumstance
Of place, time, fortune, do cohere and jump
That I am Viola.

If nothing lets means "If nothing prevents us." *Masculine usurped attire* means "manly, borrowed clothing." *Cohere and jump* means "agree." So the sentence means

> If nothing is preventing us both from being happy but my borrowed manly clothes, don't embrace me until everything that's going on— this place, this time, and my fortune—adds up and proves that I'm Viola!

Have your children take it a phrase at a time:

> *If nothing lets*
> > *to make us happy both*
> *But this*
> > *my masculine usurped attire,*
> *Do not embrace me*
> > *till each circumstance*
> *Of place, time, fortune,*
> > *do cohere and jump*
> *That I am Viola.*

What I find so unusually touching about this passage is twofold. First, I find Viola so vulnerable, so intelligent, so loving, and so hopeful that I'm rooting for her in a very deep, personal way. I desperately want her to find both her brother and that happiness that she has longed for since the moment we met her. Second, I find it very moving that this rich, complex, intricate play has pulled all its many plotlines and characters and emotions together into one final moment with such perfection.

Dr. Johnson said that *Twelfth Night* "is in the graver part elegant and easy, and in . . . the lighter scenes exquisitely humorous." If there is any such thing as a "perfect play," I think it is this one.

CHAPTER 20

Passage 12
Juliet in Love

(Juliet enters on the balcony, above)

ROMEO

But soft, what light through yonder window breaks?
It is the East, and Juliet is the sun.
Arise, fair sun, and kill the envious moon,
Who is already sick and pale with grief
That thou, her maid, art far more fair than she. . . .
It is my lady. O, it is my love! . . .
See how she leans her cheek upon her hand.
O, that I were a glove upon that hand,
That I might touch that cheek!

JULIET

O, Romeo, Romeo, wherefore art thou Romeo?
Deny thy father and refuse thy name,
Or, if thou wilt not, be but sworn my love,
And I'll no longer be a Capulet.

ROMEO

(aside)
Shall I hear more, or shall I speak at this?

JULIET

'Tis but thy name that is my enemy.
Thou art thyself, though not a Montague.
What's Montague? . . . O, be some other name!

What's in a name? That which we call a rose
By any other word would smell as sweet.

(*Romeo and Juliet,*
Act II, Scene 2, lines 1ff.)

*R*omeo *and Juliet* is the most popular play in the entire world, and
the passage above is as well known as anything ever written. It
epitomizes what we love best about Shakespeare: his language, his
characters, and in this case, probably the most enduring plot in our culture. If there was ever a literary passage that was part of the cultural DNA
of the Western experience, this is it.

One of the most remarkable things about the play is its tone, which
is unlike that of Shakespeare's other tragedies. The other tragedies are
about troubled, towering spirits, enshrouded by self-doubts, ambition, or
the uncertainties of old age. Think of *Hamlet* and *Othello, Macbeth* and
King Lear, all of them anchored by tragic heroes in troubled worlds. Their
tragedies seem inevitable from the start. *Romeo and Juliet* is different: The
first two acts play like an exuberant romantic comedy, melodramatic to
be sure, but youthful and glittering, filled with dazzling flights of language
about the breathlessness of being in love.

As your children may know already, the story is about two teenagers
who fall desperately in love with each other despite the fact that their
families are at odds. Juliet is a Capulet, Romeo a Montague, and your children should remember these names as they memorize the passage above. It
is never explained why the Capulets and the Montagues are feuding, but
the play opens with out-and-out street warfare between the two clans, and
this violent animosity becomes part of the play's continuing action.

Indeed, the theme of the play might be described as the interaction
between love and violence. These two mighty opposites meet head-on in
Romeo and Juliet, and neither one is the clear winner: Both teenagers are
claimed by violent death, and yet we sense that love has triumphed in
the end.

The play is a compelling yet lyrical interplay between Venus, the goddess of love, and Mars, the god of war, which has been a recurring theme of Western culture since Homer told the story of a Trojan War touched off by the love affair of Paris and Helen. One of my own favorite examples of this theme is the exquisite painting *Venus and Mars*, by Sandro Botticelli, that hangs in the National Gallery of Art in London. The painting, created in 1483, shows Venus in triumph. But one senses, looking carefully at the picture, that the god of war is not to be trifled with.

Venus and Mars by Botticelli

In *Romeo and Juliet*, Juliet's parents want her to marry a nobleman named Paris, and they virtually force her into agreement against her will. Romeo, in turn, would be ostracized by his family if it were known that he's in love with a Capulet. Romeo and Juliet feel alone in a world that doesn't understand them. Is it any wonder that this play appeals so strongly to our children? What teenager doesn't believe that he is misunderstood—that his parental figures are standing in the way of what he or she wants most? For my own children, *Romeo and Juliet* was the quintessential example of a story that helped them put their own anxieties and secret longings into perspective.

Romeo

Romeo and Juliet meet at a masked ball held by the Capulets. Romeo has not been invited, of course—he's a Montague. But he sneaks into the party with some of his friends, and the lightning-bolt moment occurs when he first sees Juliet across the dance floor. The instant he sees her, he exclaims,

O, she doth teach the torches to burn bright!
It seems she hangs upon the cheek of night
As rich as a jewel in an Ethiop's ear—
Beauty too rich for use, for earth too dear.

Here Shakespeare gives us a hint of what's to come: If Juliet's beauty is too dear for the Earth, then her beauty—and the love it engenders—can exist only in some other world, a world past ordinary existence, a world like heaven. She, and her love for Romeo, are too pure for the everyday world.

This speech also gives us one of the recurring images of the play: light versus dark, brightness versus night. Romeo and Juliet's love will flash across the heavens like lightning in the night sky—quickly, with intense brightness, soon to be consumed by darkness. Thus, later in the scene, Juliet warns that their love frightens her because

It is too rash, too unadvised, too sudden,
Too like the lightning, which doth cease to be
Ere one can say "It lightens."

Remind your children of the lines they heard in *A Midsummer Night's Dream: Brief as the lightning in the collied night . . . / So quick bright things come to confusion.* (The two plays were written within a year of each other.)

After the dance, Romeo lingers. He is so in love with Juliet that he can't bear to leave the Capulets' estate, so he eludes his friends and climbs into the garden under Juliet's balcony. A moment later Juliet appears. Romeo sees her and cries out to himself:

But soft, what light through yonder window breaks?

But soft means "But hold," and *yonder* means distant.

But soft, what light through yonder window breaks?

It is the East, and Juliet is the sun.
Arise, fair sun, and kill the envious moon,

Romeo is comparing Juliet to the sun, as though she were creating the light that has just spread across the garden. He then contrasts the sun with the moon. As your children know from A *Midsummer Night's Dream*, the moon is a symbol of romance. Yet Juliet is so beautiful that the romantic moon is envious of her. Have your children break the lines into phrases and memorize them one at a time:

> It is the East,
>> and Juliet is the sun.
> Arise, fair sun [i.e., Juliet],
>> and kill the envious moon,
>
> Who is already sick and pale with grief
> That thou, her maid, art far more fair [beautiful] than she.

The moon is so jealous that it is sick and has turned pale. Turn these lines into a game: "Why is the moon sick and pale with grief?" Because her maid, the sun, and by extension Juliet, is more beautiful than she is. Juliet is more beautiful than the moon itself!

> Arise, fair sun, and kill the envious moon,
> Who is already sick and pale with grief
> That thou, her maid, art far more fair than she.

Have your son or daughter really act out the next four lines. Romeo is alive with love. He is tingling with emotions. His words are bright, and they sound as clear as a trumpet call:

> It is my lady. O, it is my love!
>
> See how she leans her cheek upon her hand.
> O, that I were a glove upon that hand,
> That I might touch that cheek!

The metaphor here is beautiful in its simplicity. If he were her glove, he could be touching her cheek. He is besotted.

O, that I were a glove upon that hand,
That I might touch that cheek!

Juliet

And now it's Juliet's turn.

O, Romeo, Romeo, wherefore art thou Romeo?

Ask your children what this line means. I'll bet they get it wrong. My guess is that they'll say it means "Where are you, Romeo?" But it doesn't mean that at all. In Elizabethan times, the word *wherefore* meant "why." So Juliet is saying, "O, Romeo, Romeo, why do you have to be named *Romeo*—and therefore a Montague!"

O, Romeo, Romeo, wherefore art thou Romeo?

"O, Romeo, Romeo, why are you Romeo?!" Notice that there is no comma after the word *thou*.

Deny thy father and refuse thy name,
Or, if thou wilt not, be but sworn my love,
And I'll no longer be a Capulet.

In other words, "Deny your heritage and renounce your name. Or, if you won't do that, but if you will swear to be my love [*be but sworn my love*], then I'll renounce *my* name and no longer be a Capulet."

Deny thy father and refuse thy name,
Or, if thou wilt not, be but sworn my love,
And I'll no longer be a Capulet.

Meanwhile, Romeo is down below and says to himself

Shall I hear more, or shall I speak at this?

Juliet continues:

> 'Tis but thy name that is my enemy.
> . . . O, be some other name!
> What's in a name! That which we call a rose
> By any other word would smell as sweet.

Have your children break this section down into three parts and learn them one at a time.

> 'Tis but thy name that is my enemy.
> . . . O, be some other name!
> What's in a name!
> That which we call a rose
> By any other word would smell as sweet.

The last phrase has become one of the most famous epigrams of all time (though it is usually misquoted):

> a rose by any other word would smell as sweet.

The Rest of the Story

After the Balcony Scene, the story moves ahead at a remarkably speedy clip. That is one of the hallmarks of this play: It rushes forward—like young love—and never stops till the end. (In all the canon, only *Macbeth* has this same sense of relentless self-propulsion.)

The day after they swear their love on the balcony, the lovers are secretly married by a well-meaning friend of Romeo, Friar Laurence. The Marriage Scene ends Act II; and up until this time, the play reads like a comedy. Unfortunately for the lovers, however, events soon turn more dangerous.

Romeo meets his best friend, the volatile Mercutio, on the street, and a moment later Juliet's surly cousin Tybalt walks by. Tybalt provokes a fight and kills Mercutio. Romeo is so angry that he grabs a sword, challenges

Tybalt, and kills him—Juliet's cousin—at which point the Prince, tired of all the feuding, banishes Romeo from Verona.

That night in Juliet's bedroom, Romeo and Juliet consummate their marriage. But the next morning Romeo flees, and the lovers have little hope of ever seeing each other again. To make matters worse, Juliet's parents insist that she marry Paris in just three days' time. Friar Laurence, however, has a plan. He will give Juliet a potion to make her appear dead on the morning of her wedding; then he will get word of the trick to Romeo, and Romeo will arrive at the Capulet tomb and carry Juliet off forever. Needless to say, the plan goes awry.

Romeo never gets word of the potion. When he arrives at the tomb and finds Juliet "dead," he kills Paris, then kills himself. Then Juliet awakes, sees Romeo dead, and kills herself. The final moments of the play find the parents of the deceased lovers vowing to end their senseless feud.

Juliet's Love

Romeo and Juliet is filled with glittering language. It is Shakespeare at his most youthfully exuberant, his poetry filled with rhymes and puns and extravagant images that only a young man would dare employ so unself-consciously. For example, in the balcony scene, Juliet says to Romeo:

> My bounty is as boundless as the sea,
> My love as deep; the more I give to thee,
> The more I have, for both are infinite.

Throughout the play we witness ideas and imagery, rhythm and sound, uniting to create love poetry as beautiful as any that has ever been written. As Northrop Frye puts it, the moment Romeo and Juliet meet, "The God of Love . . . has swooped down on two perhaps rather commonplace adolescents and blasted them into another dimension."

Shakespeare has a magnificent way of showing us how it happens, and he does it, naturally, through language. Before Juliet meets Romeo, she speaks with the simple correctness of a proper young lady. In an early scene, for example, Juliet's mother asks her how she would feel about getting married, and Juliet answers without passion:

It is an honor that I dream not of.

Then comes the sea change. After the lovers are married, Juliet's voice becomes urgent with sexual desire. It almost sizzles off the page. Here is Juliet as she waits for Romeo to join her in her room after the wedding.

Gallop apace, you fiery-footed steeds,
Towards Phoebus' lodging: such a wagoner
As Phaethon would whip you to the west,
And bring in cloudy night immediately.

A *steed* is a horse; *Phoebus* is the sun god; a *wagoner* is a charioteer; and *Phaethon* was the son of Phoebus who was allowed to drive the chariot of the sun, then lost control of the runaway horses. Juliet's desire is galloping

Franco Zeffirelli's *Romeo and Juliet*, with Leonard Whiting as Romeo and Olivia Hussey as Juliet

and out of control, which is just what she hopes from the horses of the sun, so that they'll rush home and allow night to arrive.

In another part of the speech, she says that when Romeo dies, night should cut him into little stars because his brightness will make heaven look all the finer by contrast:

> Come, gentle night, come, loving, black-brow'd night,
> Give me my Romeo; and, when he shall die,
> Take him and cut him out in little stars,
> And he will make the face of heaven so fine
> That all the world will be in love with night
> And pay no worship to the garish sun.

Dazzling words coupled with remarkable thoughts. This is young Shakespeare's first masterpiece.

CHAPTER 21

Shakespeare's Life and an Overview of His Work

S hakespeare" has become such an icon for the ages, representing all that is considered literate, intellectual, and stage-worthy in our civilization, that it is easy to forget that the man himself lived a fairly normal life, at least externally. (Internally he must have lived a thousand lives, and that, in a sense, is the subject of this book.) He was born in the town of Stratford-upon-Avon in south-central England in 1564, and he died there in 1616 at the age of fifty-two.

1564–1616

Urge your children to memorize these dates. Repeat them aloud together several times. Skip a day and then go back to them. They represent the high point of the English Renaissance. They're also connected to the Renaissance in Europe: Galileo was also born in 1564, Michelangelo died in 1564, and Cervantes died in 1616.

1564–1616

These dates will be useful reference points for your children for the rest of their lives.

The specific date of Shakespeare's birth is said to be April 23, 1564, but there is no record of the exact day. We do know that he was baptized at Holy Trinity Church in Stratford on April 26, 1564; and since baptism in those days took place two to three days after birth, April 23 has been assumed to be the date of Shakespeare's birth. The choice is also symbolic: Shakespeare died on April 23, 1616 (fifty-two years later to the day), and the patron saint of England is Saint George, whose saint's day is also April 23.

True Story

Several years ago one of my plays was about to go into rehearsal at a studio of the Royal Shakespeare Company in suburban London. As we approached the door of the studio, the director turned to me and said, "Unlock the door." I looked at the lock and saw that it was one of those square silver boxes with rows of numbered buttons that you have to push in the proper sequence. I looked to the director for guidance, but he just waited patiently. This was a test. I thought for a moment and then pushed

0 4 2 3 1 5 6 4

April 23, 1564

The door sprang open, the director raised an eyebrow in approval, and we began the rehearsal.

Shakespeare's Early Life

Stratford-upon-Avon at the time of Shakespeare's birth was a prosperous market town of approximately eighteen hundred people. Shakespeare's father, John Shakespeare, was a glove maker by trade, and Shakespeare was one of seven children, two of whom died in infancy. Because John Shakespeare was a bailiff (who functioned as a kind of mayor) of Stratford when William was a youngster, we can be fairly certain that the boy attended the town's grammar school from the age of five or six. At King Edward's Grammar School, which can be visited to this day, Shakespeare would have attended classes six days a week learning Latin grammar and literature, then debate and rhetoric, and finally some Greek, from a series of teachers who were trained at Oxford University.

The school, of course, was for boys only, as were virtually all schools in the seventeenth century, and one of the school treats for the boys was to put on plays in Latin by ancient Roman authors. Certainly this was one of Shakespeare's earliest encounters with the world of drama, and it is pleasing to assume that one play in which he performed was *The Menaechmi* by the Roman comic playwright Plautus. *The Menaechmi* is about twin brothers who are so identical that they cause untold confusion for a town full of colorful characters. Shakespeare based one of his earliest plays, *The Comedy of Errors,* on this plot; only Shakespeare did Plautus one better: He created two pairs of identical twin brothers, thereby doubling the comedy and the confusion. *The Comedy of Errors* is a perfect comedy for children since it relies less on subtlety than on classic elements of farce like mistaken identity and slapstick. It is also, by any measure, the shortest play Shakespeare ever wrote, so it is particularly good for younger children.

We can readily perceive from a survey of his plays that Shakespeare was a voracious reader. His favorite book seems to have been Ovid's *Metamorphoses,* a collection of Roman mythological tales emphasizing transformation. A number of his plays and poems are based on Ovid's stories, and approximately 90 percent of all of Shakespeare's allusions to classical mythology refer to stories in *Metamorphoses.* Shakespeare also read widely in Virgil and Horace in Latin; Chaucer, Gower, and Spenser in English; and Petrarch and Boccaccio in Italian. In addition, he read a great deal of history in both English and Latin; and he seems to have spoken French with some proficiency—at least enough to write exchanges in French into some of his plays. In other words, despite never attending a university, Shakespeare was very well educated, to put it mildly.

The fact that Shakespeare's father was a bailiff of Stratford also means that Shakespeare must have seen performances by the professional acting companies that visited Stratford throughout his boyhood. This was precisely the period of English history when playwriting and playgoing were on the rise; and as new theaters were being built in London, so too bands of players roamed the countryside, bringing theater to market towns throughout England. As one distinguished historian puts it, "By the end of the century, theater-going had developed into a craze."

Shakespeare's Mature Years

When he was eighteen, Shakespeare married a local woman named Anne Hathaway, who was twenty-six at the time. They had three children: a girl named Susanna, and twins named Hamnet and Judith. Hamnet died at the age of eleven, and while there are no firsthand accounts about how Shakespeare suffered, the plays contain repeated instances where a child dies and is deeply mourned. As for Shakespeare's two daughters, Susanna

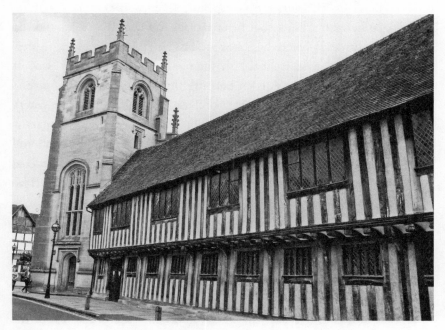

King Edward VI grammar school in Stratford

Chandos portrait of Shakespeare

and Judith both married, but Shakespeare's direct family line died out in 1670.

Compared with other dramatists of the time, we know a great deal about Shakespeare's comings and goings throughout most of his life. We have six of his signatures on legal documents, and we have quite a few records of things like loans, fines, and land acquisitions. We also have a great many contemporaneous references to the man himself, and to his writings, by fellow writers and actors. What we do not have are any diaries or letters that might have told us how Shakespeare felt about things like family and friends. We *almost* had a family recollection of Shakespeare, but it never quite transpired: In 1661 a man named John Ward, the vicar of Stratford-upon-Avon, made a note in his diary that he should visit Judith Quiney, Shakespeare's seventy-six-year-old daughter, and talk to her about her father before it was too late. But he waited too long, and Judith died before he got around to it. This is one of those literary "what ifs" that make the bookish among us grind our teeth in woe. It reminds me of Cassandra Austen burning the majority of Jane Austen's letters after Jane's death, apparently because she didn't want her sister's reputation tarnished.

From 1585 to 1592, when Shakespeare was between twenty-one and twenty-eight, we have no records of him at all. These are called the "lost years," and almost since the time of Shakespeare's death, scholars have speculated about what he was doing in those years. The speculations range from schoolteaching to practicing law to soldiering. In any case, starting in 1592 he begins to emerge in London as a playwright and actor. From this time on he is referred to in letters and other documents, and his name appears on many of the printed texts of his plays and poems.

During the period from 1592 until his retirement in 1613, Shakespeare lived and worked in London with occasional visits to Stratford to see his family. It is impossible to read anything into these domestic arrangements.

Extant signature

Was Shakespeare unhappy at home, and did he flee to London to escape his family? Or was he a devoted father and husband who had to live in London to make a living in the theater? We just don't know. All we really know about Shakespeare the man is that he was referred to more than once by his contemporaries as "gentle" Shakespeare and therefore appears to have been well liked; and that he was a successful businessman who ended up with a good deal of valuable property in Stratford, including one of the two best houses in the town.

When we first hear about Shakespeare after those "lost years" of 1585–92, he is part of a London acting company called The Lord Chamberlain's Men (later called The King's Men). After a few years he became a "sharer," or part owner, of the company; and we know from theater records of the time that he not only wrote plays for his company but also acted in them.

Throughout Shakespeare's career, professional theater was organized around individual companies of players who could perform only under the patronage of the nobility. Thus, The Lord Chamberlain's Men were in service to the Lord Chamberlain and wore his colors to official functions; in exchange, he granted them his protection and a license to perform. It was up to the companies to find their own venues for their performances, and such venues ranged from the courtyards of inns, to town squares, to the newly built permanent outdoor theaters in London with names like the Theatre, the Curtain, the Swan, the Fortune, and the Rose. The Lord Chamberlain's Men performed in many if not all of them.

London also had a few indoor theaters in Shakespeare's day (the most famous was called Blackfriars); and Shakespeare's company was frequently invited to perform at court for Queen Elizabeth, then for her successor, King James.

The interior of the New Globe Theatre

The Globe

We associate Shakespeare with one particular theater in London, the Globe, and the story of how it was constructed is so good that you should stop right now and tell it to your children. A tradesman named James Burbage had the vision to build the first-ever theater in London dedicated solely to housing theatrical productions. It was erected in 1576, and he named it, simply, the Theatre. By 1594 Shakespeare's company was in residence there, and their leading actor was Richard Burbage, James's son. Richard Burbage is a name to be reckoned with: He originated the roles of Richard III, Hamlet, Othello, and King Lear. (Not a bad resumé.)

The Lord Chamberlain's Men seemed destined to remain in the Theatre for years to come, but in 1597 the Burbages found their lease on the underlying land in jeopardy. (Not the theater building, just the land under it.) They tried to negotiate an extension, but the landlord refused to renew. What to do?

Here's where the fun comes in. On the night of December 28, 1598,

Richard Burbage and his brother Cuthbert, as well as other members of the Lord Chamberlain's Men, including, we assume, Shakespeare, dismantled the entire building and transported it southward, timber by timber, across the Thames River. There, in an area called Southwark (pronounced "SUTH-ik"), they reassembled the theater and called it the Globe.

In early 1599, the Globe Theatre opened its doors to the public, where, for the next fourteen years, it housed the premieres of everything from *Hamlet* to *The Tempest*. It burned down in 1613 during a performance of Shakespeare and Fletcher's *All Is True* (also known as *Henry VIII*), but a second Globe was rebuilt soon thereafter. That building was pulled down in about 1644, but tourists and playgoers can now visit a replica of the original Globe, which opened in 1997 only 250 yards from the site of the original.

Shakespeare's Writing

As for Shakespeare's greatest monument, the plays themselves, it is believed today that he wrote a total of thirty-eight (some scholars say thirty-nine or forty), and that a few of the lesser plays, such as *The Two Noble Kinsmen* and *Henry VIII*, were written with collaborators. (In addition, a few of the plays, including *Measure for Measure* and *Macbeth*, may have been altered slightly after Shakespeare's death by a playwright named Thomas Middleton.)

Shakespeare's plays may be seen as falling into four periods, and although these periods are somewhat arbitrary, they are convenient for giving us a sense of Shakespeare's overall output. It is impossible to be precise about the plays' exact dates, but a basic chronology is generally agreed upon. And while the brief descriptions that follow are inevitably glib because they're so short, you should use this list to familiarize yourself with the high points of the canon so that you can answer your children's questions as we proceed. A chronology of all the plays appears at the end of the book.

Exterior of the New Globe Theatre

1590–1594

The first period of Shakespeare's work stretches from about 1590 to 1594, and these early plays include:

- *Henry VI*, which is actually three plays in all, referred to as *Parts 1, 2, and 3*. Here Shakespeare virtually invented the idea of the history play. While these plays are difficult to read, filled as they are with politics and battles, they can be effective onstage.
- *Richard III*, an exuberant study of evil that is surprisingly funny and enormously entertaining. Richard kills everyone who gets in his way to achieving then holding on to the throne of England, but you can't help admiring him for his panache and eloquence.
- *Titus Andronicus*, which is full of gory doings, like a modern horror movie but with better lines.
- *The Two Gentlemen of Verona*, the least successful of Shakespeare's comedies, but the first time he has a woman dress up as a young man. It also includes good roles for a dog named Crab and his master Launce.
- *The Comedy of Errors*, about two pairs of identical twins—one pair of masters and one pair of servants—who inadvertently confuse an entire town.
- *The Taming of the Shrew*, Shakespeare's first comic masterpiece, about a bawdy, rambunctious reprobate named Petruchio who marries a shrew named Kate for her money, then comes to appreciate her.

1594–1601

During Shakespeare's second period, from about 1594 to 1601, he wrote many of the plays we associate with his greatest genius, including, among others:

- *Richard II,* a study of kingship in which a rightful king is deposed. (When Queen Elizabeth's throne was threatened in 1601 by a former favorite, the Earl of Essex, this play was revived by the Lord Chamberlain's Men, apparently to the queen's displeasure.)
- *Love's Labour's Lost,* a comedy about four noblemen who swear off women for three years in order to study. Almost immediately four desirable women, led by the Princess of France, arrive, and the men start changing their tune. It is full of complex wordplay and joyously absurd characters.
- *Romeo and Juliet,* the tragic, lyrical romance that remains Shakespeare's most popular play. Romeo and Juliet fall in love and marry despite their families' hatred for each other, and it ends in death.
- A *Midsummer Night's Dream,* Shakespeare's tribute to the world of fairies, filled with the greatest lyric poetry ever written. A quartet of lovers flee to the forest, the fairy king and queen fight over a servant, a magic flower makes people fall in love, and a tradesman named Bottom becomes an ass. Along with *Twelfth Night,* it's the greatest comedy of all time.
- *The Merchant of Venice,* called a "comedy" when it was first printed, but not a comedy at all. Shylock, a Jew, is vilified by the Gentile community because of his beliefs. In revenge, he demands a "pound of flesh" as interest on a loan, and Portia, disguised as a judge, begs him to be merciful. It is shot through with sadness.
- *Henry IV, Part 1,* the play that introduced Falstaff into the world. Prince Hal, heir to the throne, is torn between duty, represented by his father, King Henry IV, and youthful rebellion, represented by the glorious old wastrel with the big belly. Hal's nemesis is the warrior Hotspur, who is part of a rebellion against the monarchy. The play has claims to being one of Shakespeare's three or four greatest.

- *Henry IV, Part 2,* a sequel that is knottier than *Part 1* and ends with Hal's rejection of Falstaff. Falstaff's reminiscences with his old friend Justice Shallow show Shakespeare at the height of his art. It is not quite the masterpiece that *Part 1* is, but Falstaff is equally remarkable.
- *The Merry Wives of Windsor,* a farcical comedy in which Falstaff tries to seduce two married women at the same time and has to flee from a jealous husband in a laundry basket. Falstaff has none of the depth he has in the history plays, but he remains a delight, and the play is rightly an audience favorite.
- *Julius Caesar,* a play about politics and Roman history. Caesar is murdered on the Ides of March, and the play is about the political aftermath. Leave this one to adulthood.
- *Much Ado About Nothing,* one of Shakespeare's three great "high comedies," in which he took his comic art to a new level. It features the warring lovers Beatrice and Benedick, who learn, in their maturity, that they adore each other. It also involves a villain, young love, a masked ball, and a dim constable named Dogberry. It is witty, hilarious, touching, and the most surefire comedy Shakespeare ever wrote. A masterpiece.
- *As You Like It,* another of the "high comedies," this one set mostly in the Forest of Arden, where the gentle, spiritual countryside is contrasted with the bustling corrupt life of the court. Rosalind dresses up as a boy to escape a wicked uncle, and in this disguise she pursues Orlando, the man she loves. Rosalind is a self-possessed, good-natured, independent woman (Shakespeare created several such women), and she, along with Falstaff, is one of the wittiest talkers in all of Shakespeare.
- *Troilus and Cressida,* a bitter tale of love and betrayal set during the Trojan War. It is one of three plays known as "the problem plays," so named because they raise difficult moral issues that are unhappily resolved. The other two problem plays are *All's Well That Ends Well* and *Measure for Measure.*
- *Henry V,* Shakespeare's most famous history play. The eponymous hero was once Prince Hal from the *Henry IV* plays and has now grown into the warrior king who saves the English from the French.

Over the centuries it has been considered to be a play about hero-ism, but more recently it has been interpreted as an antiwar play. It is full of theater metaphors and contains some of Shakespeare's most rousing speeches.

- *Twelfth Night,* the last of the great high comedies. Viola loses her twin brother in a shipwreck and dresses as a boy, at which point the Countess Olivia falls in love with her. Meanwhile the pomp-ous steward Malvolio tries to woo his mistress. And all the while, Olivia's uncle, Sir Toby Belch, carouses with his foolish friend Sir Andrew Aguecheek. There are moments of hilarity and others of deep longing. Every part is comic perfection. For me, this is Shake-speare's greatest comedy.

1601–1608

The third period can be said to stretch from about 1600 to 1608 and in-cludes all the major tragedies, including:

- *Hamlet,* often considered the greatest play ever written. On the surface the play is about a prince of Denmark who is racked by knowledge of his mother's infidelity to his father and is determined to avenge the murder of his father by his uncle Claudius. It may well be the richest play in our literature—on every reading it gets deeper and deeper.
- *Macbeth,* the quintessential study of the moral corruption of a man's soul. Macbeth and Lady Macbeth murder their way to the throne of Scotland, but Macbeth is beset by conscience. It is dark, short, powerful, and frightening. (It also contains perhaps the only happy marriage in all of Shakespeare, that of the Macbeths. Ironic, I know.)
- *Othello.* The tragedy here is so painful that watching it is like look-ing at a fatal car accident in slow motion. It is a study of pure evil in the character of Othello's lieutenant Iago, who sets out to destroy a great man by making him mad with jealousy over his wife Desde-mona. She is entirely innocent, but Othello ends up strangling her to death and then taking his own life.

- *Antony and Cleopatra,* one of the Roman plays, a study of power, age, and sexual desire between two great rulers of the world. It is told in a long series of short scenes and can be overwhelmingly powerful. Cleopatra is one of Shakespeare's richest characters.
- *King Lear,* rightly considered one of Shakespeare's three or four greatest plays, about a king who fatally divides his kingdom between his two vicious daughters, Goneril and Regan. He goes mad with grief, then recovers, only to learn that his third daughter, the one who loved him, has been hanged. Tremendously powerful and heartbreaking.

1608–1613

The fourth and final period stretches from the end of the great tragedies to the end of Shakespeare's writing life in about 1613. It includes four plays that show Shakespeare experimenting with yet another dramatic form, one that combines tragedy, comedy, and romance. The three best are:

- *Cymbeline,* a fairy tale, with a wicked stepmother and her doltish son, as well as two noble princes raised in the wild by a kindly old man. Though respect for the play has ebbed and flowed over the centuries, the heroine, Imogen, was a favorite role of the greatest English actress of the late nineteenth century, Ellen Terry. I find the play magical and inspiring.
- *The Winter's Tale,* a story of jealousy, death, resurrection, and redemption—almost *Othello* with a happy ending. A king, Leontes, becomes unreasonably jealous of his innocent wife, and his young son dies as a result. Sixteen years later he meets the daughter he cruelly abandoned; then the wife he thought was dead comes back to life.
- *The Tempest,* Shakespeare's final play of startling greatness. It opens with a shipwreck, and the survivors take refuge on an island ruled by a powerful magician named Prospero. During the story, Prospero gives up his dreams of vengeance and comes to recognize the power of forgiveness. In the process, his daughter Miranda falls

in love with his enemy's son, and his servant Ariel, a spirit, is finally set free.

As your children learn the passages in this book, you should make them aware of Shakespeare's relative maturity when he wrote the play you're studying. The object is to develop their ears for poetry so that they ultimately become acute to the distinctive sound of each phase of Shakespeare's development. In *A Midsummer Night's Dream*, for example, it isn't hard to hear a youthful exuberance.

> *Captain of our fairy band,*
> *Helena is here at hand!*

In *Twelfth Night*, on the other hand, written in the middle years, we hear a new seriousness, comedy tinged with gravity, a sense of sadness at the passing of time.

> *In delay there lies no plenty,*
> *Then come kiss me, sweet and twenty,*
> *Youth's a stuff will not endure.*

Hamlet comes from about the same time as *Twelfth Night*, and your children will hear in it a similar voice, but one that perhaps foreshadows the depths to come.

> *What a piece of work is a man, how noble in reason, how infinite in faculties, in form and moving how express and admirable; in action how like an angel, in apprehension how like a god . . .*

In *King Lear* and *Antony and Cleopatra*, which are later than *Hamlet*, the language is more gnarled and complex, like the deep pedal tones of an organ mixing with the treble sounds of the keyboard above. Here, for example, is a famous passage from *King Lear* where the King is confronting one storm on a barren heath and another storm in his disintegrating mind:

Blow, winds, and crack your cheeks! rage! blow!
You cataracts and hurricanoes, spout
Till you have drench'd our steeples, drown'd the cocks!
You sulph'rous and thought-executing fires,
Vaunt-couriers of oak-cleaving thunderbolts,
Singe my white head.

Finally, when we come to the dramatic romances at the end of Shakespeare's life, the tone moves seamlessly, at will, from the richly poetic to the sardonic to the nostalgic and valedictory. This is Prospero's speech in *The Tempest* as magic spirits that he has conjured up return to nothingness:

Our revels now are ended. These our actors,
As I foretold you, were all spirits and
Are melted into air, into thin air;
. . .   We are such stuff
As dreams are made on, and our little life
Is rounded with a sleep.

Shakespeare to the End

In addition to the plays, Shakespeare wrote two long narrative poems, *Venus and Adonis* and *The Rape of Lucrece*, both of which were published during his early years in London. While *Venus and Adonis* was the more amusing and popular of the two, together they put Shakespeare on the literary map. His other principal nondramatic poetry consists of 154 sonnets, which circulated privately until they were published in 1609. They are generally more difficult to understand than the dramatic verse, and they address highly personal matters to do with love, marriage, mistresses, and heirs. Whether Shakespeare intended the authorial voice of the sonnets to be himself or a fictional poet with no relationship to Shakespeare's own life is a continual subject of scholarly debate.

The conclusion of Shakespeare's story takes him back to his hometown of Stratford. About 1613 he retired there and wrote little else, and it was there he died on April 23, 1616. In 1623, thirty-six of his plays were published in a single volume, known as the First Folio, eighteen of them for the first time. The publishing of Shakespeare's plays is a fascinating subject, and we'll discuss it in a later chapter. For now, when your children are rested and eager, we'll turn to one of Shakespeare's greatest tragedies, *Macbeth*.

Part Two

CHAPTER 22

Passage 13
Macbeth's Conscience

Tomorrow and tomorrow and tomorrow,
Creeps in this petty pace from day to day,
To the last syllable of recorded time;
And all our yesterdays have lighted fools
The way to dusty death. Out, out, brief candle!
Life's but a walking shadow; a poor player,
That struts and frets his hour upon the stage,
And then is heard no more: it is a tale
Told by an idiot, full of sound and fury,
Signifying nothing.

(*Macbeth*, Act V, Scene 5, lines 18–28)

After *A Midsummer Night's Dream*, *Twelfth Night*, and *Romeo and Juliet*, I thought the best way to keep my children excited about Shakespeare was to expose them to something entirely different. No more Mr. Nice Guy. It was time to get bloody. (My daughter liked the idea as much as my son did.)

Tomorrow and tomorrow and tomorrow,

This is the first line of a soliloquy spoken by Macbeth at the end of the play that bears his name. When the play begins, Macbeth, a lord of ancient Scotland, is fighting to protect his country from a rebellion. Just after

Macbeth: Act I, Scene V, painted by Richard Westall, R.A.

the final, bloody battle, Macbeth encounters three witches who prophesy that he will one day become King of Scotland.

Tomorrow and tomorrow and tomorrow,
Creeps in this petty pace from day to day,

As you tell your children the story, keep repeating these opening lines of the soliloquy until they become second nature.

Tomorrow and tomorrow and tomorrow,
Creeps in this petty pace from day to day,
To the last syllable of recorded time;

The witches' prophecy ignites ambitious thoughts in Macbeth, and soon, with the help of his wildly ambitious, ruthless wife, Macbeth has murdered Scotland's rightful king, Duncan, and seized the throne for himself. Once Macbeth becomes king, Duncan's heirs begin to suspect that Macbeth was the murderer. In response, Macbeth begins a reign of terror, murdering everyone he considers a threat to his position. This includes Macbeth's fellow soldier Banquo (who the witches prophesied would found a line of kings and is therefore a threat to Macbeth's future), as well as the wives and children of Macbeth's political enemies.

Tomorrow and tomorrow and tomorrow,
Creeps in this petty pace from day to day,
To the last syllable of recorded time;

From the beginning, Macbeth is harrowed by his conscience. His mounting sense of remorse causes him to become delusional. First he sees a dagger floating in the air, leading him to Duncan's bedchamber; then he sees the ghost of Banquo sitting at a feast. Are these visions real, or are they products of Macbeth's fevered mind? Is there a difference? What is the dividing line between imagination and reality? Does it matter if something is real to the senses as long as we perceive it to be real?

Tomorrow and tomorrow and tomorrow,
Creeps in this petty pace from day to day,
To the last syllable of recorded time;
And all our yesterdays have lighted fools
The way to dusty death.

Shakespeare raises these issues of reality versus imagination through-out the play. For example, when Macbeth sees the knife in the air, he asks:

Is this a dagger that I see before me,
. . . Art thou not, fatal vision, sensible
To feeling as to sight? Or art thou but
A dagger of the mind, a false creation
Proceeding from the heat-oppressèd brain?

By the time Macbeth delivers his last soliloquy, his enemies have his castle surrounded, and the odds against Macbeth's survival are overwhelming. Still, he insists on donning his armor one last time.

I'll fight till from my bones my flesh be hacked.
Give me my armor.

Just as Macbeth is about to fight, a woman's cry is heard in the distance. A moment later he is told that his wife is dead. Earlier we had seen Lady Macbeth sleepwalking, imagining that she could see Duncan's blood on her hands. In that distracted state, haunted by the horrific deeds that she had committed, she tried desperately to wash the blood away. (*Out, damned spot, out, I say!*) Now, on the eve of battle, Lady Macbeth dies with a cry of despair.

SEYTON

The Queen, my lord, is dead.

MACBETH

She should have died hereafter;
There would have been a time for such a word.

Tomorrow and tomorrow and tomorrow,
Creeps in this petty pace from day to day,
To the last syllable of recorded time;
And all our yesterdays have lighted fools
The way to dusty death.

Surrounded by his enemies and having heard the cry of his wife's untimely end, Macbeth could logically do a number of things from a dramatic standpoint. He could bewail his fate; he could blame his enemies; or he could turn his sword on himself. Instead, Shakespeare has him step back and pause for a moment to contemplate the pointlessness of life itself. In Western literature, this soliloquy has come to epitomize the meaninglessness and despair that lurk at the center of the human condition. It is short, profound, and terrifying.

The first line of the soliloquy is simplicity itself. Because the line is in iambic pentameter, which has five beats, the word *and* is necessarily emphasized, both times, at least a little bit. This gives the line a heavy, plodding rhythm, as if the word *tomorrow* was trudging along to its destruction.

Tomorrow _and_ tomorrow _and_ tomorrow,

The word *tomorrow* in this case has a single, strong beat: *toMORrow*.

ToMORrow _and_ toMORrow _and_ toMORrow,
Creeps in this petty pace from day to day,
To the last syllable of recorded time.

For Macbeth at this point, life is a meaningless succession of tomorrows. For how long will those tomorrows creep forward? Forever. To the very *last syllable of recorded time.*

And all our yesterdays have lighted fools
The way to dusty death.

Deliberate Ambiguity

What does this mean—*all our yesterdays?* And how can *yesterdays* light the way for fools to follow? This raises an interesting aspect of *Macbeth* that is not necessarily evident on a first reading: The language of the play, in addition to being powerful, is also frequently ambiguous. Shakespeare does this deliberately, and he does it to add a sense of mystery, murkiness, and danger to the story. This technique is explained by Shakespeare scholars Barbara Mowat and Paul Werstine:

> Each of Shakespeare's plays has its own characteristic language. In *Macbeth,* one notices particularly the deliberate imprecision of some of the play's words. Macbeth's lines "If it were done when 'tis done, then 'twere well / It were done quickly" not only play with the imprecise verb "done" but also refer to some unnamed "it." . . . We hear it again and again in Lady Macbeth's [speeches]. The sense is clear, but the language seems deliberately vague, deliberately flowery, as if designed to cover over the serpent under it. In reading *Macbeth,* one must some-times be content to get the gist of the characters' language, since in such lines as "the powers above / Put on their instruments" no precise "translation" exists.

So if at times your children find the language of *Macbeth* to be slightly confusing, don't let that trouble them. What I often say to my children, particularly when we're going to see a performance of Shakespeare, is that they shouldn't worry if they don't understand every word, or even every full speech. They should let the language roll over them, the way waves roll over you in the ocean. There will always be time to analyze later.

The Rest of the Speech

Out, out, brief candle!

Life's but a walking shadow;

Shakespeare often compares life to a lighted candle. And a *walking shadow* is a kind of ghost, isn't it? The way Banquo became a ghost in the play.

> *a poor player,*
> *That struts and frets his hour upon the stage,*
> *And then is heard no more:*

A *poor player* means an actor. As we'll discuss in a later chapter, Shakespeare frequently uses actors and the theater as metaphors in his work. *Struts* is also a good word. It suggests that Life is an actor who gets to strut around the stage thinking well of himself. This is reminiscent of another speech, in Shakespeare's *Richard II*, where a king is about to die and he compares death to a tiny actor in the brain:

> *For God's sake, let us sit upon the ground*
> *And tell sad stories of the death of kings . . .*
> > *For within the hollow crown*
> *That rounds the mortal temples of a king*
> *Keeps Death his court, and there the antic* [jester] *sits,*
> *Scoffing* [at] *his state and grinning at his pomp,*
> *Allowing him* [the king] *a breath, a little scene,*
> *To monarchize, be feared, and kill with looks,*
> *Infusing him with self and vain conceit,*
> *As if this flesh which walls about our life*
> *Were brass impregnable.*

Similarly, for Macbeth, life is

> > > *a tale*
> *Told by an idiot, full of sound and fury,*
> *Signifying nothing.*

Could Shakespeare have written anything more bleak, more filled with despair and hopelessness? I don't believe so. It is reminiscent of the twentieth-century works of Samuel Beckett, plays like *Krapp's Last Tape* and the ironically titled *Happy Days*, that view man's lot as one of absurd nothingness.

CHAPTER 23

Passage 14
Lady Macbeth and
the Imagery of Evil

The raven himself is hoarse
That croaks the fatal entrance of Duncan
Under my battlements. Come, you spirits
That tend on mortal thoughts, unsex me here,
And fill me from the crown to the toe top-full
Of direst cruelty.

(*Macbeth*, Act I, Scene 5, lines 45–50)

One of the most distinctive features of *Macbeth* is the power of its recurring imagery. Shakespeare uses four key sets of images, all of them troubling. He introduces each one early, then uses them so frequently that we can't escape them. They involve

1. darkness and the absence of light,
2. blood,
3. nature and the dislocation of nature, and
4. animals in some form of distortion, especially birds.

These recurring images give the play a feeling of evil, of otherworldly forces closing in on a fast, tight-knit world filled with ambition and violence. The play has a sense of relentless speed, like a runaway train, and Shakespeare achieves this effect by various means. Many of the scenes are short and shocking. Some open in midstream, one in the middle of a letter, others in the middle of conversations. The play itself is the third shortest in the whole canon (though the length varies depending on the edition being used).

Imagery is one of the most effective ways to get your children involved in Shakespeare's language. An image is a word or phrase that suggests a mental picture that we associate with one of our senses. So when Shakespeare refers to *blood*, we're meant to see its redness and feel its stickiness—and then we associate the word with violence and pain. The words *darkness* and *dark* and *blackness* create a whole different set of responses relating to fear and danger.

Spot the Image

Shakespeare's language is filled with images, and one of the games we played in our house was called Spot the Image. The possibilities are endless. Who can spot the most images? How many images can you find in a single exchange or a single scene? What images can you find, and why do you think Shakespeare used them? Images are concrete, visual, and easy to identify, and believe me, this is a very helpful way to keep your children interested in Shakespeare.

Let's apply the game to *Macbeth* and identify some of the images in the four clusters we've mentioned.

1. Darkness

Act I, Scene 1 opens with three witches chanting to each other in a void, and the effect is terrifying. This scene is dark in two senses. First, metaphorically, these creatures have bubbled up from the darkest level of existence. They chant, they prognosticate, they call to invisible spirits with troubling names, and they immediately plunge us into a world of evil. Second, they refer specifically to darkness in their haunting lines:

When shall we three meet again?
In thunder, lightning, or in rain? . . .
Fair is foul and foul is fair,
Hover through the fog and filthy air.

Fog is dark, and so is filthy air. We are in murky darkness from the moment the play opens—and from this point on, something remarkable happens: Almost every single scene of *Macbeth* takes place at night. In one scene, when it is day and therefore should be light, a character remarks

By the clock 'tis day,
And yet dark night strangles the traveling lamp. . . .
Darkness does the face of earth entomb.

Here, *dark night* is given human qualities. It can strangle a lamp and entomb the earth.

Night by Michelangelo

In the history of Western art, another towering genius, Michelangelo, created the same personification, anthropomorphizing night and day in two of his most famous sculptures. In the Medici tomb in Florence, Italy, the two spectacular statues *Night* and *Day* catch the same brooding, troubling aspects that Shakespeare evokes in *Macbeth*. In the illustration on page 157, notice the owl under Night's leg. Shakespeare refers to owls several times (*the owls scream*) in the course of the play.

When your children read *Macbeth*, they should visualize it in shadows and fog and recognize that these images help make the action feel dangerous.

2. Blood

In the first line of Act I, Scene 2—only the fifteenth line of the entire play—King Duncan refers to blood. He meets a *bloody man* who reports on the rebellion, telling the king that Macbeth fought bravely, *with his brandished steel, / Which smoked with bloody execution*. The word *blood* is then used again and again, more than forty times throughout the play. When Macbeth sees the apparition of the dagger in front of him, it is covered with *gouts of blood*. When Macbeth sees Banquo's ghost, it is shaking its *gory locks*. Lady Macbeth can't manage to wash Duncan's blood off her hands during the sleepwalking scene, and she remarks with harrowing simplicity,

> *Yet who would have thought the old man to have had so much blood in him.*

The most remarkable use of blood as an image occurs just after Macbeth staggers in holding the bloody daggers he has used to stab Duncan to death. He looks down at his hands, sees the blood, and exclaims:

Shakespeare's Lines	My Paraphrase
Will all great Neptune's ocean wash this blood Clean from my hand? No, this my hand will rather The multitudinous seas incarnadine, Making the green one red.	Will all the waters in the ocean clean this blood from my hands? No, my hands are so bloody, and the blood is so powerful, that the blood on my hands will turn all the seas in the world from green to red.

Shakespeare invented the word *incarnadine,* and as far as I know, it is never used again in English literature. It means "blood red," from the Latin root *carn* meaning "flesh."

3. The Dislocation of Nature

Again, the words *nature* and *natural* are used more than twenty times in the play. The basic notion is that the natural world, which is orderly and good, becomes *un*natural and distorted when evil is abroad. When Macbeth first gets the idea of killing Duncan, he realizes that it is *Against the use of nature.* Similarly, when Lady Macbeth first hears about the witches' prophecy, she fears that Macbeth is too imbued with natural human kindness.

> *Yet I do fear thy nature;*
> *It is too full of the milk of human kindness*
> *To catch the nearest way.*

From that point on, in scene after scene, as the murders are committed and the evil spreads, unnatural things begin to happen. Macbeth sees apparitions like the dagger and the ghost; he hears a disembodied voice that cries *Sleep no more! Macbeth doth murder sleep!* And he sees images of the future kings of Scotland.

4. Animals and Birds

Shakespeare associates changes in animals, especially birds, with the unnatural happenings of this evil world. Duncan's servants sleep drunkenly in *swinish sleep*. The moment Macbeth murders Duncan, *the owls shriek and the crickets cry*. When Lady Macbeth is urging her husband to fool King Duncan by looking innocent even though he's about to murder the man, she says,

> *Look like the innocent flower,*
> *But be the serpent under't.*

The most harrowing instance of animal imagery occurs soon after the murder of Duncan. Two minor characters meet and discuss how, in the face of the unnatural murder of the king, the natural world has begun to rebel. Owls are killing hawks and horses are eating each other.

Horses eating each other?! What an image! Have your children read this passage with all the foreboding it deserves:

OLD MAN

'Tis unnatural,
Even like the deed that's done. On Tuesday last
A falcon, tow'ring in her pride of place [circling in the sky],
Was by a mousing owl hawked at and killed.

ROSS

And Duncan's horses (a thing most strange and certain),
Beauteous and swift, the minions [choicest] *of their race,*
Turned wild in nature, broke their stalls, flung out [ran out],
Contending 'gainst obedience, as [as if] *they would*
Make war with mankind.

OLD MAN
'Tis said they eat each other.

ROSS

They did so, to th'amazement of mine eyes
That looked upon't.

Lady Macbeth's Remarkable Soliloquy

One of the most breathtaking speeches in the play occurs when we first meet Lady Macbeth. It is remarkable not only because of its intensity but also because it pulls together all four central images of the play.

The speech occurs in Act I, Scene 5. The scene opens with Lady Macbeth (this is the first time we've met her) reading a letter from her husband in which he tells her about the witches and their prophecies. She immediately picks up Macbeth's hints about murdering the king and decides that she'll make him follow through no matter what it takes. She says she'll

> *pour my spirits in thine ear*
> *And chastise with the valor of my tongue*
> *All that impedes thee* [stops thee] *from the golden round* [the crown].

This image of Lady Macbeth's venomous tongue in her husband's ear pouring poisonous thoughts into his brain tells us worlds about Lady Macbeth, about her evilness, her ruthlessness, and her sexual nature.

A moment later a messenger arrives telling Lady Macbeth that her husband is bringing King Duncan with him to the Macbeths' castle, and she realizes instantly that here is the perfect opportunity to murder Duncan. This is when she delivers her remarkable soliloquy. Watch for the images we discussed, and notice that the lines we're going to memorize are in bold type.

> **The raven himself is hoarse**
> **That croaks the fatal entrance of Duncan**
> **Under my battlements. Come, you spirits**
> **That tend on mortal thoughts, unsex me here,**
> **And fill me from the crown to the toe top-full**

Of direst cruelty. *Make thick my blood.*
Stop up th' access and passage to remorse,
That no compunctious visitings of nature
Shake my fell purpose, nor keep peace between
Th' effect and it. *Come to my woman's breasts*
And take my milk for gall, you murd'ring ministers,
Wherever in your sightless substances
You wait on nature's mischief. *Come, thick night,*
And pall thee in the dunnest smoke of hell,
That my keen knife see not the wound it makes,
Nor heaven peep through the blanket of the dark
To cry, "Hold, hold!"

It is a difficult speech, and here is a paraphrase of it:

Shakespeare's Lines	*My Paraphrase*
The **raven** himself is hoarse That croaks the fatal entrance of Duncan Under my battlements. Come, you spirits That tend on mortal thoughts, unsex me here, And fill me from the crown to the toe top-full Of direst cruelty.	The **raven** is hoarse from announcing the arrival of King Duncan to our castle. Come, you spirits of evil who concern yourselves with thoughts of death, take away my womanhood and fill me from head [a pun on royal crown] to toe with cruelty.
Make thick my **blood.** Stop up th' access and passage to remorse, That no compunctious visitings of **nature** Shake my fell purpose, nor keep peace between Th' effect and it.	Make my **blood** so thick that it will stop the flow of compassion through my veins, so that I feel no compunction that might arise from good **nature** or that might shake me from my cruel purpose.

Come to my woman's breasts
And take my milk for gall,
  you murd'ring ministers,
Wherever in your sightless
  substances
*You wait on **nature's***
  mischief.

Come to my breasts, you spirits of evil, and substitute bitterness for the milk that should naturally be there (or possibly suck my milk as though it were gall), wherever you are in your invisibility, serving the evil side of **nature.**

  *Come, thick **night**,*
*And pall thee in the **dunnest***
  ***smoke** of hell,*
That my keen knife see not the
  ***wound** it makes,*
Nor heaven peep through the
  blanket of the dark
To cry, "Hold, hold!"

Come, **thick night**, and cover yourself with the darkest smoke of hell so that my sharp knife can't even see the wound it makes in Duncan and so that the goodness of heaven can't even peep through the darkness and tell me to stop.

Through this and her other major speeches, Lady Macbeth shows herself to be so thoroughly evil that we almost admire her for her originality and remorselessness. Macbeth's major speeches, by contrast, are filled with self-doubt and a sense of horror at his own misdeeds. He is caught up in a relentless trek of bloodlust, where evil begets evil, and is increasingly aware of his own moral corruption.

The play ends with Macbeth's defeat at the hands of his enemies, and in the final scene, he is killed in battle and his head is brought out onstage. (That alone will encourage many children to want to see the play.)

A Puzzle

One of the central puzzles of the play involves how we feel about Macbeth's violent end. Here is a man who murdered at will out of blind ambition, killing a kinsman, a guest, and a king, yet something about him makes us feel that he was possessed of a great spirit, with the potential for another, better life. Is it the language of his speeches? His affection for his wife? His struggles with his conscience? Or did he have no choice in life? Were his evil deeds the product of Fate, or his wife, or his occupation as a soldier? These are questions you should discuss with your children.

The passage that we're memorizing in this chapter is a reminder of many of these issues. Have your children break it into sections:

> *The raven himself is hoarse*
> *That croaks the fatal entrance of Duncan*
> *Under my battlements.*
> *Come, you spirits*
> *That tend on mortal thoughts,*
> *unsex me here,*
> *And fill me from the crown to the toe*
> *top-full*
> *Of direst cruelty.*

Croaks. Unsex. Direst cruelty. These words are not soon forgotten; and the passage is so dark and foreboding that it is an ideal contrast to the comic language of Falstaff, which we'll tackle together in the next chapter.

CHAPTER 24

Passage 15
The World of Falstaff

*If sack and sugar be a fault, God help the wicked. If to be
old and merry be a sin, then many an old host that I know
is damned. If to be fat be to be hated, then Pharaoh's lean
kine are to be loved. No, my good lord, banish Peto, banish Bardolph, banish Poins, but for sweet Jack Falstaff,
kind Jack Falstaff, true Jack Falstaff, valiant Jack Falstaff,
and therefore more valiant being as he is old Jack Falstaff,
banish not him thy Harry's company, banish not him thy
Harry's company. Banish plump Jack, and banish all the
world.*

(Henry IV, Part 1,
Act II, Scene 4, lines 487–98)

This passage is spoken by Sir John Falstaff, and as the sound of his distinctive voice becomes recognizable, you will come to realize that you have entered the domain of a boisterous, dangerous, and affectionate old reprobate who may well be the greatest comic creation of all time.

Falstaff appears in three plays by Shakespeare: a history play entitled *Henry IV, Part 1*; its sequel, *Henry IV, Part 2*; and a light comedy called *The Merry Wives of Windsor*. A legend dating from the seventeenth century has it that Queen Elizabeth, after seeing the two history plays, so loved the

Merry Wives the Musical at the Royal Shakespeare Company, with Simon Callow as Falstaff and Haydn Gwynne as Mistress Page

character of Falstaff that she commanded Shakespeare to write a comedy about him, showing him in love.

The speech we're learning is one that Falstaff delivers in *Henry IV, Part 1*, defending himself against those who accuse him of being *a villainous abominable misleader of youth.*

> *If sack and sugar be a fault, God help the wicked.*

Sack was a dry white wine imported from Spain. Sack with sugar in it was a popular drink, especially among the elderly.

> *If sack and sugar be a fault, God help the wicked.*

Meaning: It's a pretty innocent thing to drink sack and sugar, as I do, and if that's the worst thing you can say about me, then I can't be too bad.

Exercise: Speaking in Character

Have your son or daughter say this line, and the following lines, in the character of Falstaff. They shouldn't overdo it and make him silly. He's not a silly man. He's funny, immoral, extravagant, cunning, affectionate, dishonest, self-aware, witty, and boundlessly inventive, but never silly. They should recite the speech with the mock gravity that Falstaff uses, always stepping outside himself to comment ruefully on the wicked world around him.

> *If sack and sugar be a fault, God help the wicked.*

> *If to be old and merry be a sin,*
> *then many an old host that I know is damned.*

Falstaff is old and merry. "Is that a sin?" he asks. If so:

> *then many an old host that I know is damned.*

A *host* is an innkeeper. Hosts were known for being merry, since it was part of their job to make customers feel welcome.

> *If to be old and merry be a sin,*
> *then many an old host that I know is damned.*

Next he tells us that he's fat—and once again he puts this so-called fault into a context that makes it sound desirable.

> *If to be fat be to be hated,*
> *then Pharaoh's lean kine are to be loved.*

Kine are cows. *Lean kine* means "skinny cows." And Falstaff is subtly referring to a passage in Genesis (41:4) where the lean cows in Pharaoh's dream are a prediction of famine. ("And the ill favoured and lean-fleshed kine did eat up the seven well favoured and fat kine. So Pharaoh awoke.") Thus Falstaff gives his defense a ring of biblical truth: "If you hate me because I'm fat, then you must love Pharaoh's lean cows, which brought about disaster."

> *If to be fat be to be hated,*
> *then Pharaoh's lean kine are to be loved.*

The Speech in Context

In order to understand the rest of the speech, we need to put it into context. The play centers on Henry IV's son, Prince Harry (known as Hal), who is heir to the throne of England. (The play takes place in the early 1400s.) Hal is a young man of impressionable age, rebellious of authority, and a lover of pranks. Instead of studying the arts of war and diplomacy, as his father wishes, he spends most of his time at a tavern in Eastcheap, a low area of London, carousing with Falstaff and his friends, who consist of a crew of ruffians (Peto, Bardolph, and Poins) and loose women (Mistress Quickly and Doll Tearsheet).

When the play opens, Falstaff—that *misleader of youth . . . that reverend Vice, that grey Iniquity*—is Hal's greatest friend. He has also become a father figure to the young prince. But Hal already has a father, the sober King Henry IV, and the underlying tension of the play is the struggle between Falstaff and King Henry IV for Hal's soul.

That this struggle creates tension may seem counterintuitive, since Shakespeare's audience knew from history that Hal, when he became King Henry V, would part ways with Falstaff. Moreover, in the course of the play, Hal makes it clear several times that he will ultimately reject Falstaff and the holiday world that Falstaff represents. Yet Falstaff is such a powerful, endearing, and enduring figure that we as audience continue to experience a tension between the two worlds pulling Hal in opposite directions.

The Great Playacting Scene

Virtually all of *Henry IV, Part 1* is memorable, but I value one scene above the rest: Act II, Scene 4, the great Playacting Scene. When it opens, Falstaff, Hal, and their friends are in Eastcheap playing tricks on one another. Falstaff has robbed some travelers, and Hal and Poins (who have robbed Falstaff in turn) are baiting Falstaff into exaggerating his own valor. Suddenly, a man from the court brings Hal an ominous message: Some of King Henry's nobles have stolen away to foment a rebellion, and the King has summoned Hal to appear before him in the morning. The country is descending into civil war, and the King wants Hal to do his duty.

When the messenger leaves, Falstaff proposes some entertainment: that he and Hal enact for their friends the drama that will occur tomorrow when Hal meets with his father and has to defend his dissolute lifestyle.

FALSTAFF

But tell me, Hal, art thou not horrible afeard? Thou being heir apparent,
could the world pick thee out three such enemies [as the rebels] . . . ?
Doth not thy blood thrill at it?

PRINCE HAL

Not a whit [not at all], i' faith. I lack some of your instinct [cowardice].

The Prince and Falstaff insult each other throughout the play like two high-spirited schoolboys who love to one-up each other.

FALSTAFF

Well, thou wilt be horribly chid [scolded] tomorrow when thou comest to
thy father. If thou love me, practice an answer.

PRINCE HAL

Do thou stand for my father [act like my father] and examine me upon the
particulars of my life.

FALSTAFF

Shall I? Content. [Good.] *This chair shall be my state* [throne], *this dagger my scepter, and this cushion my crown.*

So Falstaff puts a cushion on his head and playacts Henry IV in order to examine his "son," Prince Hal, who is played by Hal himself. Then, after about two wonderful minutes of extemporizing, they continue, but with the roles reversed: Hal plays his own father, while Falstaff plays Hal.

An Acting Opportunity

If there was ever an opportunity to involve children in Shakespeare, this is it. What child would not want to sit in a special chair with a pillow on her head for a crown, holding a dagger as if it were a scepter, playing Falstaff who, in turn, is playing the King of England and then the Prince of Wales?

The playlet opens with Falstaff representing Hal's father, the King; and the King, of course, should be condemning Falstaff for leading Hal astray. But Falstaff puts a different light on the fictional exchange:

FALSTAFF
(*as King*)

Harry, I do not only marvel where thou spendest thy time, but also how thou art accompanied. . . . And yet there is a virtuous man whom I have often noted in thy company, but I know not his name.

This is simply comedy of genius. Falstaff is pretending to be the King describing Falstaff: *a virtuous man whom I have often noted in thy company.*

PRINCE HAL
(*as himself*)

What manner of man, an it like [if it please] *your Majesty?*

FALSTAFF

(as King)

A goodly portly man, i'faith, and a corpulent [a fat one]; *of a cheerful look,
a pleasing eye, and a most noble carriage, and, as I think, his age some
fifty . . . ; and now I remember me, his name is Falstaff. . . . There is
virtue in that Falstaff; him keep with* [keep him with you], *the rest banish.*

This is too much for Hal. *Dost thou speak like a king?* he asks, amazed
and amused at Falstaff's trickery. *Do thou stand for me* [you play me], *and
I'll play my father.*

So the two men reverse roles, and Harry plays his own father, while
Falstaff pretends to be Hal. Again, do not miss this opportunity with
your children. Change pillows, change roles, arrange it whatever way
your children think best, but read the roles out loud and act the heck out
of them.

PRINCE HAL

(as King)

Now Harry, whence come you?

FALSTAFF

(as Prince)

My noble lord, from Eastcheap.

PRINCE HAL

(as King)

*The complaints I hear of thee are grievous. . . . There is a devil haunts
thee in the likeness of an old fat man. A tun* [barrel] *of man is thy
companion. Why dost thou converse with that trunk of humors, that
bolting-hutch* [sifting trough] *of beastliness, that swollen parcel of dropsies*
[disease], *that huge bombard* [wine-holder] *of sack, that stuffed cloakbag*
[suitcase] *of guts, that roasted Manningtree ox with the pudding in his
belly, that reverend Vice, that gray iniquity, that father ruffian, that vanity in years? Wherein is he good, but to taste sack and drink it? Wherein
neat and cleanly but to carve a capon and eat it? Wherein cunning but in*

craft? Wherein crafty but in villainy? Wherein villainous but in all things? Wherein worthy but in nothing?

FALSTAFF
(as Prince)

I would your Grace would take me with you [help me understand what you mean]. *Whom means your Grace?*

What a wonderful line! *I would your grace would take me with you.* What clever, mocking innocence Falstaff puts into the Prince's mouth, as though the Prince has no idea whom the King means.

FALSTAFF
(as Prince)

I would your Grace would take me with you. Whom means your Grace?

PRINCE HAL
(as King)

That villainous abominable misleader of youth, Falstaff, that old white-bearded Satan.

FALSTAFF
(as Prince)

My lord, the man I know.

PRINCE HAL
(as King)

I know thou dost.

FALSTAFF
(as Prince)

But to say I know more harm in him than in myself were to say more than I know. That he is old, the more the pity; his white hairs do witness it. . . . If sack and sugar be a fault, God help the wicked. If to be old and merry be a sin, then many an old host that I know is damned. If to

be fat be to be hated, then Pharaoh's lean kine are to be loved. No, my
good lord, banish Peto, banish Bardolph, banish Poins, but for sweet Jack
Falstaff, kind Jack Falstaff, true Jack Falstaff, valiant Jack Falstaff, and
therefore more valiant being as he is old Jack Falstaff, banish not him thy
Harry's company, banish not him thy Harry's company. Banish plump
Jack, and banish all the world.

PRINCE HAL

I do. I will.

And now we see how the speech we're memorizing fits into the puzzle.
Falstaff delivers it in defense of himself, pretending that the lines are spo-
ken by the Prince. This is Shakespeare's genius at the height of its power.
You have already taught your children the first third:

If sack and sugar be a fault, God help the wicked. If to be old and merry
be a sin, then many an old host that I know is damned. If to be fat be to be
hated, then Pharaoh's lean kine are to be loved.

Now let's teach them the rest of the speech:

No, my good lord,
banish Peto, banish Bardolph, banish Poins,

Peto	P
Bardolph	B
Poins	P

Peto, Bardolph, Poins,

The names are wonderful because they sound nothing at all like names
today. Peto. Bardolph. Poins. These rogues are now legendary.

but for sweet Jack Falstaff, kind Jack Falstaff, true Jack Falstaff, valiant
Jack Falstaff,

And here's another list: *sweet, kind, true, valiant.*

sweet,	*s*
kind,	*k*
true,	*t*
valiant	*v*

Lists like these can be tricky to memorize, so in our house we often use mnemonic devices to get us over the hump. For example, in my son's music class at the time, some of the students played instruments, but seven kids took voice.

Seven	Sweet
Kids	Kind
Took	True
Voice	Valiant

And the *o* in the word *voice* even helped us with the next adjective in the speech, *old.*

> *but for*
> **sweet** *Jack Falstaff,*
> **kind** *Jack Falstaff,*
> **true** *Jack Falstaff,*
> **valiant** *Jack Falstaff,*
>
> *and therefore more valiant*
> *being as he is*
> **old** *Jack Falstaff,*

The Subtlety of Falstaff

This last phrase epitomizes Falstaff's extraordinary wit and intelligence:

> *and therefore more valiant being as he is old Jack Falstaff,*

It is not only logical and obviously true—that when you're old, you have to be extra-valiant in order to be valiant at all—but it is also very touching: It appeals not only to the brain but also to the heart. One of the goals of this book is to introduce your children to the nuances of language, and this last phrase of the speech is a prime example.

> *and therefore more valiant*
> *being as he is **old** Jack Falstaff,*

Henry IV, Part 1 at Theatre Royal Bath, with Desmond Barrit as Falstaff and Tom Mison as Prince Hal

Peroration and Banishment

And now comes the inspiring conclusion to the speech:

> *banish not him thy Harry's company,*
> *banish not him thy Harry's company.*
> *Banish plump Jack, and banish all the world.*

Falstaff is the world, a very specific world. He is the world of truancy over duty, joy over tedium, passion over the ordinary, imagination over littleness. He is dangerous, to be sure. He breaks laws. He steals from pilgrims. He is not a Santa Claus figure full of merry fun. Like all of Shakespeare's greatest creations, he is a complex combination of moral traits, full of lights and darks.

For some Shakespeareans, Falstaff is darker than traditionally pictured. They remind us that he steals from his government and sends untested recruits off to war. He feigns death on the battlefield to save his skin, then claims heroism for further wounding a man who is dead. All the while, he proclaims (in a famous soliloquy) that notions of traditional honor have no place in his moral vocabulary. Yet Shakespeare obviously adores the old man. For Shakespeare, there is something deep within Falstaff to be admired. He represents everything in the world that is *not* buttoned-down, *not* rule-bound, *not* afraid of itself. Falstaff loves *being* Falstaff. He is full of life and wisdom, and he invents himself into something unforgettable.

As a young man, Benjamin Franklin frequently pushed a wagonload of paper around the streets of Philadelphia to show that he was an industrious printer. In fact, the paper had no destination; Franklin was doing it to create the illusion that he was industrious. Like all great men and women, he was inventing his own legend. Falstaff does the same thing right before our eyes: He invents the legend of Falstaff. And in the process, he talks better than any other character in English literature.

Repetition

Your children may ask: Why does Falstaff repeat the phrase *banish not him thy Harry's company?*

> *banish not him thy Harry's company,*
> *banish not him thy Harry's company.*
> *Banish plump Jack, and banish all the world.*

Could it have been a printing error? Yes, possibly. But I don't think so. I think it's a deliberate poetic choice on Shakespeare's part to make the ending of the speech more moving; to give the actor playing Falstaff a chance to make his plea twice, with a different reading each time; and to emphasize the importance of the banishment issue.

Abraham Lincoln and the Mangling of Shakespeare

The sixteenth president of the United States was a great lover of Shakespeare. He enjoyed reading the plays, and he saw them onstage as often as possible. But one of the things he could not understand was why the producers of his day cut out the Playacting Scene from *Henry IV, Part 1*.

Cut out?

From Shakespeare?

One thing that surprises most of us today is the extent to which directors and producers have changed Shakespeare's texts over the past four hundred years. In Shakespeare productions these days, the director will commonly decide to make a few cuts. Shakespeare's plays are long (a full-text *Hamlet* runs over four hours), and some sections are so confusing to us in the present day (like many of the jokes made by Shakespeare's jesters) that small, judicious cuts can arguably be justified.

However, starting in the eighteenth century, many producers "improved" Shakespeare's plays to accord with their own beliefs about what the plays "should" be saying and what they thought the public wanted. Thus, for many years, *King Lear* was performed with a happy ending tacked on—with Lear recovering, Cordelia getting married, and the three sisters happily reuniting. The greatest actor-producer of the eighteenth century, David Garrick, added fifty extra lines at the end of *Romeo and Juliet* so that the lovers could have a love scene together in the Capulets' tomb before Romeo gasped his last. *The Winter's Tale* was performed with only three of its five acts because the first two were considered "unnecessary." And for much of the nineteenth century many people read a version of Shakespeare that was "bowdlerized" into *The Family Shakespeare*—that is, cut down by a brother and sister named Bowdler who took out every blasphemous and sexually suggestive word that a father, reading aloud to his family, would consider embarrassing or improper. Today we consider such changes barbarous, but for more than a hundred years they were commonplace.

Thus, in Abraham Lincoln's day, it was common to leave out the "play extempore" from Act II, Scene 4 of *Henry IV, Part 1*. In 1863 Lincoln saw such a production and invited the actor who played Falstaff, James Hackett, back to the White House after the performance. He wanted to know "why one of the best scenes in the play, that where Falstaff & Prince Hal alternately assume the character of the King, is omitted in the representation." Lincoln's secretary of state, John Hay, reported that "Hackett says it is admirable to read but ineffective on stage." Lincoln, along with centuries of theatergoers, disagreed.

CHAPTER 25

Passage 16
Falstaff's Voice

*Before I knew thee, Hal, I knew nothing, and now am I,
if a man should speak truly, little better than one of the
wicked.*

(Henry IV, Part 1, Act I, Scene 2, lines 99–101)

*Why, Hal, 'tis my vocation, Hal. 'Tis no sin for a man to
labor in his vocation.*

(Henry IV, Part 1, Act I, Scene 2, lines 110–11)

*There lives not three good men unhanged in England, and
one of them is fat and grows old.*

(Henry IV, Part 1, Act II, Scene 4, lines 133–35)

*I am not only witty in myself, but the cause that wit is in
other men.*

(Henry IV, Part 2, Act I, Scene 2, lines 9–11)

We have heard the chimes at midnight, Master Shallow.

(Henry IV, Part 2, Act III, Scene 2, lines 221–22)

There are many memorable aspects of *Henry IV, Part 1*: It has an exciting story about a rebellion, an extravagant set of characters, and a profound theme involving the struggle for the soul of the Prince of Wales. It has a strong political point of view and stirring battle scenes, and it's very, very funny. But the most unforgettable part of the play is Falstaff, and his greatness lies in his distinctive voice. I want your children to recognize that voice, and I want them to use this chapter as a jumping-off point so that they learn to become acute to the *sounds* of Shakespeare.

Let's begin by listening to the following passage. Each of you should take a role and read your parts aloud:

FALSTAFF

An old lord of the council rated me the other day in the street about you, sir, but I marked him not, and yet he talked very wisely, but I regarded him not, and yet he talked wisely, and in the street, too.

PRINCE HAL

Thou didst well, for wisdom cries out in the streets and no man regards it.

FALSTAFF

. . . Before I knew thee, Hal, I knew nothing, and now am I, if a man should speak truly, little better than one of the wicked. . . .

PRINCE HAL

I see a good amendment of life in thee, from praying to purse-taking.

FALSTAFF

Why, Hal, 'tis my vocation, Hal. 'Tis no sin for a man to labor in his vocation.

The exchange comes from Falstaff and Hal's first scene together in the tavern. Their banter is a form of competition, the kind my brother and I indulged in when we were growing up. The difference is that Falstaff and Hal raise the language of banter to a high art.

An old lord of the council rated me the other day in the street about
you, sir,

Here, Falstaff is saying that he bumped into someone on the street who
was a worthy citizen—a lord of the King's Council—who criticized him for
spending time with Prince Hal. In recounting the incident (which he may
be making up), Falstaff adopts a kind of mock disapproval. As one legendary Shakespeare commentator, A. C. Bradley, puts it, Falstaff makes "truth
appear absurd by solemn statements, which he utters with perfect gravity
and which he expects nobody to believe." His voice is full of pretended
self-pity and pity for the wicked world. He is always acting.

Notice also how Falstaff falls into repetition. It is one of his linguistic
hallmarks: He takes his time to say things. He circles around a subject so
artfully that we hardly notice it at first, but he is creating a work of beauty
with his tongue; he is fashioning his sentences the way an oil painter creates a masterpiece, layer after layer:

but I marked him not, and yet he talked very wisely, but I regarded him
not, and yet he talked wisely, and in the street, too.

The Prince replies:

Thou didst well, for wisdom cries out in the streets and no man
regards it.

And here we have another one of those remarkable epigrams that Shakespeare drops into the dialogue like an extra piece of candy that we didn't
expect. It is an allusion to *Proverbs*, 1:20:

Wisdom cries out in the streets and no man regards it.

Falstaff then remarks:

Before I knew thee, Hal, I knew nothing, and now am I, if a man
should speak truly, little better than one of the wicked.

Do we believe Falstaff here, even for an instant? That before he knew Hal he was innocent and knew nothing? Of course not. But we delight in Falstaff blaming Hal in a jocular way for his own state of corruption and dissipation. Have your children commit it to memory:

> *Before I knew thee, Hal, I knew nothing,*
> *and now am I, if a man should speak truly,*
> *little better than one of the wicked.*

Prince Hal answers him sarcastically:

> *I see a good amendment of life in thee, from praying to purse-taking.*

This sentence means, in essence, "Look how you've changed. You used to pray, but now you rob people and take their purses." Which is a perfect setup for Falstaff's magnificent reply:

> *Why, Hal, 'tis my vocation, Hal. 'Tis no sin for a man to labor in his vocation.*

Meaning: "But Hal, purse stealing is my life's work. It's my job. Surely it's not a sin for a man to work at his job!"

Use This Line!

In our house, this line has become one of our favorites, and our kids use it whenever we catch them doing something that they know they shouldn't be doing.

Scenario 1

Our daughter, Olivia, stays up past her bedtime and her mother catches her in bed with her computer.

MOM

Olivia, what do you think you're doing?

OLIVIA

Why, Mom, 'tis my vocation, Mom. 'Tis no sin for a girl to labor in her vocation.

Scenario 2

Our son, Jack, is horsing around on his cell phone when he should be studying.

DAD

Get off the cell phone or I'll kill you.

JACK

Why, Dad, 'tis my vocation, Dad. 'Tis no sin for a boy to labor in his vocation.

Go over these scenarios with your children—act them out—and the words will stay with you forever. You do, however, run the risk of hearing this remark more than you'd like.

Falstaff's Voice

It is difficult to exaggerate Falstaff's wittiness and sheer intelligence. The critic Harold Bloom believes that Falstaff "speaks what is still the best and most vital prose in the English language," and I agree with him. Bloom calls Falstaff "the Socrates of Eastcheap," which is witty in it-self; and of the two dozen or so greatest characters in Shakespeare, he remarks that

> Falstaff, Rosalind, Hamlet, and Cleopatra are something apart in world literature: through them Shakespeare essentially invented human per-

sonality as we continue to know and value it. Falstaff has priority in this invention.

In order for your children to get some real inkling of the quality of Falstaff's prose, I want you to have them say aloud all of the following quotations. These are merely twelve of the dozens of wonderful lines spoken by Falstaff throughout the two history plays. You heard some of them in the previous chapter, and here are some more to add to your children's store of knowledge.

Indeed, you come near me now, Hal, for we that take purses go by the moon.

Marry then, sweet wag, when thou art king, let not us that are squires of the night's body [robbers who steal at night] *be called thieves of the day's beauty. Let us be Diana's foresters* [Diana was goddess of the moon], *gentlemen of the shade, minions of the moon.*

I prithee, sweet wag, shall there be gallows standing in England when thou art king?

If the rascal have not given me medicines to make me love him, I'll be hanged. It could not be else; I have drunk medicines. [Notice the repetition.]

The next one is a terrific joke: Hal and Falstaff are waiting for some travelers on the road, and Hal tells Falstaff to lie down and put his ear to the ground to hear if the travelers are coming. Falstaff answers:

Have you any levers to lift me up again, being down?

Cut the villains' throats! Ah, whoreson caterpillars, bacon-fed knaves, they hate us youth. [Falstaff is an old man but speaks of himself as a youth.]

There lives not three good men unhanged in England, and one of them is fat and grows old.

I tell thee what, Hal, if I tell thee a lie, spit in my face, call me horse.

Hal asks Falstaff how long since he was able to see his own knee. Falstaff answers:

My own knee? When I was about thy years, Hal, I was not an eagle's talon [claw] in the waist. I could have crept into any alderman's thumb-ring. A plague of sighing and grief. It blows a man up like a bladder.

If I be not ashamed of my soldiers, I am a soused gurnet [a pickled fish].

From *Henry IV, Part 2:*

Men of all sorts take a pride to gird at me. The brain of this foolish-compounded clay, man, is not able to invent anything that intends to laughter more than I invent, or is invented on me. I am not only witty in myself, but the cause that wit is in other men. I do here walk before thee like a sow that hath overwhelmed all her litter but one.

And finally, this also from *Henry IV, Part 2,* when Falstaff is visiting a country town in Gloucestershire and reminisces with a doddery old friend of his youth:

SHALLOW
O, Sir John, do you remember since we lay all night in the windmill in Saint George's Field?

FALSTAFF
No more of that, good Master Shallow, no more of that.

SHALLOW
Ha, 'twas a merry night. And is Jane Nightwork alive?

FALSTAFF

She lives, Master Shallow.

SHALLOW

She never could away with me [endure me].

FALSTAFF

Never, never. She would always say she could not abide Master Shallow.

SHALLOW

Nay, she must be old. She cannot choose but be old. . . .

FALSTAFF

We have heard the chimes at midnight, Master Shallow.

Of the twelve passages above, there are three lines that I would like your children to memorize:

There lives not three good men unhanged in England, and one of them is fat and grows old.

I am not only witty in myself, but the cause that wit is in other men.

We have heard the chimes at midnight, Master Shallow.

This final line has become so well known as a kind of philosophical commentary on the passing of time that the great actor Orson Welles used it as the title of his movie about Falstaff, *Chimes at Midnight.*

The more your children repeat these and other quotations, the closer they will get to the essence of Shakespeare's greatness. There is simply no substitute for Shakespeare's actual words, either in study or in performance. That's why this book is based on memorization. Memorization is the key to understanding Shakespeare's artistry.

The Greatest Shakespeare Game of Them All

As you've almost certainly noticed by this time, some of the banter be-tween Falstaff and Hal is based on insults. They insult each other through-out the two history plays, and their mutual wordplay is dazzlingly creative.

You should point this out to your children and have them read aloud the following list of insults. Then give them a subject and have them try to invent insults as good as Shakespeare's. My children loved doing this, though they found it to be a lot harder than it looked. It's pretty easy to call somebody a numbskull or an idiot. But it takes real creative spirit to come up with insults like these:

SPOKEN BY HAL

You fat-kidneyed rascal

This sanguine coward

This bed-presser

This horse-back breaker

This huge hill of flesh

That trunk of humors

That bolting-hutch of beastliness

That swollen parcel of dropsies

That huge bombard of sack

That stuffed cloakbag of guts

That Mannington tree ox with the pudding in his belly

Thou claybrained guts

Thou knotty-pated fool

SPOKEN BY FALSTAFF

You gorbellied knaves

You starveling

You elfskin

You dried neat's tongue

You bull's pizzle

You stockfish

You tailor's yard [yardstick]

You sheath
You bowcase
You vile standing tuck [rapier]
Whoreson caterpillars
Bacon-fed knaves

Hal's Language

Falstaff is Hal's spiritual father, and Hal is Falstaff's masterpiece. He has created Hal in his own image, at least spiritually, and one of the ways we know this is through Hal's use of language. He mimics Falstaff's language the way a child mimics the father he loves. This is one of the subtlest and cleverest things that Shakespeare does in the play: He tricks us into identifying the men with each other through Hal's imitation of Falstaff. We hear it in the insults listed above; and we hear it, even more vividly, in the very first words we hear out of Hal's mouth—one of the most astonishing speeches in all of Shakespeare. Act I, Scene 2 of *Henry IV, Part 1* begins when Falstaff wakes up in the tavern and sees Prince Hal sitting beside him. You and your son or daughter should each take a part:

FALSTAFF
Now, Hal, what time of day is it, lad?

PRINCE HAL
Thou art so fat-witted with drinking of old sack, and unbuttoning thee after supper, and sleeping upon benches after noon, that thou hast forgotten to demand that truly which thou wouldst truly know [forgotten to ask what you really want to know]. *What the devil hast thou to do with the time of day?*

In other words, you are so old, fat, and slovenly, why on earth would you want to know the time?

Now listen carefully to Hal's comparison of the elements of time (such as minutes, clocks, sundials, and the sun) to the things that Falstaff actually cares about, like drink, food, and women:

PRINCE HAL

Unless hours were cups of sack [liquor], *and minutes capons* [fowl],
and clocks the tongues of bawds [loose women], *and dials the signs of*
leaping-houses [bawdy houses], *and the blessed sun himself a fair hot wench*
in flame-colored taffeta [silk fabric], *I see no reason why thou shouldst be*
so superfluous to demand [so ridiculous to ask] *the time of day.*

FALSTAFF

Indeed, you come near me now, Hal, for we that take purses, go by the
moon.

The fact that Falstaff takes no offense at Hal's outburst and admits
that *you come near me now, Hal* (meaning "you're probably right, Hal")
endears us to Falstaff immediately. Falstaff knows that Hal is being boy-
ishly juvenile, and he makes room for it. He indulges Hal, treating him
as an equal, letting him spout off without reproach. For parents, there is
a lesson here.

Note: Listen especially to the line where Hal compares the sun (a symbol of royalty) to a desirable woman in a bright silk gown: *and the blessed*
sun himself a fair hot wench in flame-colored taffeta. Have your children say
it aloud and repeat it. (The word *blessed* is pronounced "BLESS-èd" with
two syllables.)

> *and the blessed sun himself a fair hot wench in*
> *flame-colored taffeta*

It is a line that any writer in the world would give his right arm to have
written.

Hotspur

A character we haven't touched on yet is Hotspur, one of the rebels who
tries to depose the king. He is a young man, also named Harry, and he

is everything that Hal isn't: He is ambitious, brave, political, and a soldier to his bones. Hal is very aware that the world—including his own father—makes comparisons between Hal's lackadaisical ways and Hotspur's serious ones; and a significant part of the plot of Henry IV, Part 1 is the rivalry between the two Harrys, a rivalry that leads to a final confrontation on the battlefield at the end of the play. Here is Hal's father, the King, as he thinks about the comparison of his son with Hotspur:

> O that it could be proved
> That some night-tripping fairy had exchanged
> In cradle-clothes our children where they lay. . . .
> Then I would have his Harry, and he mine.

What a terrible thing to say about your own son. Is it any wonder that Hal is neurotic and seeks a surrogate father in Falstaff?

Hotspur is notable not only for his competition with Hal but also for his incessant talking. While his words are remarkable, he is known to his fellow rebels as someone who can't stop talking—a trait that jeopardizes their cause. Hotspur speaks romantically and heroically, rather like Romeo, and says things like

> By heaven, methinks it were an easy leap
> To pluck bright honor from the pale-faced moon—

Yet he is reckless in a way that makes him a liability to his own cause. Have your children listen for the difference between Hal's speeches (which, as we've seen, sound quite a bit like Falstaff's witty talk) and Hotspur's brave, boasting, romantic speeches. Have them repeat Hotspur's lines that we just quoted:

> By heaven, methinks it were an easy leap
> To pluck bright honor from the pale-faced moon—

and compare them to this wry, funny comment by Hal on what *he* thinks of Hotspur:

he that kills . . . some six or seven dozen . . . Scots at a breakfast,
washes his hands and says to his wife "Fie upon this quiet life! I want
work!"

Hotspur is also crucial to the plot of *Henry IV, Part 1.* In fact, while
Falstaff gives the play its soul, Hal's relationship to Hotspur drives the action. Interestingly, Hal and Hotspur do not meet face to face until Act V
(at which point they fight each other at the Battle of Shrewsbury); but as
the playwright William Gibson observes in his book on how Shakespeare
shaped his plays, the crowning action of *Henry IV, Part 1* is the final encounter between the two young men. As Gibson puts it, "It is almost a
lovers' meeting [between] two diamonds, fated to collide." In the end, in
the final battle, Hal kills Hotspur in hand-to-hand combat and thus vin-
dicates himself in his own eyes. Falstaff subsequently awakes from playing
dead at the battle, wounds the body of Hotspur with his own sword, and
then takes credit for killing *this gunpowder Percy.*

The End of the Story

By this time, your children will want to know the conclusion of the story
between Falstaff and Hal. We know that in the end Hal chooses his re-
sponsibility to his country over that *vanity in years* Sir John Falstaff, but
how does he do it? Is he kind or cruel? I am sorry to report that at the end
of *Henry IV, Part 2,* just after Hal is crowned King of England, he rejects
Falstaff publicly, in front of the world, and banishes him from his presence
forever without a shred of kindness. Here is the scene after the coronation
as Falstaff waits joyfully along the procession route, fully expecting Hal to
embrace him:

(Enter the king and his train.)
FALSTAFF
God save thy Grace, King Hal, my royal Hal. . . . God save thee, my
sweet boy!

KING HENRY V (WHO WAS PRINCE HAL)

I know thee not, old man. Fall to thy prayers.
How ill white hairs becomes a fool and jester.
I have long dreamt of such a kind of man,
So surfeit-swelled, so old, and so profane;
But being awaked, I do despise my dream.

The scene is painful, yet the outcome was inevitable. England's warrior-king was a hero to Shakespeare's audience because he turned away from his youthful indiscretions and then went on to save the kingdom from England's traditional enemy, the French. And in fact, Shakespeare prepares us several times for this terrible reality.

One instance occurs at the end of the great Playacting Scene. After Falstaff makes his plea for himself—*Banish plump Jack and banish all the world*—Hal says, *I do. I will.* It is a chilling moment, and we know instantly what will happen in the end.

Another instance occurs at the end of Act I, Scene 2 of *Part 1*—the scene we've already looked at, where Hal and Falstaff first appear together and Falstaff asks what time it is. At the end of the scene, Hal delivers a soliloquy that tells us exactly how he'll act when he becomes king. Of course, part of us doesn't want to believe it, yet we know in our hearts that the rejection is inevitable. Children forge their own destinies. The wheel turns. The world can be cruel.

Here is Hal's soliloquy from that scene. It is rightly famous for the beauty of its language and the conviction of the speaker. But when we know what it leads to—the rejection of Falstaff—it takes on a political reality that puts it in shade.

PRINCE HAL
*(alone, after agreeing to go on one of
Falstaff's illegitimate escapades)*

Shakespeare's Lines	*My Paraphrase*
I know you all, and will a while uphold The unyok'd humor of your idleness. Yet herein will I imitate the sun, Who doth permit the base contagious clouds To smother up his beauty from the world That when he please again to be himself, Being wanted, he may be more wond'red at By breaking through the foul and ugly mists Of vapors that did seem to strangle him.	I know what you're all thinking, and for a while I'll continue to be irresponsible like the rest of you. But by doing this, I'm imitating the sun, who allows the clouds to cover his beauty, so that when he decides to show himself, he'll be even more wondered at because he'll be breaking through those foul and ugly clouds that seemed to be strangling him.
If all the year were playing holidays, To sport would be as tedious as to work; But when they seldom come, they wish'd for come, And nothing pleaseth but rare accidents.	If we could always be on holiday, year-round, then to have fun would seem like work. But when holidays seldom come, then we look forward to them, and nothing is as pleasing as a rare surprise.

So when this loose behaviour I
  throw off
And pay the debt I never
  promisèd,
By how much better than my
  word I am,
By so much shall I falsify
  men's hopes;
And like bright metal on a
  sullen ground,
My reformation, glitt'ring o'er
  my fault,
Shall show more goodly and
  attract more eyes
Than that which hath no foil
  to set it off.

I'll so offend to make offence
  a skill,
Redeeming time when men
  think least I will.

So when I throw off this bad
behavior that you see now,
and I pay my debt to society,
I'll be as good as my word; and
like a bright piece of metal on
a dark background, my change
of behavior shining over my
faults will show even more
clearly. It will seem even more
brilliant than good behavior
that has always been good and
is not in contrast to the old
bad behavior.

So for now, I'll act so badly
that I'll raise it to the level of
a skill; and then I'll redeem
myself when everyone is least
expecting it.

CHAPTER 26

Passage 17
Rosalind

Why, what means this? Why do you look on me?
I see no more in you than in the ordinary
Of nature's sale-work.—'Od's my little life,
I think she means to tangle my eyes, too. –
No, faith, proud mistress, hope not after it.
'Tis not your inky brows, your black silk hair,
Your bugle eyeballs, nor your cheek of cream
That can entame my spirits to your worship. . . .
But, mistress, know yourself. Down on your knees
And thank heaven, fasting, for a good man's love,
For I must tell you friendly in your ear,
Sell when you can; you are not for all markets.

(*As You Like It*, Act III, Scene 5, lines 46ff.)

Rosalind is another one of those Shakespeare characters whom your children simply have to know. Like her female counterparts in other Shakespeare comedies—Katherine in *The Taming of the Shrew*, Helena in *A Midsummer Night's Dream*, Viola and Olivia in *Twelfth Night*, Beatrice in *Much Ado About Nothing*, and Imogen in *Cymbeline*—she is smart, sassy, witty, resilient, good-natured, and full of life. And she might just be the best talker of all of them.

The play that Rosalind prances through like a colt is *As You Like It*, a comedy that celebrates simple country life over the scheming, political life at court. While the play is verbally sophisticated, it's also perfect for introducing children to Shakespeare because the story is so dramatic and the characters so vivid. These include two doughty heroines, a band of Robin Hood–like nobles, romantic shepherds, a funny parson, a country wench, and a wisecracking jester. The plot has equally strong dramatic scenes, including a wrestling match, a lion on the prowl, and a quadruple wedding.

Toward the beginning of the play, which opens at the court of France, Rosalind attends a wrestling match and falls in love with one of the contenders, a young nobleman named Orlando. Orlando's jealous brother has rigged the match so that Orlando will be killed. (Brothers rarely get along in Shakespeare.) Orlando, however, wins the match but then, fearing for his life, flees to the Forest of Arden with his faithful old servant Adam, a role that Shakespeare himself was reputed to have played. (There was a real Forest of Arden in England in Shakespeare's day, and it's still there, but the one in the play is an idealized forest supposedly in France.)

To everyone's surprise, Rosalind is soon banished from court by her uncle, the Duke, who fears her popularity with his people. She too flees to the Forest of Arden, where her father lives in exile. Her cousin Celia, who is her best friend, insists on going with her, and they decide to disguise themselves for purposes of safety. Rosalind dresses up as a boy and calls herself "Ganymede," and Celia dresses up as Ganymede's sister, calling herself "Aliena." Along with them comes the court jester, Touchstone, who is certainly the funniest of all the jesters in Shakespeare.

What an image Shakespeare creates! Two high-spirited young women in disguise, wandering into the romantic Forest of Arden with a city-wise jester by their side. *Now am I in Arden, the more fool I,* declares Touchstone with skepticism.

> *When I was at home I was in a better place, but travelers must be content.*

Touchstone is like a modern stand-up comedian with a cynical outlook. But in the course of the play, he falls for a country wench and marries her (with lecherous intentions, to be sure), and in the end, even he is affected by the spirit of Arden.

As You Like It at the Old Vic with Juliet Rylance
as Rosalind and Thomas Sadoski as Touchstone

The Passage at Hand

One of the adventures that Rosalind experiences in the forest brings us
to the passage at hand. Rosalind and Celia overhear a young shepherd,
Silvius, declaring his love for a pretty shepherdess, Phebe, who scorns his
love. Silvius is so ardent and Phebe so disdainful that Rosalind simply cannot watch them without interfering. To the surprise of the two shepherds,
she strides out of the trees and starts lecturing Phebe on good manners
and good sense:

ROSALIND

(as Ganymede, coming forward)

And why, I pray you? Who might be your mother

[Are you really such a great lady]

That you insult, exult, and all at once,
Over the wretched? What though you have no beauty . . . ,
Must you therefore be proud and pitiless?

Rosalind then continues with the lines that we're about to memorize:

Why, what means this? Why do you look on me?

Evidently, Phebe is looking at Rosalind in a strange way. As usual, Shakespeare is telling us right in the text how to play the scene.

Why, what means this? Why do you look on me?
I see no more in you
                    than in the ordinary
Of nature's sale-work.

Meaning "I see nothing more in you than in the ordinary products made by nature for general sale"—for example, fruit from a farmer. Highlight for your children that Rosalind uses a commercial image here—which will double back in a few verses in a very funny way. Also point out how Shakespeare leaves out the word *products* in order to make the verse scan so beautifully. Not:

I see no more in you than in the ordinary products
Of nature's sale-work.

But rather:

I see no more in you than in the ordinary
Of nature's sale-work.

And now comes the funniest moment in the speech. Rosalind suddenly understands why the shepherdess Phebe is looking at her so strangely:

Because Rosalind is dressed as a boy,
and Phebe just fell in love with her!

Shakespeare pulled the same trick in *The Two Gentlemen of Verona*. He'll pull it again in *Twelfth Night* and yet again in *Cymbeline*. If you're Shakespeare and you're having your female lead dress up as a boy, you're going to do something wonderful with it in the course of the plot.

Playacting

If you're working with your daughter on this passage, she should now put on a cap, dress up as a boy, and play Rosalind. I can't imagine any girl from five to fifteen not having fun with this passage. My daughter used to love it.

If you're working on this passage with your son, all the better. Tell him to think of himself as a boy actor pretending to be a female character who is dressing up as a boy for purposes of the plot. As we'll discuss in a moment, that is exactly the way it was done in Shakespeare's day.

Back to the Passage

> *Why, what means this? Why do you look on me?*
> *I see no more in you than in the ordinary*
> *Of nature's sale-work.*

And this is the precise moment when Rosalind sees Phebe falling in love with her:

> *'Od's my little life,*
> [an expression of surprise]
> *I think she means to tangle my eyes, too!*

What a phrase: *she means to tangle my eyes, too.* Could there possibly be a lovelier, cleverer, more poetic way of saying "she means to get my heart entangled through her pretty glance, just the way she entangled the heart of Silvius"?

> *'Od's my little life,*
> *I think she means to tangle my eyes, too!*

Rosalind then tells Phebe how far that will get her:

> No, faith, proud mistress, hope not after it.

We now come to three transitional lines that are beautiful and witty and have such a strong rhythm underneath that they're easy to learn:

> 'Tis not your inky brows, your black silk hair,
> Your bugle eyeballs, nor your cheek of cream
> That can entame my spirits to your worship.

Once again we have a list of qualities, something that your children have now become good at memorizing:

> inky brows [eyebrows]
> black silk hair
> bugle [shiny black, like a bead] eyeballs,
> cheek of cream

> brows, hair, eyeballs, cheek

Like the exercise we practiced when Bottom described his dream in *A Midsummer Night's Dream*, have your child touch each part of his or her face in rhythm with the sounds of each phrase: *brows, hair, eyeballs, cheek.*

> 'Tis not your **inky brows,**
> your **black silk hair,**
> Your **bugle eyeballs,**
> nor your **cheek of cream**

> That can entame my spirits to your worship.

Rosalind is right. She's not the sort of man who can be "entamed" by anybody. She's not a man at all, and so she definitely can't be tamed by this snooty and headstrong albeit beautiful girl.

The Ultimate Put-down

And now we come to the cleverest part of the whole speech. Rosalind returns to the commercial imagery that she set up earlier (*the ordinary of nature's sale-work*) and plays on it:

> But, mistress, know yourself. Down on your knees
> And thank heaven, fasting, for a good man's love,
> For I must tell you friendly in your ear,
> Sell when you can; you are not for all markets.

In our household, this last has become another one of those signature lines that we use whenever we can squeeze it in.

MOM

I think I look rather good in this new bathing suit. What do you think, dear?

OLIVIA

Sell when you can; you are not for all markets.

DAD

How's my haircut?

JACK

Sell when you can; you are not for all markets.

Cruel, but funny.

Now let's teach your children these last four lines:

> But, mistress, know yourself.
> > Down on your knees
> And thank heaven, fasting,
> > for a good man's love,

Notice the addition of the word *fasting*. It implies that Phebe should be so grateful for a good man's love—the love offered her by the shepherd Silvius—that she should be thanking heaven as fervently as a monk who fasts for religious reasons. Shakespeare implies all of that with a single word, and it is just the sort of choice that makes him such a remarkable poet. He implies a world of meaning with this single word—and at the same time the word defines Rosalind's character: It tells us that she has a wry, incisive, yet good-natured sense of humor.

> For I must tell you friendly in your ear,
> Sell when you can; you are not for all markets.

Friendly in your ear is beautiful as well, isn't it? Now put those last four lines together:

> But, mistress, know yourself. Down on your knees
> And thank heaven, fasting, for a good man's love,
> For I must tell you friendly in your ear,
> Sell when you can; you are not for all markets.

Rosalind's Wit

Like Falstaff, Rosalind is tremendously witty. She and Beatrice in *Much Ado About Nothing* really begin the entire line of glamorous, witty females whom we admire so much over the next four centuries of plays and movies. (Viola in *Twelfth Night* is equally entrancing, but not in the same sassy way. She is more heartfelt and vulnerable. Helena in *A Midsummer Night's Dream* is a precursor to Rosalind and Beatrice, though this is rarely recognized.)

As we did with Falstaff, we want to get your children used to hearing what Rosalind sounds like. Here is another one of her characteristic speeches, fully as witty as the one we just memorized. It occurs toward the end of the play, after Orlando expresses surprise that his formerly evil brother Oliver has fallen in love with Celia. Rosalind (still dressed as the boy Ganymede) explains to Orlando:

[Y]our brother and my sister no sooner met but they looked, no sooner looked but they loved, no sooner loved but they sighed, no sooner sighed but they asked one another the reason, no sooner knew the reason but they sought the remedy; . . . They are in the very wrath of love, and they will together. Clubs cannot part them.

Is it any wonder that Orlando falls so desperately in love with Rosalind? Anyone who speaks with that much wit is worth a world of sacrifices. See if your children can learn the last two lines on the spot. It's worth every second of the two minutes it will take them:

They are in the very wrath of love, and they will together. Clubs cannot part them.

The Boy Actors

As your children may know already—and this is one of those popular facts that happens to be true—there were no women actors in the English theater of Shakespeare's day. Women were not allowed to act onstage in the Elizabethan and Jacobean eras, and this situation did not change until 1660, well after Shakespeare's lifetime. Thus, when Shakespeare created Rosalind and Celia—and Juliet and Viola and Ophelia and Desdemona—they were all portrayed by boy actors, probably in the age range of twelve to seventeen. We don't know their ages for certain, but they had to be young enough that their voices hadn't changed yet.

The boy actors in companies like the Lord Chamberlain's Men were apprentices to older actors, and there were usually two to four of them in a company of about twenty-six men at any one time. Usually Shakespeare's plays contain no more than eight important speaking parts, reflecting the number of sharers (owners) in the company. The rest of the men and boys were hired by the company, swelling the company's ranks to about twenty-six. Most plays were performed by fifteen or so actors per play, many of them doubling roles.

While we know the names of a few of the boy actors, we don't know for certain which roles each one played and whether one or another was *the* great boy actor who originated any of the most famous female leads. (Evidence suggests that one of the greatest boy actors was a young man named John Rice, who probably originated the roles of Lady Macbeth and Cleopatra.) It seems clear, however, that the very existence of the boy actors prompted Shakespeare to create so many girl-dressed-as-boy plots. Viola, Rosalind, Portia, and Imogen would have been very convincing as boys because they *were* boys.

In *As You Like It,* this cross-dressing gets an extra twist: The boy actor portrays the girl Rosalind—who in turn dresses up as the boy Ganymede— who in turn pretends to be the girl Rosalind so that Orlando can practice wooing her. A Polish literary critic, Jan Kott, wrote a groundbreaking book entitled *Shakespeare Our Contemporary* in 1965, in which he comments on the sexual ambiguity that Shakespeare created in his cross-dressing comedies, especially in *As You Like It,* where the boy actor

> disguised as a girl plays a girl disguised as a boy. Everything is real and unreal, false and genuine at the same time. And we cannot tell on which side of the looking glass we have found ourselves. As if everything were mere reflection. . . . The love scenes in the Forest of Arden have the logic of dreams. . . . Disguise is a dangerous game [and the] most dangerous disguise of all is the one where sex is changed.

One speculates that Shakespeare's older female roles, like the Nurse in *Romeo and Juliet,* were played by mature actors, since the deeper voice and the physical look would have been more in keeping. But it is probable that even the middle-years roles, like Lady Macbeth and Cleopatra, were played by boy actors. If so, these young men must have been very well trained and immensely skilled.

Exercise

If your son is game, it will be fun for him to work up one of Rosalind's passages and act it out as though he were one of Shakespeare's boy actors preparing a convincing stage performance as a young woman. This is done in acting schools all the time, and if you have a son who is genuinely interested in acting, it would be a wonderful way for him to begin honing his profession. Viola's Willow Cabin Speech from *Twelfth Night* would be a good place to start.

Reviewing

One of the things you'll want your children to do, in addition to simply memorizing the passages one after the other, is finding a way to retain the passages, keeping them freshly at their fingertips for years to come. In our family, we found success in this area by doing three things.

First, we found that retention was directly related to how well we memorized each passage in the first place. The passages where our kids finished up still hesitating somewhere along the way never really stuck. But the passages that they could rattle off by rote, at high speeds without hesitations, stayed with them for years and years. "Speed runs" (which we use in the theater all the time, rattling off entire plays before opening night) are highly recommended. Do them often, and make them fun.

Second, simple reviews every now and then are a great help. After you've finished memorizing Passage 17 above, go back to Passage 9 or 10 and recite it aloud together. Start doing this at the end of every session. Especially now that you're over halfway through this book, start reviewing passages randomly and regularly. Most aspects of learning are a product of repetition, none more so than memorization.

Finally, in our house we've tried to find funny ways to trigger passages when the kids were least expecting it. You've seen some examples throughout the book. "How fast can you run upstairs and clean up your vile and horrific-looking room before I murder you?" *Swifter than arrow from the Tartar's bow.* Or if we're watching the news on TV and we see something about a love story: "Do you remember what Caesario would do if he loved Olivia in his master's flame?" *Make me a willow cabin at her gate.* "What does the Royal Wedding remind you of (in addition to owning Buckingham Palace)?" Theseus and Hippolyta. "And what did Theseus say to Hippolyta, which also happened to open the whole play?" *Now fair Hippolyta, our nuptial hour draws on apace.* Great praise always followed a right answer, as well it should have. By learning Shakespeare, your kids are going the extra mile, and they deserve to be admired for it.

CHAPTER 27

Passage 18
This Wide and Universal Theatre

Thou seest we are not all alone unhappy.
This wide and universal theatre
Presents more woeful pageants than the scene
Wherein we play in.

(*As You Like It*, Act II, Scene 7, lines 142–45)

We are about to make a quantum leap into the heart of Shakespeare. The passage printed at the beginning of the next chapter has become a classic over the past four hundred years, and as we dig into it, we'll learn that it deserves its status as much as Beethoven's Fifth Symphony and Michelangelo's Sistine Chapel ceiling; they are all classics because of the quality of their artistry. The passage printed above is the introduction to the longer passage, and it is equally worth memorizing.

To understand the power of the great Ages of Man Speech, your children must understand its setting. Certainly the lines are remarkable as a stand-alone reverie on the passage of time, but their significance is enhanced by their context in the play's narrative.

As your children know from the last chapter, Orlando has fled to the Forest of Arden to escape the murderous intentions of his brother. With him has come a servant, old Adam, who has served the family since Orlando was a boy. The two men are suffering for want of food, and Adam is on the brink of starvation. (Reminder: Recite all these lines aloud with your children, even when the lines are not part of the passage that they're memorizing.)

ADAM

Dear master, I can go no further. O, I die for food. Here lie I down and measure out my grave. Farewell, kind master.

Orlando replies with words that reveal the goodness of his heart. He has an innate humanity that reminds me of Theseus in A *Midsummer Night's Dream*:

ORLANDO

For my sake be comfortable. Hold death awhile at the arm's end. I will here be with thee presently [soon], *and if I bring thee not something to eat, I will give thee leave* [allow you] *to die. But if thou diest before I come, thou art a mocker of my labor.*

Orlando runs off to find food for Adam, and as the scene changes to the encampment of Duke Senior (Rosalind's father), we find the Duke speaking to his followers. As we have learned earlier in the play, Duke Senior has

many merry men with him; and there they live like the old Robin Hood of England. They say many young gentlemen flock to him every day and fleet the time carelessly, as they did in the golden world.

Duke Senior and his followers are waiting for one of their number to arrive, a man named Jaques (with the English pronunciation "JAY-kwees"). He is one of the pantheon of great Shakespeare characters whom your children must get to know. Jaques's primary characteristic is a kind of world-weary melancholy that affects every word he utters. As he says of himself:

I can suck melancholy out of a song as a weasel sucks eggs.

When Jaques enters, he is bursting with excitement (which for Jaques is unusual) because he has met Touchstone in the forest and finds the jester amusing in the extreme. Jaques cries:

> A fool, a fool, I met a fool i' th' forest,
> A motley fool. A miserable world!
> [Motley is the diamond-pattern cloth worn by jesters.]

He is amused that this fool is so *deep-contemplative*. He discovered this when he saw Touchstone pulling a sundial from his pocket:

> And looking on it with lack-luster eye,
> Says very wisely . . .
> "'Tis but an hour ago since it was nine,
> And after one hour more 'twill be eleven.
> And so from hour to hour we ripe and ripe,
> And then from hour to hour we rot and rot,
> And thereby hangs a tale."

As *You Like It* is full of brilliant talkers, and Jaques and Touchstone are two of them.

At this point in the story, as the Duke and his friends are about to eat their rustic supper, Orlando rushes in, brandishing his sword:

> Forbear, and eat no more! . . .
> He dies that touches any of this fruit
> Till I and my affairs are answerèd.

Question: Ask your children what they think Duke Senior's response will be to this desperate man who rushes into his camp brandishing a sword and demanding food.

Answer: To Orlando's surprise, Duke Senior responds with courtesy:

DUKE
Sit down and feed, and welcome to our table.

Orlando answers, amazed:

Speak you so gently? Pardon me, I pray you.
I thought that all things had been savage here . . .
If ever you have looked on better days,
If ever been where bells have knolled [tolled] to church,
If ever sat at any good man's feast,
If ever from your eyelids wiped a tear
And know what 'tis to pity and be pitied,
Let gentleness my strong enforcement be,
[Let me use gentleness as though it were force,]
In the which hope I blush and hide my sword.

Could Orlando possibly have answered with a more beautiful speech? Repeat it aloud with your children—right now—and remind them that here is a man who has been humbled by kindness.

Orlando now explains that he and old Adam are starving, and that Adam is waiting alone not far away. This prompts the kindly Duke to promise that no one will eat anything until Orlando returns with Adam. Orlando rushes off, and it is at this point that the Duke says to his followers the words that we're about to memorize:

Thou seest we are not all alone unhappy.
This wide and universal theatre
Presents more woeful pageants than the scene
Wherein we play in.

Make sure that your children learn this touching introduction to the more famous passage that follows.

Thou seest we are not all alone unhappy.

"You see that there are others who suffer as we do."

This wide and universal theatre
Presents more woeful pageants than the scene
Wherein we play in.

"The world is like a big theater, and in it there are scenes even more woeful than ours."

> This wide and universal theatre
> Presents more woeful pageants
> > than the scene
> Wherein we play in.

Theater as Metaphor

Your children should be aware, particularly as we tackle the Ages of Man Speech in the next chapter, that throughout his writing career, Shakespeare used the theater as one of his central metaphors for the life of mankind. We saw it in *A Midsummer Night's Dream* as the Mechanicals put on a play to solemnize the Duke's wedding; we saw it in *Macbeth* (*a poor player who struts and frets his hour upon the stage*); and we saw it in *Henry IV, Part 1*, where Falstaff and Hal put on their play in the tavern. Similarly, we'll see it in several of the passages to come: in the great Prologue to *Henry V* (*O, for a muse of fire*); in Hamlet's speech to the players (*Speak the speech, I pray you*); and, finally, in the moving summation of Shakespeare's art in *The Tempest* (*Our revels now are ended*).

That Shakespeare should refer to the theater so often in his plays makes all the sense in the world. Shakespeare was a playwright, an actor, and a theater shareholder. His whole professional life revolved around the theater—and we're about to encounter the greatest example of theater-as-metaphor in all of English literature.

CHAPTER 28

Passage 18, Continued
The World as a Stage

All the world's a stage,
And all the men and women merely players.
They have their exits and their entrances,
And one man in his time plays many parts,
His acts being seven ages.

At first the infant,
Mewling and puking in the nurse's arms.
Then the whining schoolboy with his satchel
And shining morning face, creeping like snail
Unwillingly to school.

And then the lover,
Sighing like furnace, with a woeful ballad
Made to his mistress' eyebrow.

Then a soldier,
Full of strange oaths and bearded like the pard,
Jealous in honor, sudden and quick in quarrel,
Seeking the bubble reputation
Even in the cannon's mouth.

And then the justice,
In fair round belly with good capon lined,
With eyes severe and beard of formal cut,
Full of wise saws and modern instances;
And so he plays his part.

The sixth age shifts
Into the lean and slippered pantaloon
With spectacles on nose and pouch on side,
His youthful hose, well saved, a world too wide

For his shrunk shank, and his big, manly voice,
Turning again toward childish treble, pipes
And whistles in his sound.
                              Last scene of all,
That ends this strange eventful history,
Is second childishness and mere oblivion,
Sans teeth, sans eyes, sans taste, sans everything.

(*As You Like It*, Act II, Scene 7, lines 146–73)

The First Half

In this famous passage, Jaques describes the life cycle of every man and woman who has ever lived to old age. He begins by observing, simply:

All the world's a stage,
And all the men and women merely players [actors].

Its simple rhythm mirrors the simplicity of the statement. Notice that it is in perfectly regular iambic pentameter.

All the **world's** a **stage**,
And **all** the **men** and **women** **merely** **players**.

And yet perhaps this opening statement is not quite as simple as it seems. The existence of a play implies the existence of a playwright—a prime mover in the background—and that therefore we are all following a script. Shakespeare underlines this idea by reminding us that the actors in this play

have their exits and their entrances.

We all arrive on this scene called life, and we will all, ultimately, leave it with a final exit.

Notice also how the opening of this speech starts in the middle of a line:

DUKE SENIOR

This wide and universal theatre
Presents more woeful pageants than the scene
Wherein we play in.

JAQUES

All the world's a stage . . .

This gives the opening a sense of surprise and immediacy. It means that we have to say it as though we're jumping onto a passing train. I think that Shakespeare did it so that his speech about life would sound less bombastic. He wanted the now-famous passage to sneak up on us and sound conversational.

Practice the opening of the passage in this way with your children. You play Duke Senior and have your son or daughter play Jaques. Make sure that they start the speech *All the world's a stage* as an extension of your line, *Wherein we play in.*

1. The Infant

At first the infant,
Mewling and puking in the nurse's arms.

Mewling means "making baby noises." Also point out to your children that this "age," like all but one of the ages in the speech, begins in the middle of a line. Again, I think Shakespeare does this to make the speech move along dynamically and not pompously. Notice also how Jaques gives every age a slightly sardonic twist because that's how he views the world. Here the baby is not only making baby noises, he's also puking.

2. The Schoolboy

> *Then the whining schoolboy with his satchel* [backpack or rucksack]
> *And shining morning face, creeping like snail*
> *Unwillingly to school.*

What a perfect picture of this poor boy dragging to school every day. I'm especially fond of the phrase *shining* **morning** *face*. Not only does it tell us that the boy's face has been scrubbed clean for school, but it also implies that by evening it won't be so shining: It will be dirty from the mayhem of a long school day. To pack so much information into such little space is a mark of Shakespeare's poetic genius. Also notice the internal rhyme *whining* and *shining*, which makes the sentence easier to memorize.

3. The Lover

> *And then the lover,*
> *Sighing like furnace, with a woeful ballad*
> *Made to his mistress' eyebrow.*

Shakespeare starts these lines from the premise that it is typical of a young man or woman to write poems to his or her loved one. Fair enough. And it is equally typical that a lover sighs in longing for the object of such youthful obsession. But to sigh *like furnace* is an exceptionally witty, Jaques-like thing to say. A furnace is full of hot air and expels that air with loud groans.

Equally witty is the notion that a lover would write his woeful ballad *to his mistress' eyebrow*. Lovers adore everything about their loved ones, and here the lover is so obsessed by his beloved that he's writing an entire poem about her *eyebrow*.

4. The Soldier

> *Then a soldier,*
> *Full of strange oaths and bearded like the pard* [leopard],
> *Jealous in honor, sudden and quick in quarrel,*

Seeking the bubble reputation
Even in the cannon's mouth.

Shakespeare paints the picture of a soldier who has just been off to war. He is full of *strange oaths* because he has been in foreign parts. He is bearded like a leopard because that was the look that soldiers cultivated in Elizabethan times: an exotic look with just those few hairs sticking out of their chins.

The soldier here is also jealous of his honor—in other words, he's just waiting to be challenged so he can fight. He moves with sudden movements, and he is quarrelsome because he's anxious—indeed, overanxious—to prove his worth.

Jealous in honor, sudden and quick in quarrel,
Seeking the bubble reputation

Not seeking "high reputation" or "worthy reputation" but *the bubble reputation.*

BUBBLE?

Bubble is a good word to discuss with your children. It has a subtlety that they might otherwise miss. Shakespeare is reminding us that reputations are fleeting and subject to bursting, and that everything that the soldier is quarreling about is ephemeral and likely to change overnight. Famously, there have been many economic bubbles over the years, and when the market bursts, the economy explodes and readjusts. Shakespeare suggests all this and more in a single phrase: *the bubble reputation.*

5. The Justice

And then the justice,
In fair round belly with good capon lined,
With eyes severe and beard of formal cut,
Full of wise saws and modern instances;
And so he plays his part.

Justice means "justice of the peace," which was a lower court judge or magistrate. It is a job for someone in middle age who has earned a level of respectability. Shakespeare portrays the justice as having a comfortably large belly, which is lined with capon (a small edible bird).

Of all seven descriptions, I find this one the most vivid. I feel that I know this man. I have seen him in country towns. He is one of the local worthies who goes to a club, eats well, and tells good stories. His beard is of *formal cut*. He is no longer *bearded like the pard*—that was youthful and daring. Also, he is full of *wise saws and modern instances*. A *saw* is a saying, and a *modern instance* would be the kind of example that he, as a justice, would hand down from the bench. Finally, at the end of this description, Shakespeare brings the opening section to a close with a nice, steady cadence of finality: *And* **so** *he* **plays** *his* **part.**

Your children are now over halfway through the speech, and they've learned five of the seven ages. Point out to them the accuracy of the picture that Shakespeare has painted of the march of time. Nothing can stop the process as it moves along from innocence to self-awareness to wisdom—and then, as we'll see in a moment, to the feeble existence of old Adam in the play. It is the way of the world.

The Second Half

6. The Pantaloon

> *The sixth age shifts*
> *Into the lean and slippered pantaloon*
> *With spectacles on nose and pouch on side,*
> *His youthful hose, well saved, a world too wide*
> *For his shrunk shank, and his big, manly voice,*
> *Turning again toward childish treble, pipes*
> *And whistles in his sound.*

A *pantaloon* is a feeble and rather ridiculous old man. The literal meaning of the word *pantaloon* is the baggy trousers that old men often wear;

and the word is also used for one of the stock characters in a form of sixteenth-century Italian stage comedy called commedia dell'arte. In that tradition, Pantaloon was the foolish old fellow who was losing his memory because age was overtaking him. (Shakespeare paints a perfect portrait of him in Justice Shallow in *Henry IV, Part 2.*)

Have your children notice in particular that the age *shifts* into the pantaloon. How exceptionally clever to imply that the age itself slips *into* the pair of trousers while at the same time saying the age moves from the justice to the foolish old man.

The sixth age shifts

Into the lean and slippered pantaloon
With spectacles on nose and pouch on side,
His youthful hose, well saved, a world too wide
For his shrunk shank,

Other words to point out include *pouch*, which is a purse, and *youthful hose*, which are the stockings that the old man would have worn when he was young. Touchingly, he has saved them, and they are now too big for him: They are too wide for his *shrunk shank*. Shakespeare has chosen to emphasize the *w* sound (*well . . . world . . . wide*) to approximate an old man's speech.

*His youthful hose, **well** saved, a **world** too **wide***

And he has chosen the words *shrunk shank* in order to make us slow down as we say the line, just as the pantaloon is slowing down as he walks.

Shakespeare then contrasts the sound of a young man with the sound of an old man:

*and his **big, manly voice***
[which sounds big and manly with its strong consonants]
*Turning again toward **childish treble, pipes***
And whistles in his sound.

Every great actor whom I have ever heard recite this speech has used the words *pipes*, *whistles*, and *sound* to subtly emphasize the whistling sound of an elderly person's speech.

> *pipessss and whisssstlessss in his ssssound*

Have your children try it that way. Have them pretend, with dignity, that their speech sounds like that of an old man or woman. Their voices should move higher into the treble (upper) range, and we should hear, just slightly, the whistling *s*'s.

7. Second Childishness

> Last scene of all,
> *That ends this strange eventful history,*
> *Is second childishness and mere oblivion,*
> *Sans teeth, sans eyes, sans taste, sans everything.*

The last scene of this play called life is second childishness, when we lose everything but our last breath. We descend into *mere oblivion*, or nothingness. The word *mere* is simple but telling. In the end, even our oblivion is paltry and insignificant. *Sans* (pronounced in English to rhyme with *pans*) means "without." (*Sans* is the French word for "without" but is pronounced differently in French.) Treat the last line as a list. Use gestures to memorize it, as we've done before.

> *Sans* **teeth**,
> *sans* **eyes**,
> *sans* **taste**,
> *sans* **everything**.

This final line, with its repetition of *sans*, has a relentlessness to it. Remind your children that it is reminiscent of Macbeth's

> *Tomorrow and tomorrow and tomorrow*

Ironically, this witty, melancholy speech appears in one of Shakespeare's sunniest comedies. But that is also typical of Shakespeare. None of his comedies is all lightness and humor. Even *The Merry Wives of Windsor* gets serious for a moment about adultery; and even *The Comedy of Errors* has a plot that puts an old man's life in danger. The Ages of Man Speech ends in melancholy partly because of Jaques's melancholic perspective, but also because Shakespeare was fearlessly true to life. Throughout his plays we see not only comedy and not only tragedy but also, always, the truth.

CHAPTER 29

Passage 19
O, for a Muse of Fire!

O, for a muse of fire that would ascend
The brightest heaven of invention!
A kingdom for a stage, princes to act,
And monarchs to behold the swelling scene!
Then should the warlike Harry, like himself,
Assume the port of Mars, and at his heels,
Leashed in like hounds, should famine, sword, and fire
Crouch for employment. But pardon, gentles all,
The flat unraisèd spirits that hath dared
On this unworthy scaffold to bring forth
So great an object. Can this cockpit hold
The vasty fields of France? Or may we cram
Within this wooden O the very casques
That did affright the air at Agincourt?
O pardon, since a crookèd figure may
Attest in little place a million,
And let us, ciphers to this great account,
On your imaginary forces work.
Suppose within the girdle of these walls
Are now confined two mighty monarchies,
Whose high uprearèd and abutting fronts
The perilous narrow ocean parts asunder.
Piece out our imperfections with your thoughts.
Into a thousand parts divide one man,
And make imaginary puissance.
Think, when we talk of horses, that you see them
Printing their proud hoofs i' th' receiving earth,

> For 'tis your thoughts that now must deck our kings,
> Carry them here and there, jumping o'er times,
> Turning th' accomplishment of many years
> Into an hourglass; for the which supply,
> Admit me chorus to this history,
> Who, prologue-like, your humble patience pray
> Gently to hear, kindly to judge our play.

(Henry V, Prologue to Act I)

One aspect of Shakespeare's genius resides in the fact that he rarely, if ever, repeated himself. He was always coming up with new solutions to age-old problems, new ways of beginning plays, ending plays, creating new subject matter, and tackling new themes.

Just look at the comedies alone. *Love's Labour's Lost*, one of the early comedies, is filled with profusions of exquisite, intricate love poetry, then ends with the death of the heroine's father, thereby adding a somber note to the final scene. Meanwhile, *The Taming of the Shrew*, written in the same period, uses a rough, vernacular style to tell the story of a misogynist who meets his match amid episodes of knockabout comedy and mistaken identity. In *Much Ado About Nothing* we have a pair of witty, jaded lovers, as well as a dark-hearted villain caught by the local constabulary; *As You Like It* contains rival brothers, romantic shepherds, a court jester, and a lion; and in *Cymbeline* Shakespeare creates a fairy tale princess, an evil stepmother, two princes raised in a cave, and the beheading of a villainous suitor. On and on it goes. In each play Shakespeare sets himself a new challenge, and his invention simply never flags.

In *Henry V*, which was written in 1599 (at about the same time as *As You Like It*, and just before *Hamlet*), Shakespeare does something new yet again: He starts each of the five acts with an actor (called the Chorus) speaking directly to the audience as a sort of narrator who sets the scene. Four of these Prologues function as narrative links between acts. The Prologue to Act I, however, is entirely different. It has very little to do with the play *Henry V* but everything in the world to do with Theater with a capital *T*.

In the Prologue to Act I, the Chorus says, in essence, that he needs great inspiration to make his play convincing to the audience since it does not *actually* take place on the fields of France, there are not *actually* thousands of soldiers in view, and the play does not *actually* span the many years that it pretends to. He reminds us that we're in a theater and that we must use

our imaginations.

That's what this Prologue is about, and that, in essence, is what the works of Shakespeare are about.

The Mystery of the Theater

One of the mysteries of literature is how simple words on a page can get us thinking about our humanity across time and space: how a story written in the sixteenth century can be as inspiring and relevant as if it were written yesterday. Similarly, one of the mysteries of the theater is how words spoken on a stage can transport us to other worlds, convincing us that we are partaking of other lives playing out in front of us, all the while knowing that those lives are being portrayed by actors. Like language itself, theater is always operating on two levels:

1. the level where we are convinced we are seeing what the play says we're seeing, like a battle on a field in France, and
2. the level where we know full well that we are in a room called a theater watching five actors pretending to be a whole army.

The Act I Prologue is meant to remind us of this two-level mystery.

In the 1950s, the playwright and novelist J. B. Priestley wrote an essay in which he recounted the experience of taking his children to the theater. He noticed that when they were very young, they sat in their seats and looked around, very aware that they were in this strange room called a theater. But "a year or two later these same children may be a wonderful audience."

> What has happened? They have arrived at dramatic experience. And . . . we can say that this experience has for them an unusual intensity . . . difficult to recapture in later life, just because they are fully and eagerly responsive on both our necessary levels. For they are rapturously concerned with the characters and action of the piece being presented, but at the same time they are more intensely conscious than adults are of not being physically involved in the scene. . . . So two wonderful things are happening at once; and I cannot help feeling that it is the child surviving in us who makes us fully responsive to the Theatre.

I was recently rereading *A Midsummer Night's Dream*, and I was delighted to see Shakespeare making exactly the same point five years before he wrote *Henry V*. In Act V of the *Dream*, as the Mechanicals are putting on their play *Pyramus and Thisbe*, Hippolyta remarks that *This is the silliest stuff that I ever heard*. Theseus replies:

> *The best in this kind are but shadows; and the worst are no worse, if imagination amends them.*

He's saying that even the best actors can only be shadows of the characters they're portraying; and the worst actors are no worse, as long as our *imagination* takes over and makes them real in our minds. So this profound view of the theater—and of life—was on Shakespeare's mind well before he wrote his great Prologue to *Henry V*.

Learning the Speech: The First Half

> *O, for a muse of fire that would ascend*
> *The brightest heaven of invention!*

The Chorus begins by invoking a *muse*, a goddess of artistic inspiration. In Greek mythology, there were nine Muses, one each for comedy, tragedy, dance, etc. They were thought to inspire great thoughts that would spur on artistic creation. Here the Chorus cries out O, *for a muse of fire*. He wants inspiration that will rise up as powerfully as *fire* and ascend to the *heaven* of *invention*.

> A **kingdom** *for a stage,*
> **princes** *to act,*
> *And* **monarchs**
> *to behold the swelling scene!*
> [A list, a list!]

The Chorus not only wants a *muse of fire* to inspire him. He also wants a real kingdom, real princes, and real monarchs to be part of his play. If he had such a muse, such a stage, and such actors, he could present a grander vision of history.

> *Then should the warlike Harry, like himself,*
> *Assume the port of Mars, and at his heels,*
> *Leashed in like hounds, should famine, sword, and fire*
> *Crouch for employment.*

In Roman mythology, Mars was the god of war. And if King Henry did assume the port of Mars—that is, climb up to the door of war—he would have three formidable qualities at his heels, three of the external manifestations of war: famine, sword, and fire. He would be in charge of these qualities, as if they were *hounds* on their leashes, crouching next to him, waiting for their *employment*.

Art Project

If your children like art, have them try to draw or paint King Henry V assuming the port of Mars with three hounds leashed in at his heels. If I had any drawing talent at all, I'd be the first one in line with my pad and pencil. Shakespeare has created an image here that is so palpable and clear that who in the world wouldn't want to paint it? I've trolled the Internet looking for just such an image by an established artist, and surprisingly, I couldn't find one to show you.

Aside

One subject that we haven't touched on yet is the representation of scenes from Shakespeare in the history of art. As you can imagine, many great artists have used Shakespeare's plays as their inspiration. One of my own favorites is Henry Fuseli (1741–1825), who painted in a number of subject areas but became renowned for his Shakespeare paintings. Here is one of his most famous, of Titania and Bottom in *A Midsummer Night's Dream*:

Titania and Bottom by Henry Fuseli

In the Bibliography, I've listed a good source by Jane Martineau for looking at Shakespeare in art. It's a wonderful subject for your children to pursue.

And if any of them are good painters, Henry at the port of Mars is clearly a subject that could make them famous.

Back to the Speech

> But pardon, gentles all,
> The flat unraisèd spirits that hath dared
> On this unworthy scaffold to bring forth
> So great an object.

The Chorus now asks pardon for his actors (*unraisèd spirits*) who have dared to portray so great an object as the story of Henry V on *this unworthy scaffold*—this stage, which is nothing but a wooden structure: "Gentle audience, please pardon our actors who dare to play this great story on this unworthy stage."

> Can this cock-pit hold
> The vasty fields of France?

I love this image: A *cock-pit* is a round area where cockfights were staged in Shakespeare's day. He's comparing his theater, the Globe, with a cock-pit, since both were round (or essentially round; in fact, the Globe was multisided).

He elaborates on this roundness two lines later. Note: The word *casques* means "helmets"; and Agincourt is the town where a famous battle against the French took place.

> Or may we cram
> Within this wooden O the very casques
> That did affright the air at Agincourt?

The phrase *this wooden O* is Shakespeare's description of his own theater. Just imagine it: A man is standing on the stage, surrounded on three sides by the audience, and as he speaks, he gestures to everything that surrounds him calling it *this wooden O*. Shakespeare is here obliterating the separation of the world of the play and the world of the audience. He is saying, "Here we are in this theater, this wooden O: How can we cram into this place the soldiers and the horses and everything else that the word *helmets* implies?"

> O pardon, since a crookèd **figure** may
> Attest in little place a **million**,
> And let us, **ciphers** to this great **account**,
> On your imaginary forces work.

Here is Shakespeare punning again. He uses the word *figure* in two senses: A *figure*, in addition to being a person, is also a number. Moreover, a number that is a *cipher* is a zero. And a zero is a placeholder that can become part of a million if you move the decimal point. So one *crookèd figure* can become part of a million—and one lone person can turn into a million people in our imaginations. In addition, an *account* is both a story and a sum of mathematical figures. So a single figure can become a million if you let the Chorus *On your imaginary forces work*. Brilliant.

The Second Half

The second half of the speech is quite straightforward. It does, however, contain some unfamiliar words and phrases, so let me paraphrase it. Please make sure your children read the real speech first, then the paraphrase.

Shakespeare's Lines	My Paraphrase
Suppose within the girdle of these walls Are now confined two mighty monarchies,	Suppose that here, within the confining walls (*girdle*) of the theater, there are two mighty kingdoms (England and France).

Whose high uprearèd and
    abutting fronts
The perilous narrow ocean
    parts asunder.

The *fronts* of these kingdoms
face each other across the
English Channel (a *perilous
narrow ocean*) but still within
the *girdle* of the theater.

Piece out our imperfections
    with your thoughts.

With your thoughts, fill in
what you don't see.

Into a thousand parts divide
    one man,
And make imaginary
    puissance.

In your minds, divide one
man into a thousand men and
thereby make an imaginary
army.

Think, when we talk of
    horses, that you see them
Printing their proud hoofs i'
    th' receiving earth,

When we talk about horses,
see them in your minds, paw-
ing the earth,

For 'tis your thoughts that
    now must deck our kings,

because it's your thoughts that
make our actors into kings.

Carry them here and there,
    jumping o'er times,
Turning th' accomplishment of
    many years
Into an hourglass;

With your thoughts, carry our
kings everywhere, even jumping (like horses) over time and
turning the accomplishments
of years into the short time
measured with an hourglass.

             for the which supply,
Admit me chorus to this
    history,
Who, prologue-like, your
    humble patience pray
Gently to hear, kindly to judge
    our play.

And to repay me for telling
you all this (supplying you
with this information), allow
me to be the Prologue-like
Chorus to this play, and I ask
you to be patient and gentle
and to judge our play kindly.

Once your children understand this half of the speech, help them memorize it a phrase at a time. The Quotation Pages will help more than ever on this one because it's so long. After that it's just a matter of repetition.

Henry V has turned out to be one of Shakespeare's most popular plays, less, I think, because of the quality of the plot and characters than because it contains so many muscular speeches. Shakespeare's other popular history plays are remembered for other qualities: *Richard III* for the funny, ruthless, spiderlike megalomaniac at the center who will do anything to become King of England; *Richard II* for the sensitivity of the hero; and *Henry IV, Part 1* for Falstaff and his relationship to the coltish Prince Hal. *Henry V* is a different kind of play. It's about heroism and war and the tragedy of war—and it's also about the magic of Theater.

CHAPTER 30

Henry the Patriot

enry V is the last great history play written by Shakespeare. He wrote ten history plays in all, and this was the ninth, so he was certainly a master of the form by the time he tackled it. The play tells the story of the man we first knew as Prince Hal in *Henry IV*. Historically, Henry V was known as England's savior, the man who rallied his troops and saved the country from the hated French. With this in mind, Shakespeare makes him into an almost god-like creature who personally walks among his men on the night before the Battle of Agincourt, then leads them into the fray and defeats the enemy.

Shakespeare and the Question of Interpretation

Your children should be aware of a movie version of *Henry V* produced in 1944 toward the end of World War II, starring and directed by Sir Laurence Olivier. It became popular in part because of its overt patriotism, which boosted the morale of the English as they fought through the final months of the war to defeat Hitler. A more recent film of *Henry V* was made in 1989 by Kenneth Branagh, who also starred and directed. Branagh takes a much grittier approach and portrays Henry less as an untainted hero and more as a realist. In the Olivier version, the war and heroism are idealized;

Henry V at Shakespeare's Globe Theatre with Nigel Cooke as Exeter, Jamie Park as Henry, James Lailey as Westmoreland, and Brendan O'Hara as Fluellen

in the Branagh version, we see the horrors of war and experience the violence of human sacrifice.

Your children should of course see both of these films, if nothing else, for their sheer entertainment value. But there is also a twofold lesson here.

First, Shakespeare's plays, like all great works of art, are open to interpretation. That is a hallmark of art that has real value. If a work is static and never changes, then it can never tell us very much about how we change over our lifetimes, and how mankind changes over time. As Hamlet says, it is the artist's job to hold the mirror up to nature.

When we experience a work of art that has genuine value—when we look at a significant painting or watch a performance of a well-written play—we see it differently depending on who we are by nature and where we are in the trajectory of our own experience. Great art changes with us as we and the world grow older.

Second, Shakespeare's work is particularly susceptible to this openness of interpretation, more so than the work of other dramatists. The critic

Stanley Wells calls this a "self-renewing quality" of Shakespeare's work, "as if [Shakespeare] himself had had the wisdom to leave his plays slightly unfinished, to hold back from final decisions so that future ages could read into them preoccupations of their own times. . . . Perhaps there is, somehow, a more mythic quality about Shakespeare that enables his plays to speak to generation after generation."

One of the joys of watching Shakespeare on film is to see how interpretations have changed over the years, especially in terms of a single play, and I urge you to watch a few Shakespeare plays on film with your children. Literally hundreds of films of Shakespeare's plays have been made over the years, and I've listed a few of my favorites in the Bibliography.

Henry's Famous Speeches

Henry V is exciting and well told, but what makes it particularly memorable is the language of Henry's heroism. Your children may well recognize two of Henry's most famous speeches from the play, as they have become emblems of bravery and patriotism throughout the world.

Speech 1: The Rallying Cry

The first is Henry's rallying cry during the battle to conquer the city of Harfleur. Here is a cut version of the speech that would be perfect for a recitation contest—or just for the fun of learning it.

Shakespeare's Lines	My Paraphrases
Once more unto the breach, dear friends, once more, Or close the wall up with our English dead! In peace there's nothing so becomes a man As modest stillness and humility, But when the blast of war blows in our ears, Then imitate the action of the tiger;	Fight through the opening in the enemy's lines [the breach] again and again, or, if that fails, then close the breach with our dead bodies. If this were peacetime, we would be modest and quiet, but when it's wartime we should imitate tigers!
Stiffen the sinews, summon up the blood, Disguise fair nature with hard-favored rage. . . . Now set the teeth and stretch the nostril wide, Hold hard the breath, and bend up every spirit To his full height. On, on, you noblest English! . . . Be copy now to men of grosser blood, And teach them how to war.	Stiffen your muscles and disguise your peaceful natures with looks of rage so you can frighten the enemy. Bare your teeth and stretch your nostrils, hold your breaths and raise your spirits to their full height. On, you noble Englishmen! Show lesser men how to fight!

And you, good yeomen,
Whose limbs were made in
England, show us here
The mettle of your pasture.
Let us swear
That you are worth your
breeding, which I doubt not,
For there is none of you so
mean and base
That hath not noble luster in
your eyes.

And all of you who come from England, show us the value of your origins, that you are worthy of your country, which I don't doubt. For none of you is of such lowly birth that you don't still have some nobility about you.

I see you stand like greyhounds
in the slips,
Straining upon the start. The
game's afoot.
Follow your spirit, and upon
this charge
Cry, "God for Harry,
England, and Saint George!"

I see you waiting like greyhounds just before a dog race, straining your leashes so that you can start. The game is about to begin. So follow your spirit and go forward crying "God for Harry, England, and Saint George!"

Speech 2: The Saint Crispin's Day Speech

Another famous speech from *Henry V* is known as the Saint Crispin's Day Speech, and it occurs just before the Battle of Agincourt. Henry's nobles are having a discussion among themselves, worrying that the French outnumber them five to one. One of the nobles, the Earl of Westmoreland, wishes aloud that some of the idle men at home in England were with them now in France to help them fight:

> *O that we now had here*
> *But one ten thousand of those men in England*
> *That do no work today.*

Henry's famous speech is in reply to Westmoreland. Again, here is a slightly cut version that is perfect for recitation contests.

Shakespeare's Lines	My Paraphrases
If we are marked to die, we are enough To do our country loss; and if to live, The fewer men, the greater share of honor. God's will, I pray thee wish not one man more.	If we are destined to die, there are enough of us to be a loss to our country; but if we're going to live, then the fewer we are, the more glory we'll earn. So please don't wish for any more of us.
By Jove, I am not covetous for gold, Nor care I who doth feed upon my cost; It yearns me not if men my garments wear; Such outward things dwell not in my desires. But if it be a sin to covet honor, I am the most offending soul alive. No, 'faith, my coz, wish not a man from England. . . .	By heaven, I don't covet gold, I don't care who eats at my expense, and I don't care if men wear my clothing. Such outward things don't bother me. But if it's a sin to covet honor, then I'm the most covetous person alive. No, don't wish for any more men from England. . . .

Rather proclaim it, Westmore-
land, through my host,
That he which hath no stom-
ach to this fight,
Let him depart. His passport
shall be made,
And crowns for convoy put
into his purse.
We would not die in that
man's company
That fears his fellowship to die
with us.

Rather, make an announce-
ment to my troops that if
anyone doesn't have the
stomach for the fight ahead,
let him leave. We'll give him a
passport and some money. We
don't want to die in the company of any man who doesn't
want to die with us.

This day is called the Feast of
Crispian.
He that outlives this day and
comes safe home
Will stand o'tiptoe when this
day is named
And rouse him at the name of
Crispian. . . .

Today is the Feast of Saint
Crispin. Anyone who lives
through this day and gets
home safely will stand on
his tiptoes and raise a cheer
whenever, in the future, he
hears the word Crispin. . . .

Old men forget; yet all shall be
forgot,
But he'll remember with
advantages
What feats he did that
day. . . .

Old men forget things; indeed,
everything will be forgotten,
but the men who have fought
with us today will remember
"with advantages" what they
did today. . . .

This story shall the good man teach his son, *And Crispin Crispian shall ne'er go by,* *From this day to the ending of the world,* *But we in it shall be rememberèd—*	Good men will tell the story of this day to their sons, and the anniversary of this day will never go by without our being remembered for our valor—
We few, we happy few, we band of brothers; *For he today that sheds his blood with me* *Shall be my brother; be he ne'er so vile,* *This day shall gentle his condition;*	We happy few, we band of brothers. I call you brothers because whoever sheds his blood with me today, no matter how lowly his origins, will be my brother, because by fighting today he becomes more noble.
And gentlemen in England now abed *Shall think themselves accursed they were not here,* *And hold their manhoods cheap whiles any speaks* *That fought with us upon Saint Crispin's day.*	And noblemen who are in bed right now back in England will feel deprived and will think less of themselves because they never got to fight by our side on Saint Crispin's Day.

What a speech! What a rallying cry of sheer patriotism! One of my favorite sections of the speech is this:

> *Old men forget; yet all shall be forgot,*
> *But he'll remember, with advantages,*
> *What feats he did that day.*

Shakespeare starts the line with a fond observation about mankind as it grows older:

Old men forget;

Then he adds the observation that in the sands of time, all that we do will be forgotten:

yet all shall be forgot

Then he adds a joke, a warm, human, touching joke:

*But he'll remember, **with advantages,*** *What feats he did that day.*

The old man won't just brag about his exploits in the war; he'll exaggerate the exploits *with advantages.* Only Shakespeare could pack this much wisdom, humor, and humanity into three short lines.

You should also point out to your children that the whole notion of centering the speech on Saint Crispin's Day is a bit of happenstance. The text of the speech can be confusing otherwise. Why Saint Crispin? Was he a famous fighter or hero? Not at all. The Battle of Agincourt happened to fall on a saint's day in the calendar (October 25) honoring Saint Crispin, the patron saint of cobblers and leather workers. Shakespeare seized on this fact as a way of identifying the day for rhetorical purposes.

Many a middle-schooler has won a recitation contest with this speech and for all the right reasons. It is long enough to show effort; it is complex enough to show intellectual accomplishment; and if recited well, there is no more stirring speech in the English language.

CHAPTER 31

Hooray for Heminges and Condell

I n addition to William Shakespeare, there are two other heroes in this book, and their names are John Heminges and Henry Condell. It's a scandal that there aren't statues of these two men in front of every library in the world, and I hope that you and your children will help me rectify this situation.

Heminges and Condell were close friends, fellow theater owners, and acting colleagues of Shakespeare, but their greatest achievement was that they published the first edition of Shakespeare's complete plays in 1623, seven years after his death. The book was formally titled *Mr. William Shakespeares Comedies, Histories, & Tragedies*, and it is known as the First Folio. The remarkable thing is that without the First Folio, we would not have *eighteen* of Shakespeare's plays. Since none of Shakespeare's manuscripts survive, and none of these plays appeared first in surviving "quarto" editions, these eighteen plays would have been lost forever had it not been for these two men. We wouldn't have *Twelfth Night, As You Like It, The Tempest, Julius Caesar, The Taming of the Shrew, Antony and Cleopatra*, and twelve others.

And it is not just these eighteen plays that were saved. Some of Shakespeare's plays that *were* published in his lifetime were printed in such corrupt versions that they are almost unrecognizable as Shakespeare plays. The First Folio was published to set the record straight and make certain that authorized, quality texts of all of Shakespeare's plays were available to the public. Thanks to Heminges and Condell, the course of literary history was changed forever.

To appreciate the full accomplishment of Heminges and Condell, your children should understand a little about the publishing history of Shakespeare's plays. When Shakespeare wrote a play, it was purchased outright by the acting company for which it was written. Thus most of Shakespeare's plays were eventually owned by the Lord Chamberlain's Men, which then became the King's Men. Shakespeare himself no longer owned his plays; and moreover, he had no right to protect the integrity of his words because at this time there were no copyright laws as we know them today.

When Shakespeare's plays were performed, some of them were so popular that Shakespeare's company decided to make additional money by

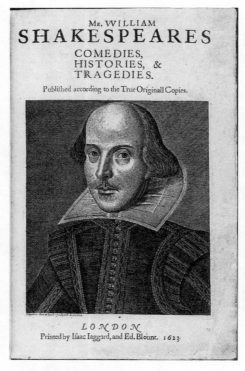

The title page of the First Folio

selling them to publishers, who printed them in editions called quartos. A quarto is the equivalent of a modern paperback. It is called a quarto because the pages are made by folding a large sheet of paper twice (into a quarter of its original size), then binding the book on one side and cutting the pages open. A folio is twice as big because the sheets were folded only once. A folio was often bound with a leather cover and was equivalent to a modern coffee-table book.

Scholars have divided the quartos into two kinds. The "bad quartos" were apparently patched together from various sources, such as partial scripts, actors' memories, or the scribblings of plagiarists who were planted in the audience; the "good quartos" were usually printed directly from the author's or a scribe's manuscripts, or from the manuscripts used as prompt-books. Prior to the printing of the First Folio, some of Shakespeare's plays were available only as bad quartos, and some of them are pretty bad indeed. Take, for example, Hamlet's famous soliloquy, which appears like this in the good quarto:

> To be, or not to be—that is the question:
> Whether 'tis nobler in the mind to suffer
> The slings and arrows of outrageous fortune,
> Or to take arms against a sea of troubles
> And, by opposing, end them. To die, to sleep—
> No more—and by a sleep to say we end
> The heartache and the thousand natural shocks
> That flesh is heir to—'tis a consummation
> Devoutly to be wished.

The bad quarto of Hamlet reads like this:

> To be, or not to be, I there's the point,
> To Die, to sleepe, is that all? I all:
> No, to sleepe, to dreame, I mary there it goes,
> For in that dreame of death, when wee awake,
> And borne before an everlasting Judge,
> From whence no passenger ever returned.

Heminges and Condell's mission, as advertised on their title page, was to present all of Shakespeare's plays "Published according to the True Originall Copies." In their introduction to the volume, they wrote that they wished that the author himself had lived "to have set forth and overseen his own writings," but since he did not, it fell to his friends, "the office of their care, and pain, to have collected and published them." Later scholarship has shown that Heminges and Condell did indeed go to great pains to ensure that the plays as printed in the First Folio were accurate. They based some texts on Shakespeare's original manuscripts or on transcripts of those manuscripts; they based others on manuscripts used in the theater; and many were based on "good quarto" printings. Thus—and it is worth reiterating—it is thanks to Heminges and Condell that we have eighteen Shakespeare plays that we would not otherwise have at all; and we also have several additional plays that would not otherwise have been preserved for posterity in reliable form.

Your children should also understand that it was not self-evident that someone would print Shakespeare's complete plays either during his lifetime or soon after his death. The First Folio marks the first time anyone ever took the trouble to publish the complete plays of a contemporary author, and it attests to the esteem in which Shakespeare was held in his own day. (The closest equivalent at the time was Ben Jonson, who self-published his own *Works* in 1616.)

It is now believed that only about 750 copies of the First Folio were printed, and of them, about 240 survive. Over one-third of these copies are held by the Folger Shakespeare Library in Washington, D.C. (of which I am a trustee), and you can go into the Exhibition Hall of the Folger Library any day of the week and see a First Folio on display. You can even turn the pages electronically on a screen above the book.

One Last Frightening Anecdote

In addition to our gratitude to Heminges and Condell, we should all be thankful that the fire that destroyed the Globe Theatre in 1613 took place during a performance. As David and Ben Crystal point out in their inspired book *The Shakespeare Miscellany*, because the Globe burned down during a performance, it was possible to save many of the company's assets, which almost certainly included many Shakespeare scripts that were later used as sources for the First Folio. No such luck attended the Fortune Theatre (despite its name): It also burned down—in 1621—but it did so at midnight, when no one was around to help save what was in it. As a consequence, all its contents were destroyed. My heart skips a beat just thinking about it.

Part Three

CHAPTER 32

Passage 20
What a Piece of Work Is a Man

I have of late, but wherefore I know not, lost all my mirth,
forgone all custom of exercises, and, indeed, it goes so
heavily with my disposition that this goodly frame, the
earth, seems to me a sterile promontory; this most excellent
canopy, the air, look you, this brave o'erhanging firmament,
this majestical roof, fretted with golden fire—why, it ap-
peareth nothing to me but a foul and pestilent congregation
of vapors.

What a piece of work is a man, how noble in reason,
how infinite in faculties, in form and moving how express
and admirable; in action how like an angel, in apprehen-
sion how like a god: the beauty of the world, the paragon
of animals—and yet, to me, what is this quintessence of
dust?

(Hamlet, Act II, Scene 2, lines 318–32)

*H*amlet could well be the greatest play ever written, just as everyone says it is. It is a ghost story, a mystery, and a thriller, filled with murders, revenge, poison, a war, a troupe of actors, a play-within-a-play, love, madness, suicide, pirates, a funeral, and a final duel that leaves the stage strewn with dead bodies. Is there any child who wouldn't want to be part of this world for a few hours? I can't imagine it.

The passage that we're about to memorize is delivered by Hamlet to two of his friends (though they turn out to be less than friends), Rosencrantz and Guildenstern. It occurs about a third of the way through the play, and at this point in the action Hamlet is in torment. His father, the King of Denmark, has died suddenly, and his mother, Gertrude, has married his uncle Claudius with unseemly speed. Hamlet blames his mother for her lust and disloyalty to his father, and he is in mental agony over these feelings. And then there's the Ghost.

The play opens with a ghost, the Ghost of Hamlet's Father, haunting the battlements of Elsinore Castle, seeking revenge. When Hamlet meets the Ghost, the Ghost tells him that Claudius, the Ghost's own brother, murdered him in order to seize the throne.

The two scenes where the Ghost confronts Hamlet at night on the battlements and exhorts his son to *revenge his foul and most unnatural murder*—Act I, Scenes 4 and 5—are two of the most exciting scenes in all of literature, and I urge you to sit and read them with your children from beginning to end. If that seems too daunting (depending on the age of your children), describe the scenes and read them some of the best passages aloud. For example:

In Scene 4, when Hamlet sees the Ghost for the first time, he cries:

> *Angels and ministers of grace, defend us!*
> *Be thou a spirit of health or goblin damned,*
> *Bring with thee airs from heaven or blasts from hell,*
> *Be thy intents wicked or charitable,*
> *Thou com'st in such a questionable shape*
> *That I will speak to thee. I'll call thee "Hamlet,"*
> *"King," "Father," "Royal Dane." O, answer me!*

Angels and ministers of grace, defend us! Ask your daughter to imagine seeing a real-life ghost taking shape in front of her. How would she react? Would she fall backward? Gasp? Find it hard to breathe? Would she then cry out:

> *Angels and ministers of grace, defend us!*

What a glorious cry of terror and wonder. Have your daughter enact the whole speech, ending with the cry:

"*King*," "*Father*," "*Royal Dane*." *O, answer me!*

A moment later the Ghost beckons Hamlet to follow him to another part of the castle. Hamlet's friends try to hold him back out of fear for his safety. Split up the parts, and let your son play Hamlet:

MARCELLUS

You shall not go, my lord.

HAMLET
Hold off your hands!

HORATIO

Be ruled. You shall not go.

HAMLET
My fate cries out
And makes each petty arture [artery] in this body
As hardy [strong] as the Nemean Lion's nerve.
Still am I called. Unhand me gentlemen.
By heaven, I'll make a ghost of him that lets me [tries to stop me]!
I say, away!—
[to Ghost:]
Go on. I'll follow thee.

(Ghost and Hamlet exit.)

Don't fail to point out how Shakespeare uses a pun, even at this moment of high emotion: *I'll make a ghost of him that lets me!* It is characteristic of Shakespeare to play games with language in the most unexpected places.

When the Ghost and Hamlet are alone together (in Scene 5), the Ghost explains himself, his voice deep with wretchedness. This time have your child play the Ghost:

GHOST

I am thy father's spirit,
Doomed for a certain term [period] to walk the night
And for the day confined to fast in fires
Till the foul crimes done in my days of nature [time of living]
Are burnt and purged away. . . .
If thou didst ever thy dear father love—

HAMLET

O God!

GHOST

Revenge his foul and most unnatural murder.

HAMLET

Murder?

GHOST

Murder most foul . . .

The Ghost then explains to Hamlet that everyone thinks he died in his orchard from being stung by a serpent, but the truth is that Claudius killed him by pouring poison into his ear. Again, your child should play the Ghost.

GHOST

　　　　　　　　But know, thou noble youth,
The serpent that did sting thy father's life [kill thy father]
Now wears his crown.

HAMLET

O, my prophetic soul! My uncle!

GHOST

Ay, that incestuous, that adulterate beast,
. . . won to his shameful lust

The will of my most seeming-virtuous queen.
O Hamlet, what a falling off was there!

The Ghost fills Hamlet's ear with the details of his own murder the way Claudius filled King Hamlet's ear with poison. This paradox underscores an important question: Is the Ghost lying or telling the truth? Are his words reliable or poisonous? This is something that Hamlet will spend the next two acts of the play trying to find out.

At the end of Scene 5, the morning light begins to dawn:

GHOST
Fare thee well at once.
The glowworm shows the matin [morning] *to be near . . .*
Adieu, adieu, adieu. Remember me.
(He exits.)

HAMLET
O all you host of heaven! O earth! What else?
. . . Remember thee?
Yea, from the table [tablet] *of my memory*
I'll wipe away all trivial, fond records, . . .
O most pernicious woman! [his mother]
O villain, villain, smiling, damned villain! [his uncle]
. . . That one may smile and smile and be a villain.

From this point on in the story, Hamlet's actions become quirky and unsettling. One of the interesting questions of the play is whether Hamlet is merely pretending to be mad or is, in fact, going mad with grief. The first we hear of his madness is in the very next scene, Act II, Scene 1, when Ophelia, a young woman at court, tells of a frightening occurrence. She has just had a visit from Hamlet, and she reports the encounter to her meddlesome father, Polonius, who is the King's chief counselor. Have your son or daughter recite Ophelia's speech aloud:

OPHELIA
O my lord, my lord, I have been so affrighted! . . .
My lord, as I was sewing in my closet [room],

Lord Hamlet, with his doublet all unbraced [his coat unfastened],
No hat upon his head, his stockings fouled [dirty], . . .
Pale as his shirt, his knees knocking each other,
And with a look so piteous in purport [in meaning]
As if he had been loosèd out of hell
To speak of horrors—he comes before me.

POLONIUS

Mad for thy love?

OPHELIA

My lord, I do not know.

Kenneth Branagh and Kate Winslet from the
movie version of *Hamlet*

Polonius, who is a terrible gossipmonger, reports Hamlet's supposed love madness to Claudius, who has sent for two of Hamlet's old school friends, Rosencrantz and Guildenstern, and now gets them to spy on Hamlet and report on his actions.

The passage that your children are about to memorize occurs during Hamlet's first encounter with his old "friends," and I have chosen it for two reasons. First, it is here that Hamlet most clearly describes the feeling of melancholy that has overwhelmed him as he tries to deal emotionally with the death of his father and the treachery of his mother. Second, it is an example of Shakespeare's prose at its very height.

Memorizing prose is a bit different from memorizing poetry. We don't have the rhythms of poetry to rely on; therefore memorizing prose often requires more repetition. If your children are still on the young side when you tackle this passage, you might confine yourselves to the second half. Either way, you should approach the passage one phrase at a time.

> *I have of late* [recently],
> *but wherefore* [why] *I know not,*
> *lost all my mirth* [cheerfulness]

Your children will remember from *Romeo and Juliet* that *wherefore* means "why." Hamlet doesn't know quite why he has lost his mirth:

> *I have of late, but wherefore I know not,*
> *lost all my mirth,*
> *forgone all custom of exercises* [stopped exercising]
> *and, indeed, it goes so heavily with my disposition*
> *that this goodly frame, the earth,*
> *seems to me a sterile promontory;*

Hamlet thinks of the earth as a lonely piece of land jutting out into the sea. Repeat this section in parts, then as a whole, until the passage is second nature.

I have of late, but wherefore I know not, lost all my mirth, forgone all custom of exercises, and, indeed, it goes so heavily with my disposition that this goodly frame, the earth, seems to me a sterile promontory;

Hamlet now elaborates on his view of the earth:

this most excellent canopy, the air, look you, this brave o'erhanging firmament, this majestical roof, fretted with golden fire—why, it appeareth nothing to me but a foul and pestilent congregation of vapors.

In other words, the sky (this *firmament*, this *roof*), which is adorned (*fretted*) with stars (*golden fire*), is nothing to him but a dirty gathering of unclean smog (*a foul and pestilent congregation of vapors*).

Notice that the passage has a double meaning. Hamlet is referring to the sky, and the actor playing Hamlet is referring to the Globe Theatre. As you can see from the picture below, the *majestical roof fretted with golden fire* is the painting on the ceiling over the playing area, a depiction of the zodiac showing the sun, the moon, and the familiar planets.

The Merry Wives of Windsor, with Christopher Benjamin as Falstaff, Serena Evans as Mistress Page, and Sarah Woodward as Mistress Ford

Once again Shakespeare is reminding his audience that theater encompasses two experiences at once: the story being portrayed and the actors playing it.

Hamlet now launches into his breathtaking description of humanity.

> *What a piece of work is a man, how noble in reason, how infinite in faculties, in form and moving how express and admirable; in action how like an angel, in apprehension how like a god: the beauty of the world, the paragon of animals—and yet, to me, what is this quintessence of dust?*

Again, have your children take it a phrase at a time:

> *What a piece of work is a man,*
> *how noble in reason,*
> *how infinite in faculties,*
> *in form and moving how express and admirable;*
> *in action how like an angel,*
> *in apprehension* [understanding] *how like a god;*
> *the beauty of the world,*
> *the paragon* [the perfect, best example] *of animals—*
> *and yet to me what is this quintessence* [very essence] *of dust?*

Whenever I read this passage, I wonder if Hamlet isn't trying to intimidate Rosencrantz and Guildenstern. He knows by now that they have been summoned by the King to spy on him. They've admitted it. So is he showing off a bit? Dazzling them with language to keep them off balance? Whether he is or not, Hamlet is clearly troubled by the fact that his friends are now his enemies, and the mood he expresses here will continue to pervade the play.

> *and yet to me what is this quintessence of dust?*

This wonderful, admirable man is in despair.

CHAPTER 33

Passage 21
Who's There?

Who's there?

(*Hamlet*, Act I, Scene 1, line 1)

*H*amlet begins with two soldiers, outdoors, guarding a castle at night. They're nervous because they're waiting for a ghost to appear. They have seen the ghost before, and they have invited Hamlet's best friend, Horatio, to see it for himself. Here's how the play opens:

BARNARDO

Who's there?

FRANCISCO

Nay, answer me. Stand and unfold yourself [tell me who you are].

BARNARDO

Long live the King!

FRANCISCO

Barnardo?

BARNARDO

He. . . . 'Tis now struck twelve. Get thee to bed, Francisco.

FRANCISCO
For this relief much thanks. 'Tis bitter cold,
And I am sick at heart. . . .

HORATIO
What, has this thing appeared again tonight?

Recite this as a dialogue with your children and really act it out. You are two soldiers and a student, isolated in the dark of night, deeply frightened because at any moment a ghost might materialize in front of you. You have seen the ghost before, and it was terrifying. Notice especially the opening line of the play:

Who's there?

This is all your children are going to memorize this week. Two words. They've been working hard at Shakespeare, and they probably need a break.

Who's there?

One eminent critic calls these two words "the most tingling line in the world's drama." These seemingly casual words embody one of the central questions of the whole play: Who is out there listening? Will he change our fate or seal it? Is there a Greater Power who is watching? If there really is a ghost, and it's not just a figment of Hamlet's fevered imagination, is it a force of good or evil? What is *this thing* that might appear tonight? Is it Hamlet's father still walking the earth until he is avenged? Is it the devil? Or is it Hamlet's conscience? His fears? His doubts? Worst of all, is nobody there and are we alone in the universe?

Who's there?

Hamlet's Voice

Like all the very best characters created by Shakespeare, like Falstaff and Rosalind, Viola, Benedick, and Lady Macbeth, Hamlet has his own distinctive voice. Hamlet's voice is that of a man who understands everything about life but has been deeply injured by it. The voice is tragic and ironic at the same time. Also, Hamlet has a remarkable sense of humor—remarkable because it is so intelligent, so clear, and so deep. One great Shakespearean critic, Mark Van Doren, has said that Hamlet "is that unique thing in literature, a credible genius." Here are some of the things that Hamlet says in the course of the play:

> *O God, I could be bounded in a nutshell and count myself a king of infinite space, were it not that I have bad dreams.*

> *There's a divinity that shapes our ends,*
> *Rough-hew them how we will.*

> *Tis now the very witching time of night*
> *When churchyards yawn and hell itself breathes out*
> *Contagion to the world: now could I drink hot blood,*
> *And do such bitter business as the day*
> *Would quake to look on.*

> *There is special providence in the fall of a sparrow.*

> *Let [the Players] be well used, for they are the abstract and brief chronicles of the time.*

> *I must be cruel, only to be kind.*

> *You would pluck out the heart of my mystery; you would sound me from my lowest note to the top of my compass.*

> *There are more things in heaven and earth, Horatio,*
> *Than are dreamt of in your philosophy.*

> *To be honest, as this world goes, is to be one man pick'd out of ten thousand.*

[speaking of his father:]
He was a man, take him for all in all,
I shall not look upon his like again.

[Hamlet's dying words to his friend Horatio:]
If thou didst ever hold me in thy heart,
Absent thee from felicity awhile,
And in this harsh world draw thy breath in pain
To tell my story.

These are the words of a genius, written by a genius. A. C. Bradley wrote of Hamlet's eloquence, "After Hamlet, this music is heard no more. It is followed by music vaster and deeper, but not the same."

Bonus Passage

In the second scene of the play, Hamlet sees his schoolmate Horatio for the first time since returning to Denmark for his father's funeral. Horatio, who is Hamlet's only true friend in the play, remarks:

HORATIO
My lord, I came to see your father's funeral.

HAMLET
I prithee, do not mock me, fellow student.
I think it was to see my mother's wedding.

HORATIO
Indeed, my lord, it followed hard upon [quickly].

HAMLET
Thrift, thrift, Horatio. The funeral baked meats
Did coldly furnish forth the marriage table.

I consider the final lines of this exchange to comprise as witty a remark as I have ever heard, and this remark sets the tone for Hamlet's discourse for the rest of the play. It is all wit on the surface and all tragedy beneath.

> *Thrift, thrift, Horatio. The funeral baked meats*
> *Did coldly furnish forth* [provide cold foods for] *the marriage table.*

It points up Claudius's treachery and Gertrude's infidelity while outwardly "pretending" that the situation—saving cold meat for the next meal—is the most natural, practical thing in the world. Which it is, if you aren't saving it from a funeral banquet for the widow's wedding feast.

> *Thrift, thrift, Horatio. The funeral baked meats*
> *Did coldly furnish forth the marriage table.*

Say the lines aloud one more time with your children, and I bet they'll know them by heart.

CHAPTER 34

Passage 22
The Advice of Polonius

Give thy thoughts no tongue,
Nor any unproportioned thought his act.
Be thou familiar, but by no means vulgar.
Those friends thou hast, and their adoption tried,
Grapple them unto thy soul with hoops of steel,
But do not dull thy palm with entertainment
Of each new-hatched, unfledged comrade. Beware
Of entrance to a quarrel, but, being in,
Bear 't that th' opposèd may beware of thee.
Give every man thy ear, but few thy voice.
Take each man's censure, but reserve thy judgment.
Costly thy habit as thy purse can buy,
But not expressed in fancy (rich, not gaudy),
For the apparel oft proclaims the man, . . .
Neither a borrower nor a lender be,
For loan oft loses both itself and friend,
And borrowing dulls the edge of husbandry.
This above all: to thine own self be true,
And it must follow, as the night the day,
Thou canst not then be false to any man.

(*Hamlet*, Act I, Scene 3, lines 65–86)

This is one of the best-known passages in all of Shakespeare, and it's a classic for a reason: It is full of good sense and expressed with perfection. Read it through, and you'll see that it is a set of precepts—principles for living a practical, honest, moral life. Ironically, the passage is delivered by Polonius, who is the meddlesome father of Ophelia and the wily chief counselor to Claudius.

The context is simple: Polonius's son, Laertes, is returning to college and his ship is waiting in the harbor. Polonius pulls Laertes aside and gives him some fatherly advice about how to comport himself when he reaches his destination.

(1)   *Give thy thoughts no tongue,*

In other words, don't just blurt out (give tongue to) your thoughts and say anything that comes into your head. Be thoughtful. Act maturely.

Nor any unproportioned thought his act.

Don't act on *unproportioned* thoughts. Don't be reckless. Don't act on a decision if it's not well considered.

Give thy thoughts no tongue,
Nor any unproportioned thought his act.

(2)   *Be thou familiar,*

Be open and friendly with people (*familiar*),

but by no means vulgar.

But don't be so friendly that you become offensive.

Be thou familiar, but by no means vulgar.

Point out to your children that throughout this speech, Polonius emphasizes the importance of proportion. He's saying that balance is the key to a wise, honorable life. We'll see this idea return over and over in the next several lines.

(3)   *Those friends thou hast, and their adoption tried,*
            Grapple them unto thy soul with hoops of steel,

In other words, "As for the friends you already have and who have passed the test of friendship [*their adoption tried*], hold them as close to you as if a hoop of steel were encircling you both. But"—and here is that issue of proportion again—

But do not dull thy palm with entertainment
Of each new-hatched, unfledged comrade.

Don't cheapen yourself (*dull thy palm*) with friendliness to every new person you meet who has not yet proven himself worthy of it (*each new-hatched, unfledged comrade*). *New-hatched* and *unfledged* are examples of bird imagery. *New-hatched* refers to a baby bird; and *unfledged* refers to a bird that hasn't yet developed mature feathers.

Those friends thou hast, and their adoption tried,
Grapple them unto thy soul with hoops of steel,
But do not dull thy palm with entertainment
Of each new-hatched, unfledged comrade.

(4)   *Beware / Of entrance to a quarrel, but, being in,*
            Bear 't that th' opposèd may beware of thee.

Be careful about entering into a fight (*a quarrel*), but once you're in one, be so brave that your opponent is scared of you (*beware of thee*). Notice how Shakespeare puns on the word *beware*. You beware a fight; but once you're in it, make sure that your opponent may *beware* [be wary] of you. Shakespeare frequently turns the same word into two different parts of speech. It is one of his hallmarks. Notice also the rhyme between *beware* and *bear*, as well as all the hard *b*'s that sound so quarrelsome.

(5)   *Give every man thy ear, but few thy voice,*

Listen to everyone (*Give every man thy ear*), but don't talk too much (*but few thy voice*). Again, this piece of advice is filled with irony, since Polonius is one of the great babblers of all time.

(6)   *Take each man's censure, but reserve thy judgment,*

Listen to the opinions of others (*censure*), but don't be judgmental yourself (*reserve thy judgment*).

(7)   *Costly thy habit as thy purse can buy.*

Buy clothes that you can afford,

But not expressed in fancy (rich not gaudy),

but don't make them too *fancy*—too imaginative or decorative.

For the apparel oft proclaims the man,

Because what you wear is often how people judge you.

This bit of advice is ideal for children, but they usually don't want to hear it. What you wear and how you look gives strangers a first impression about who you are. It may be unjust, but it is a fact of life.

(8)   *Neither a borrower nor a lender be,*
        For loan oft loses both itself and friend,
        And borrowing dulls the edge of husbandry.

I always find this part of the passage especially clever, partly for what it says, and partly for how it is expressed. *Neither a borrower nor a lender be* means just what it says: Don't borrow money and don't lend money. Polonius tells us why in the next two lines:

First, *loan oft loses both itself and friend*: When you loan money to someone, you often lose not only the money itself but also the friend you loaned it to. They don't want to see you because they feel guilty about not paying you back.

Second, *borrowing dulls the edge of husbandry*: Having extra money that you haven't earned (and that you have to pay back) often makes you less able to manage your own accounts. *Husbandry* means management of your resources—keeping track of your household expenses. Borrowing gives you a sense of having more money than you actually have and therefore leads to overspending.

> *Neither a borrower nor a lender be,*
> *For loan oft loses both itself and friend,*
> *And borrowing dulls the edge of husbandry.*

(9)   *This above all: to thine own self be true,*
          And it must follow, as the night the day,
          Thou canst not then be false to any man.

And here's the big finish to the speech: *to thine own self be true*. Like every great writer, Shakespeare proportions his work so that it has a beautiful shape, and part of that shape involves building to this moment: *to thine own self be true*.

Tell your children to think of the entire passage as a whole and notice that it falls into three parts:

1. It starts simply (*Give thy thoughts no tongue,*).
2. Then it has a middle section containing one good piece of advice after another (listen to people, don't pass judgment on others, don't quarrel, be brave, etc.).
3. And then it ends with the most profound piece of advice in the passage—one that illuminates and deepens the rest:

> *This above all, to thine own self be true.*
> *And it must follow, as the night the day,*
> *Thou canst not then be false to any man.*

Simplicity, simplicity. Just as Shakespeare uses simple things to break our hearts in emotional passages—Lear's button, Desdemona's handkerchief—so at times he uses simple language to make his most profound statements.

True Story

The day before my daughter left for college—which happened yesterday as I write these words (and yes, it's true, they grow up faster than you ever believed possible)—we sat down together for the traditional father-daughter talk. And, as I had imagined for years, we discussed, among other things, Polonius's advice to Laertes. I started to recite the lines that Polonius says just before he begins the passage that your children just learned:

> POLONIUS
> *Yet here, Laertes? Aboard, aboard, for shame.*
> *The wind sits in the shoulder of your sail*
> *And you are stayed for. There. My blessing on thee.*
> *And these few precepts, in thy memory,*
> *Look thou character.*
> [See that you inscribe these pieces of advice in your memory.]

When I got as far as *Aboard, aboard for shame,* my daughter started reciting the words from memory—all of them, from *Give thy thoughts no tongue* right through to *thou canst not then be false to any man.* I am not exaggerating one iota. We had recited it so many times over the years that it was simply in her muscle memory. As she recited it, I started to cry. I'm sorry, but I just did. It was the greatest going-away present she could have ever given me.

As of about twenty hours ago, my daughter is a college girl, and I hope she's following Polonius's advice.

CHAPTER 35

Hamlet's Soliloquies

amlet is vast, both emotionally and in sheer stage time. It is the
longest of all Shakespeare's plays: Using the First Folio as a guide,
Hamlet contains 3,906 lines, while *Twelfth Night* contains 2,579,
Macbeth has 2,529, and Shakespeare's shortest play, *The Comedy of Errors*,
contains 1,918. In *Romeo and Juliet*, Shakespeare refers to *the two hours'
traffic of our stage*, but most of his plays take a great deal longer than that
to perform.

Hamlet has an unusually high number of plot twists, and giving your
children a sense of the whole play, both structurally and emotionally, is a
challenge. However, one way to approach it is to teach your children something about each of Hamlet's major soliloquies and use them as markers
along the narrative trail. *Hamlet* is the play in which Shakespeare makes
the soliloquy into an art form, and by understanding the placement and
meaning of the soliloquies, we can start to see the arc of the play.

As a reminder: We call a speech a soliloquy when a character onstage
addresses that speech to the audience, or to himself as if he were thinking
aloud. Usually the character is alone onstage, but if he is not, the other
characters onstage cannot hear him.

The soliloquy is a stage convention, a technique that playwrights
have developed to tell their stories with as much truth and depth as they
can muster. This technique may seem unreal, if by reality we mean naturalism. But naturalism is only one kind of theatrical technique, and it is

often the least effective kind. A soliloquy is theatrical in the best sense: It allows the character onstage to convey his innermost thoughts directly to the audience, and it is therefore a way for the playwright—and the audience—to dig as deeply as possible into the reality beneath the mere action.

Hamlet delivers five major soliloquies in the course of the play. They are the pinnacle of literary art in the English language, and your children should become familiar with them. I will now confess that as a boy I memorized all of them. I saved up my money and bought the cast album of a famous production of *Hamlet* that had been on Broadway in the mid-1960s starring Richard Burton, directed by John Gielgud. (It still holds the record for the longest run of *Hamlet* on Broadway.) I listened to the vinyl recording until it literally wore out; but I was a bit of a fanatic about all this ("Do ya think, Dad?" my children have asked), and your children needn't be. However, they should learn to recognize the opening lines, as well as the significance, of all of Hamlet's major soliloquies—and by doing so, they'll learn a great deal about the story, themes, and character of the play as a whole. In the course of this overview, we'll pick one of the soliloquies and memorize part of it together.

Bear in mind as we look at Hamlet's soliloquies that they are essentially Shakespeare's way of acquainting us with Hamlet's interior struggle between, on the one hand, obeying the Ghost's instructions about revenge and, on the other, following the demands of his own nature, which are rational, moral, and nonviolent. This struggle illuminates the philosophical themes that abound in Hamlet—themes of appearance and reality, the demands of conscience and morality, the nature of action, the relationship of our self to the world. Also, Hamlet's dilemma has come to symbolize basic structural differences in how we look at the world, especially the dichotomy between Romanticism, with its appeal to the emotions, and Enlightenment, with its appeal to the intellect.

Your children should also recognize that the whole notion of a soliloquy as a theatrical device to illuminate the inner struggle of a character essentially begins with *Hamlet*. Shakespeare's plays prior to *Hamlet* contain long speeches delivered alone onstage, and many of them are masterpieces, but they are rarely about the character's inner torment.

Hamlet, with Sir Laurence Olivier as Hamlet and Jean Simmons as Ophelia

Hamlet's First Soliloquy:
O that this too, too sullied flesh

Hamlet's first soliloquy occurs in the second scene of Act I, within minutes of the beginning of the play. As usual, Shakespeare wastes no time introducing us to his protagonist and the emotional heart of the story.

Remind your children that in Act I, Scene 1, two guards, along with Hamlet's best friend, Horatio, have seen the Ghost of Hamlet's father walking along the battlements of the castle. (*Who's there?*) They decide they must tell Hamlet about it, and they hurry off. A moment later, in Scene 2, we meet Hamlet's uncle and mother, Claudius and Gertrude, newly married, surrounded by their court; and a few moments later we meet Hamlet himself and begin to understand his mental agony.

Scene Work

As I have pointed out before, Shakespeare rarely pussyfoots around with his story. He usually begins his plays by plunging us straight into the action. This same technique holds true in microcosm, in Shakespeare's scenes. His scenes usually have no preamble: The characters often enter the scenes in mid-discussion. This is why his plays always feel so dynamic. If you have a budding playwright on your hands, this is a great lesson to be learned and remembered.

Similarly, when my children have taken music lessons over the years, their best teachers have emphasized how certain phrases should begin with the kind of breath control and attack that makes you feel as if you are jumping onto a moving train. There should be no resting between such phrases: Keep the energy up, and the art takes care of itself. It's the same with playwriting. Keep the story moving, and a lot of other problems solve themselves. Remind your children that the arts are related—music, drama, sculpture, painting—and that solutions are often similar from genre to genre.

Back to the First Soliloquy

So, at the beginning of Act I, Scene 2, Claudius and Gertrude are making a public appearance. Claudius deals briefly with a political issue, then grants permission to Laertes to return to France. Crucially, throughout these affairs of state, Hamlet is onstage, silent and alone, dressed in black, brooding on his father's death and his mother's disloyalty. Claudius finally turns to Hamlet and says:

> But now my cousin [nephew] Hamlet and my son, . . .
> How is it that the clouds still hang on you?

Thus, cruelly but with pretended innocence, Claudius reminds Hamlet of his position—he is both nephew and stepson at the same time; and he speaks disparagingly of Hamlet's mood: *How is it that the clouds still hang on you?*

When Gertrude chimes in and asks Hamlet why the recent events seem to have affected him so deeply, Hamlet answers: *'Seems,' madam? Nay, it is. I know not 'seems.'* He then assures her that his black clothes, his sighs, his tears, and his other outward shows of grief are indeed *actions that a man might play* [actions that someone might pretend],

> *But I have that **within** which passes* [is beyond] *show,*
> *These but the trappings and the suits of woe.*

It is the feelings that Hamlet has *within himself* that matter, he says; and the moment Claudius, Gertrude, and the court depart, as he sits onstage alone in his grief, Hamlet tells us what those feelings are:

> *O that this too, too sullied flesh would melt,*
> *Thaw, and resolve itself into a dew,*
> *Or that the Everlasting had not fixed*
> *His canon 'gainst self-slaughter!*

That is the opening of Hamlet's first soliloquy, and if you think your children are up for it, stop right now and teach it to them. You will never, ever regret it.

> *O that this too, too sullied flesh would melt,*
> *Thaw, and resolve itself into a dew,*
> *Or that the Everlasting had not fixed*
> *His canon 'gainst self-slaughter!*

Here is the whole soliloquy. You should begin by having your children read the real words; then read them the paraphrase to make sure they understand everything. Do it a sentence at a time so that they can follow without confusion.

Shakespeare's Lines	My Paraphrase
O that this too, too sullied flesh would melt, Thaw, and resolve itself into a dew, Or that the Everlasting had not fixed His canon 'gainst self-slaughter!	Oh, if only my unclean flesh would melt away into watery dew; or if only God had not written his holy law to forbid suicide.
O God, O God, How weary, stale, flat, and unprofitable Seem to me all the uses of this world!	Oh God, oh God, how useless the world seems!
Fie on 't, ah fie! 'Tis an un-weeded garden That grows to seed. Things rank and gross in nature Possess it merely.	Fie! It's like a garden grown over with nothing but foul weeds.
That it should come to this: But two months dead—nay, not so much, not two. So excellent a king, that was to this Hyperion to a satyr; so loving to my mother That he might not beteem the winds of heaven Visit her face too roughly. Heaven and earth, Must I remember?	My father has been dead for less than two months! He was like Hyperion (the sun god), compared to this lustful satyr (a mythological creature who was half goat, half man). My father was so loving to my mother that he would not allow the winds themselves to blow too hard on her cheeks. Oh, must I remember?!

Why, she would hang on him
As if increase of appetite had
   grown
By what it fed on. And yet,
   within a month

She would hang on my father
as if her appetite for him grew
bigger the more she had of
him.

(Let me not think on 't;
   frailty, thy name is woman!)
. . .

I don't want to think about
it. Another word for *frailty* is
woman!
. . .

(O God, a beast that wants
   discourse of reason
Would have mourned longer!),
   married with mine Uncle,
My father's brother, but no
   more like my father
Than I to Hercules.

Oh God, a beast that lacks
the ability to reason would
have mourned longer than my
mother did before marrying
my uncle, a man who is no
more like my real father than
I am like Hercules.

                Within a month,
Ere yet the salt of most unrigh-
   teous tears
Had left the flushing of her
   gallèd eyes,
She married.

Within that month, before
even the salt of her wicked
tears had stopped turning her
eyes red, she married!

O most wicked speed, to post
With such dexterity to inces-
   tuous sheets!
It is not, nor it cannot come
   to good.
But break, my heart, for I
   must hold my tongue.

O such wicked speed, to rush
so easily to the sheets of in-
cest! Good cannot come of
this, but my heart must break
because I must not speak
aloud of it.

If we listen closely, we realize that Hamlet's anguish is based primarily on shock at his mother's lust and infidelity. She has vaulted incestuously into her brother-in-law's bed: *A beast would have mourned longer!* cries Hamlet. She is *rank and gross* like an *unweeded garden*—and Hamlet uses the same metaphor when he confronts his mother in the famous Closet Scene in Act III:

> *Repent what's past; avoid what is to come;*
> *And do not spread the compost on the weeds*
> *To make them ranker.*

This realization of his mother's betrayal changes everything for Hamlet. He can never look at a woman the same way again. Suddenly for Hamlet, all women, including Ophelia, are false. (*Frailty, thy name is woman!*) And for the moment, he can do nothing to resolve his wounded feelings. He hasn't met the Ghost yet and doesn't suspect at this point that he has a murder to avenge. Therefore, his heart must *break, . . . for I must hold my tongue.* By understanding this soliloquy, your children will have a very good handle on the whole opening of the play.

CHAPTER 36

Passage 23
O, What a Rogue and Peasant Slave Am I!

O, what a rogue and peasant slave am I! . . .
    I have heard
That guilty creatures sitting at a play
Have, by the very cunning of the scene,
Been struck so to the soul that presently
They have proclaimed their malefactions.
For murder, though it have no tongue, will speak
With most miraculous organ. I'll have these players
Play something like the murder of my father
Before mine uncle. I'll observe his looks;
I'll tent him to the quick. If he do blench,
I know my course. The spirit that I have seen
May be the devil, and the devil hath power
T' assume a pleasing shape; yea, and perhaps,
Out of my weakness and my melancholy,
As he is very potent with such spirits,
Abuses me to damn me. I'll have grounds
More relative than this. The play's the thing
Wherein I'll catch the conscience of the King.

(Hamlet, Act II, Scene 2, lines 577ff.)

We know what happens next in the story: That night—the same night as Hamlet's first soliloquy—Hamlet goes to the battlements of the castle and meets the Ghost of his father. The Ghost tells Hamlet that he, the Ghost, was poisoned by his brother Claudius, and he urges Hamlet to avenge his murder. End of Act I.

Act II contains one of the greatest scenes in all of Shakespeare, Scene 2, where events tumble forth one after another. In essence, four things happen in this scene:

1. Claudius and Gertrude get two of Hamlet's old school friends, Rosencrantz and Guildenstern, to spy on Hamlet, and Hamlet discovers what they're up to.

2. Hamlet begins to *act* as though he were mad, but he seems to do it out of anger and contempt for Polonius, not because of real insanity. As Polonius himself admits, *Though this be madness, yet there is method in't.*

3. A group of traveling actors visit Elsinore Castle and perform an excerpt from one of Hamlet's favorite plays. When it is over, Hamlet realizes, to his shame, that he has shown less passion in avenging his father's death than the players have shown in enacting a mere play about the Trojan War.

4. Hamlet sets a trap to find out if Claudius did, in fact, murder his father.

The genius of Hamlet's second soliloquy, which ends the scene, is that it encapsulates all the action of the play up to this point, and, at the same time, it is wildly emotional. This makes it an ideal passage for your children to memorize.

I have suggested that your children memorize only the last third of the soliloquy not because the whole thing isn't miraculous, but out of concern that your children might feel defeated if they tried to learn the whole thing. However, if your children are up for it, do, absolutely, help them memorize the whole soliloquy. This is the first long passage of Shakespeare I learned myself, and I suppose I was about twelve when I did it. Kids are sponges, and if you go into the exercise with the whole soliloquy as a given, you're apt to get excellent results. In any case, I'll explain the whole soliloquy now, and you and your children can decide how much of it to memorize.

Certainly, at a minimum, they must memorize the opening line. We want them to know the opening lines of all five of the great soliloquies, and they already know the opening sentence of the first one:

> *O that this too, too sullied flesh would melt,*
> *Thaw, and resolve itself into a dew,*
> *Or that the Everlasting had not fixed*
> *His canon 'gainst self-slaughter!*

The opening sentence of the second soliloquy is shorter:

> *O, what a rogue and peasant slave am I!*

Hamlet is heartsick. He is about to compare himself to the actor—the Player King—who has just poured out his heart in a fiction, while he, Hamlet, should be acting upon a real-life betrayal. Read the soliloquy to your children a section at a time, and explain what it means as you go.

DO NOT BE DAUNTED BY ITS LENGTH OR ITS SEEMING
DIFFICULTY. IF YOU TAKE IT A SENTENCE AT A TIME,
IT WILL BECOME PERFECTLY CLEAR.
THE PURPOSE OF YOUR WORK WITH YOUR CHILDREN IS
TO DEMYSTIFY SHAKESPEARE.
PERSEVERE!

Shakespeare's Lines	My Paraphrase
O, what a rogue and peasant slave am I!	Oh, what a useless lowly person I am!

*Is it not monstrous that this
  player here,
But in a fiction, in a dream of
  passion,
Could force his soul so to his
  own conceit
That from her working all his
  visage wanned,
Tears in his eyes, distraction
  in his aspect,
A broken voice, and his whole
  function suiting
With forms to his conceit—
  and all for nothing!*

Isn't it monstrous that this
actor who was acting out a
fiction could do it so well
that he actually grew pale,
shed tears, seemed distracted,
spoke with a broken voice,
and did everything to play his
part—and yet he did it without any real-life need!

*For Hecuba!
What's Hecuba to him, or he
  to Hecuba,
That he should weep for her?
  What would he do
Had he the motive and the
  cue for passion
That I have?*

He did it in the course of
telling us about Hecuba (the
wretched heroine of Greek
tragedy who wept for Troy and
for her lost children). Why
should he weep for Hecuba
when she is nothing to him?
What would he do if he had
my reasons for passion?

*He would drown the
    stage with tears
And cleave the general ear
  with horrid speech,
Make mad the guilty and ap-
  pall the free,
Confound the ignorant and
  amaze indeed
The very faculties of eyes and
  ears.*

He would weep so much that
the stage would be flooded
with tears, and he would
speak with such horrid power
that ears would split. He
would make the guilty go insane, terrify the innocent, and
astound our eyes and ears.

Yet I,
A *dull and muddy-mettled*
  rascal, peak
Like John-a-dreams, unpreg-
  nant of my cause,
And can say nothing—no, not
  for a king
Upon whose property and
  most dear life
A damned defeat was made.

Yet I, a dull-spirited dreamer,
mope around unfulfilled
by my cause and can't say
anything—not even for a king
whose life and property were
stolen.

    Am I a coward?
Who calls me "villain"?
  breaks my pate across?
Plucks off my beard and blows
  it in my face?
Tweaks me by the nose? gives
  me the lie i' th' throat
As deep as to the lungs? Who
  does me this?
Ha! 'Swounds, I should take
  it! For it cannot be
But I am pigeon-livered and
  lack gall
To make oppression bitter, or
  ere this
I should have fatted all the
  region kites
With this slave's offal. Bloody,
  bawdy villain!
Remorseless, treacherous,
  lecherous, kindless villain!
O, vengeance!

Am I a coward? Who calls
me a villain? Hits me? Pulls
my beard? Tweaks my nose?
Challenges me? Calls me a
liar? Who?! God's wounds (an
oath), I should take it! Because I'm obviously as meek as
a pigeon and lack the guts to
feel real bitterness. Otherwise
I would have made all the
birds (*kites*) in this region fat
by feeding them Claudius's
internal organs (*offal*). Bloody,
lustful, remorseless, treacherous, unnatural villain! O,
vengeance!

Why, what an ass am I! This	O, what an ass I am. What
is most brave,	a coward, that I, the son of
That I, the son of the dear	a dear, murdered father, who
father murdered,	have been told by a ghost to
Prompted to my revenge by	take revenge, can only talk
heaven and hell,	and curse about it like a har-
Must, like a whore, unpack	lot. Fie! Wait. Hmm . . .
my heart with words	
And fall a-cursing like a very	
drab,	
A scullion! Fie upon 't, foh!	
About, my brains!—Hum,	

And now we come to the next portion of the soliloquy that your children should memorize.

> *I have heard*
> *That guilty creatures sitting at a play*
> *Have, by the very cunning of the scene,*
> *Been struck so to the soul that presently* [instantly]
> *They have proclaimed their malefactions* [crimes].

This passage is so clear and straightforward that it hardly needs paraphrasing. Hamlet has heard that a cleverly placed scene in a play will strike so into the soul of a guilty audience member that that person will admit his crimes.

> *For murder, though it have no tongue, will speak*
> *With most miraculous organ.*

"Because murder will speak out in a miraculous way." Hamlet personifies murder and compares it to a living being who can speak.

> *I'll have these players*
> *Play something like the murder of my father*

Before mine uncle. I'll observe his looks;
I'll tent [probe] him to the quick [deeply]. If he do blench [turn pale],
I know my course.

So Hamlet is going to have the players put on a play that is *something like* the murder of his father. In fact, we've learned earlier in the scene that the play is called "The Murder of Gonzago," and that it will have an additional speech in it that Hamlet has written. During the performance of this play, Hamlet will observe his uncle's looks. If Claudius flinches, Hamlet will be certain that Claudius is guilty of murder, and Hamlet will know his course: that he must kill Claudius.

Hamlet now delivers the most interesting lines of the soliloquy:

> *The spirit that I have seen*
> *May be the devil, and the devil hath power*
> *T' assume a pleasing shape; yea, and perhaps,*
> *Out of my weakness and my melancholy,*
> *As he is very potent with such spirits,*
> *Abuses me to damn me.*

Here Hamlet admits that the Ghost may not have been the Ghost of his father, but may have been the devil. After all, the devil does have the power to *assume a pleasing shape*. As your children will recall, Hamlet considered this possibility before:

> *Angels and ministers of grace, defend us!*
> *Be thou a spirit of health, or goblin damned?*

So here Hamlet is asking again: Was the Ghost *really* a ghost? Or was he the devil? Or was he something in Hamlet's mind? Was he a manifestation of Hamlet's suspicions? Of his madness? Remember, Horatio and the two guards also saw the Ghost in Act I, Scene 4. So the Ghost could not have been totally in Hamlet's mind.

On the other hand, only Hamlet heard the Ghost speak. So perhaps the call for revenge was only in Hamlet's mind. Hamlet recognizes this possibility, and so he needs confirmation of the murder. That confirmation will come when he observes his uncle watching "The Murder of Gonzago." (Hamlet later refers to this play as "The Mousetrap.")

> *The spirit that I have seen*
> *May be the devil, and the devil hath power*
> *T' assume a pleasing shape; yea, and perhaps,*
> *Out of my weakness and my melancholy,*
> *As he is very potent with such spirits,*
> *Abuses me to damn me.*

And now comes the famous ending to the soliloquy. I'm sure that you and your children have heard it before:

> *I'll have grounds*
> *More relative [relevant] than this. The play's the thing*
> *Wherein I'll catch the conscience of the King.*

What an ending to a remarkable speech. It leaves us on tenterhooks, longing to see what happens next. And the alliteration and rhyme are perfection: *catch/conscience, thing/King.* This is genius at its full stretch. No one in history, before or since, has written better than this.

> *The play's the thing*
> *Wherein I'll catch the conscience of the King.*

CHAPTER 37

The End of the Story

The next section of the story begins with a soliloquy, and that soliloquy begins with the most famous line in the English language: *To be or not to be, that is the question.* We'll discuss that speech in detail in the next chapter. For now let's review the whole story of *Hamlet*, using the soliloquies to help us understand the organization of the play.

Like most stories, *Hamlet* has a three-part arc:

Part 1

Hamlet begins with a young prince whose father has died and whose mother has vaulted into his uncle Claudius's bed with unseemly speed. We meet Hamlet in the second scene of the play, where he delivers his first soliloquy.

Soliloquy 1

> *O that this too, too sullied flesh would melt . . .*

In this soliloquy (which we discussed in chapter 35), Hamlet tries to deal psychologically with his mother's betrayal. Not long afterward he is confronted by his father's Ghost, who reveals that he was murdered by Claudius. The Ghost enjoins Hamlet to avenge him. Hamlet struggles internally with how to cope with the Ghost's demands. Part 1 ends with Hamlet's second soliloquy, where Hamlet decides to set a trap to find out if his uncle is in fact guilty.

Soliloquy 2

O, what a rogue and peasant slave am I!

We discussed this soliloquy in chapter 36.

Part 2

This section of the play opens with the third soliloquy.

Soliloquy 3

To be or not to be, that is the question:

Hamlet's inner struggle has led him to thoughts of suicide. The soliloquy appears toward the beginning of Act III, Scene 1, as Claudius and Polonius watch Hamlet from a hiding place. They have prearranged with Ophelia to stage a meeting with Hamlet *as 'twere by accident*, so that the two men can observe Hamlet's behavior.

As soon as *To be or not to be* is over, the action rattles along briskly from one incident to the next. The trap for Hamlet's uncle is sprung during the play called "The Murder of Gonzago," when Claudius rushes out of the room. A few moments later Hamlet is walking through the castle and by chance overhears Claudius confessing his crimes, wanting to pray to God but unable to do so for reasons of conscience. Claudius soliloquizes:

> *O, my offense is rank, it smells to heaven;*
> *It hath the primal eldest curse upon't,*
> *A brother's murder. . . .*
>   *O, what form of prayer*
> *Can serve my turn? "Forgive me my foul murder"?*
> *That cannot be, since I am still possessed*
> *Of those effects for which I did the murder:*
> *My crown, mine own ambition, and my queen.*

Now, for the first time, Hamlet (and we) are absolutely certain that Claudius did in fact murder old Hamlet. At this moment, at the end of Claudius's soliloquy, when Claudius finally starts to pray for forgiveness, Hamlet almost kills his uncle but decides against it. This is the occasion for Hamlet's fourth soliloquy.

Soliloquy 4

> *Now might I do it pat, now he is a-praying,*

In this soliloquy, Hamlet talks himself into not killing Claudius while Claudius is praying, because then Claudius's soul would go to heaven. Hamlet reasons that he would rather kill Claudius while Claudius is sinning so that his soul will go to hell. At least that's what Hamlet says. But his hesitation seems to go deeper and be part of his moral repugnance to cold-blooded murder.

> *Now might I do it pat, now he is a-praying,*
> *And now I'll do't. (He draws his sword.)*
>   *And so he goes to heaven;*
> *And so am I revenged.*

But, thinks Hamlet:

>   *am I then revenged,*
> *To take him in the purging of his soul,*

When he is fit and season'd for his passage?
No!

Hamlet decides that he would rather kill Claudius

When he is drunk asleep, or in his rage,
Or in the incestuous pleasure of his bed;
At gaming, swearing, or about some act
That has no relish of salvation in't;

Remember, if Hamlet went ahead and killed Claudius at this point, he would prevent the eight deaths that follow by the end of the play. But Hamlet doesn't know that, and, as the great literary critic Northrop Frye says, "Hamlet is too civilized for stealthy murder."

Hamlet at the Royal Shakespeare Company, with David Tennant as Hamlet and Patrick Stewart as Claudius

In the next scene, Hamlet confronts his mother and begs her to abstain from his uncle's bed.

QUEEN

Hamlet, thou hast thy father much offended.

HAMLET

Mother, you have my father much offended.

QUEEN

Come, come, you answer with an idle tongue.

HAMLET

Go, go, you question with a wicked tongue.

Things that are said in this famous Closet Scene (which is often staged in Gertrude's bedroom) have prompted some critics to compare Hamlet's struggle to aspects of the Oedipus complex. That complex, based on Sigmund Freud's famous theory of psychoanalysis, maintains that males compete with their fathers for their mothers' affection. The theory here is that Hamlet is psychologically prevented from killing Claudius because Claudius is fulfilling Hamlet's own Oedipal desires by killing his father and marrying his mother. But that is only one of the dozens of critical theories about *Hamlet* that have been posited over the years, and the complexity and depth of the play are so stunning that it is subject, quite rightly, to a whole world of interpretation.

While Hamlet is in his mother's private chamber, he hears a spy behind the curtain and runs him through with his sword. Hamlet thinks he has stabbed Claudius, but it turns out to be Polonius, who was indeed spying on the prince. It is at this moment that the Ghost of Hamlet's Father revisits the play. He enters the room and exhorts Hamlet not to forget his promise to kill Claudius. Hamlet converses with the Ghost, but Gertrude cannot see the Ghost—she sees Hamlet talking to the thin air—and therefore believes that Hamlet really has gone mad. As Hamlet berates Gertrude for her lustful behavior, Gertrude cries:

O Hamlet, thou hast cleft [cut] *my heart in twain* [in two], and Hamlet answers,

> *O throw away the worser part of it,*
> *And live the purer with the other half.*

(If your children ever use the word *worser* for "worst," they can now defend themselves by reminding you that Hamlet said it first.)

Claudius, now aware of the threat to his life, sends Hamlet to England and tries to have him killed. While on his way, Hamlet sees an army marching past and hears of the brave deeds of the Prince of Norway who is leading his men into war. Hamlet compares his own cowardice to the bravery of the Norwegian prince and his followers, and this is the trigger for Hamlet's final soliloquy.

Soliloquy 5

> *How all occasions do inform against me.*

Like the other soliloquies, this one is filled with Hamlet's inner struggle: his effort to cope with his own inaction at a time when action is called for. The example of the soldiers going off to fight *even for an eggshell* makes him ashamed of himself, and the soliloquy ends with a declaration of future action no matter what:

> *O, from this time forth,*
> *My thoughts be bloody or be nothing worth!*

This renewed determination to avenge his father's murder ends Part 2 of the play and catapults us into Part 3.

Part 3

Events move quickly now. On his way to England, Hamlet escapes (his ship is boarded by pirates!), and he makes his way back to Denmark to confront his destiny. Meanwhile, at Elsinore, Ophelia goes mad with grief over her father's death (and, presumably, the loss of Hamlet's love) and dies by drowning herself in a stream. Her brother Laertes has by now returned from France, and when he hears that Hamlet is on his way back to Denmark, he vows to kill him to avenge the deaths of his father and sister.

Laertes and Claudius now hatch a plan together: Laertes will challenge Hamlet to a duel, and Laertes's sword will be tipped with poison. Meanwhile, in case that fails, Claudius will put poison in a cup of wine for Hamlet to drink.

Hamlet does return from England, and he nears Elsinore on the day of Ophelia's funeral. In one of the greatest scenes in the play, Hamlet chats with the grave digger, a comic fellow who doesn't give a fig for death—he's seen too much of it. This is where Hamlet, famously, finds the skull of his father's jester in the ground, holds it up, and says *Alas, poor Yorick.* Although this moment has become a cliché, the Yorick speech is in fact tremendously moving. It is another example of a great genius writing a speech for another great genius.

HAMLET
(taking the skull)
Alas, poor Yorick! I knew him, Horatio—a fellow of infinite jest, of most excellent fancy. He hath borne me on his back a thousand times. . . . Here hung those lips that I have kissed I know not how oft [often]. *Where be your gibes* [jokes] *now? your gambols* [dances]*? your songs? your flashes of merriment that were wont* [likely] *to set the table on a roar? Not one now to mock your own grinning? Quite chapfallen?*

When Laertes and the other mourners show up for the funeral, Laertes jumps into Ophelia's open grave, Hamlet comes forward, and they grapple with each other.

The next day they meet for the duel, where things almost turn out as Claudius planned. But not quite. When Hamlet and Laertes begin their duel, Gertrude insists on drinking from the nearby (poisoned) cup of wine—and dies from it. Meanwhile Hamlet is scratched by the poisoned sword and realizes the trick. He changes swords with Laertes and stabs him. Then he attacks Claudius, stabs him with the sword, and forces him to drink the rest of the poison from the cup. As you can tell, even from this short description, it is one of the most thrilling scenes in all of literature, and your children should watch it. The breathless sense of peril that it creates is astonishing.

As Hamlet is dying, Horatio, Hamlet's loyal friend, grabs the cup of poison and tries to drink it himself so that he can join Hamlet in death. Hamlet wrestles it out of Horatio's hand:

HAMLET

Give me the cup. Let go! By heaven, I'll h'at [have it].
O God, Horatio, what a wounded name,
Things standing thus unknown, shall I leave behind me!
If thou didst ever hold me in thy heart,
Absent thee from felicity [happiness] *awhile*
And in this harsh world draw thy breath in pain
To tell my story.

Have your children act out this speech. Hamlet is dying. He's saving his best friend from dying with him. His soul is in torment over the wounded reputation he leaves behind him, and yet perhaps his soul is finally at rest because he has, at last, killed his father's murderer. What great heroics can here be played.

The play ends a few moments later, after the Prince of Norway enters and claims the crown of Denmark. He does honor to Hamlet; and the final image of the play is of Hamlet in death, having at last avenged the murder of his father.

CHAPTER 38

Passage 24
The Most Famous Words
in the World

To be, or not to be; that is the question:
Whether 'tis nobler in the mind to suffer
The slings and arrows of outrageous fortune,
Or to take arms against a sea of troubles,
And, by opposing, end them. To die, to sleep—
No more—and by a sleep to say we end
The heartache and the thousand natural shocks
That flesh is heir to—'tis a consummation
Devoutly to be wished. To die, to sleep—
To sleep, perchance to dream. Ay, there's the rub,
For in that sleep of death what dreams may come,
When we have shuffled off this mortal coil,
Must give us pause.

(*Hamlet*, Act III, Scene 1, lines 64–76)

These words are so famous that they've become a cliché. Actors find it hard to speak them because audiences have heard them so many times before. Even professionals tend to dismiss the speech, resigned that no one is going to listen because they think they know what it says. But the speech is famous for a reason. It is staggeringly well written and immensely touching, and you should take time to read it to your children and explain what it means. As you do, have them memorize at least the first third, which will take them through the most famous part of the speech and get them to its central meaning.

Let's begin by reviewing the whole speech, making sure we understand all the words. Go over it slowly with your children, reading them Shakespeare's words, then the paraphrase.

Shakespeare's Lines	My Paraphrase
To be, or not to be—that is the question: Whether 'tis nobler in the mind to suffer The slings and arrows of outrageous fortune, Or to take arms against a sea of troubles And, by opposing, end them.	To live or not to live. Is it more honorable to live or to end one's life? Is it nobler to suffer by living through all of the slings and arrows that life shoots at you, or is it better to fight against that sea of troubles by ending your life?
To die, to sleep— No more—and by a sleep to say we end The heartache and the thousand natural shocks That flesh is heir to—'tis a consummation Devoutly to be wished.	Dying is an ending (a consummation) to be wished for. It means we can sleep through all those thousand shocks that we humans must suffer (that flesh is heir to).

To die, to sleep—
To sleep, perchance to dream.
  Ay, there's the rub,
For in that sleep of death what
  dreams may come,
When we have shuffled off
  this mortal coil,
Must give us pause.

The sleep of death might mean that we can dream. But there's an obstacle (*the rub*): Perhaps when we have died—when we have *shuffled off this mortal coil*, untangled ourselves from human affairs—our dreams will be nightmares. That gives us pause.

    There's the respect
That makes calamity of so
  long life.
For who would bear the whips
  and scorns of time,
Th' oppressor's wrong, the
  proud man's contumely,
The pangs of despised love,
  the law's delay,
The insolence of office, and
  the spurns
That patient merit of th' un-
  worthy takes,
When he himself might his
  quietus make
With a bare bodkin?

That's the consideration that makes us put up with suffering for such a long time. Because who could bear all the evils of life—the tortures of time, oppression, insulting language (*contumely*) from the overproud, the pangs of unrequited love, the delays of the law, the insolence of people in office, and being spurned by unworthy people whom you try to be patient with? Why bear all this when you can make peace through death (*quietus*) with the help of a mere unsheathed dagger (*bodkin*)?

Who would these fardels bear, *To grunt and sweat under a* * weary life,* *But that the dread of some-* * thing after death,* *The undiscovered country* * from whose bourn* *No traveler returns, puzzles* * the will,* *And makes us rather bear* * those ills we have* *Than fly to others that we* * know not of?*	Who would bear these bur- dens (*fardels*) of grunting and sweating under a weary life, if it weren't for the dread of something worse after death—the *undiscovered coun- try* from which travelers never return? That dread of death paralyzes (*puzzles*) our will and makes us bear what we suffer rather than fly to what we don't know.
Thus conscience does make * cowards of us all,* *And thus the native hue of* * resolution* *Is sicklied o'er with the pale* * cast of thought,* *And enterprises of great pith* * and moment* *With this regard their currents* * turn awry,* *And lose the name of action.*	Thus awareness, or conscious- ness (*conscience*), makes us all into cowards, and thus our resolution is made weaker by our thinking; and great enter- prises (like killing ourselves) aren't acted upon.

The First Sentence

Hamlet is in such despair that he is asking himself whether it is worth the trouble to go on living. Scholars take at least two views of Hamlet's questioning in this speech. Is he asking himself the question because he is at this moment contemplating suicide? Because he is ready to grab a *bare bodkin* and stick it into his heart? Or is he reasoning with himself, asking himself the philosophical question, weighing the pros and cons of suicide in a more intellectual way as he has been trained to do by his studies at Wittenberg?

Unlike the soliloquy *Oh, what a rogue and peasant slave am I!* with its exclamation point and sense of anger, or *Oh that this too, too sullied flesh would melt, / Thaw or resolve itself into a dew,* with its music of mental agony, this soliloquy sounds more measured and intellectual. Hamlet seems to be asking himself the reasonable, logical question: Is it nobler—more honorable—to suffer all the things that life throws at you, the slings and arrows of fortune? Or is it nobler to fight against those troubles by ending your own existence?

> *To be, or not to be—that is the question:*
> *Whether 'tis nobler in the mind to suffer*
> *The slings and arrows of outrageous fortune,*
> *Or to take arms against a sea of troubles*
> *And, by opposing, end them.*

The Second Sentence

In the second sentence, Hamlet simply notes to himself that if by dying (or "sleeping") we could actually end all the heartaches of life, then it would, in fact, be the perfect solution. It would be a solution *devoutly to be wished.*

> *To die, to sleep—*
> *No more—and by a sleep to say we end*
> *The heartache and the thousand natural shocks*
> *That flesh is heir to—'tis a consummation*
> *Devoutly to be wished.*

The Third Group of Sentences

Now Hamlet raises the *rub*—the obstacle. The rub is that if you sleep, you might dream (*perchance to dream*). And the dreams that come during that sleep of death *give us pause.* They do so because they might be nightmares—a world that is even worse than living. As Hamlet calls it later in the soliloquy, that world, that dread of something after death, is *an undiscovered country* from which *no traveler returns*. And that possibility—that death would bring us the nightmares of hell—makes us hesitate (*must give us pause*). It stops us from killing ourselves. Thus *conscience*, or awareness of this problem, makes cowards of us all, and therefore we don't take action and commit suicide.

> *To die, to sleep.*
> *To sleep, perchance to dream. Ay, there's the rub,*
> *For in that sleep of death what dreams may come,*
> *When we have shuffled off this mortal coil,*
> *Must give us pause.*

Memorizing

Naturally, if any of your children want to learn the whole speech, they should go for it. Despite the familiarity of the opening line, the speech as a whole is magnificently romantic and strikes a real chord with children. At thirteen or fourteen, children are thinking about life and death, and this speech can represent a rite of passage, like a song by the Rolling Stones but with better grammar. So encourage them to learn as much of it as they can, but at a minimum, they should learn the first three sections.

CHAPTER 39

Hamlet and the Theater

There is a final aspect of *Hamlet* you should discuss with your children, and that is Hamlet's relationship to the world of acting, including his famous speech to the players.

As your children well know by this time, Shakespeare frequently used the theater as a metaphor for the whole of life. We see it particularly in Shakespeare's comedies and histories—we've examined many of them together—but here, in *Hamlet,* we see Shakespeare use the theater in a tragedy and in even greater depth than in his other plays. We see it in the way Hamlet speaks, in the things he speaks about, in his metaphors, in his personal love for actors, and in the way the entire plot hinges on a theater performance ("The Murder of Gonzago").

There are three things your children should especially notice.

1. Hamlet as Actor

The first has to do with the manner in which Hamlet relates to the other characters. Hamlet acts in front of them. He is a natural-born actor, just as Falstaff, Rosalind, and Richard III are. He cajoles people along by assuming the character of the Hamlet they want to see. This aspect of his character goes a long way toward explaining his madness with Polonius and Ophelia. The literary critic Mark Van Doren makes this point:

Hamlet is an actor. Like any character in whom Shakespeare was greatly interested, he plays a role. He plays indeed many roles, being supreme in tragedy as Falstaff was supreme in comedy. His long interest in the theater has taught him how, but his best tutors now are the pressure of circumstances and the richness of his own nature. Like Falstaff, he shows the man he is by being many men.

Read this excerpt from Act II, Scene 2 aloud, and listen to Hamlet acting with Polonius. Hamlet is acting the role of the cultured, intellectual madman while at the same time—knowing that Polonius has been spying on him—toying with Polonius contemptuously:

POLONIUS

Do you know me, my lord?

HAMLET

Excellent well. You are a fishmonger. . . . I would you were so honest a man.

POLONIUS

Honest, my lord?

HAMLET

Ay, sir. To be honest, as this world goes, is to be one man picked out of ten thousand. . . . Have you a daughter?

POLONIUS

I have, my lord.

HAMLET

Let her not walk i' th' sun. Conception is a blessing, but as your daughter may conceive, friend, look to 't.

POLONIUS

. . . What do you read, my lord?

HAMLET

Words, words, words.

POLONIUS

What is the matter, my lord?

HAMLET

Between who?

POLONIUS

I mean, the matter that you read, my lord.

HAMLET

*Slanders, sir; for the satirical rogue says here that old men have
grey beards, that their faces are wrinkled, their eyes purging thick
amber . . . and that they have a plentiful lack of wit, together with most
weak hams; . . . for yourself, sir, shall grow old as I am, if, like a crab, you
could go backward.*

POLONIUS

*(aside) Though this be madness, yet there is method in 't. . . . . My lord,
I will take my leave of you.*

HAMLET

*You cannot, sir, take from me any thing that I will more willingly part
withal—except my life, except my life, except my life.*

2. Hamlet and the Players

The second thing about Hamlet and the theater that always moves me
is the way Hamlet changes, almost instantly, from melancholy Dane to
bright, giddy theater lover the instant the traveling players arrive at Elsinore Castle. The scene where we see this most clearly is that amazing
Act II, Scene 2 again.

As your children know, Hamlet learns in this scene that Rosencrantz and Guildenstern are spies for his mother and uncle, and this realization confirms his feelings of injustice and isolation. At this very moment, the players, who are his old and valued friends, arrive with a flourish of trumpets.

The instant the players enter the room, Hamlet changes, brightening instantly with pleasure and relief. We hear it immediately in his voice as he greets them. Suddenly his speech pattern is buoyant and jumps from one "welcome" to the next. He uses pun after pun, playing with words in a giddy manner. And then, like a young boy who can't wait to open his next present, he insists that the players perform a speech immediately:

HAMLET

You are welcome, masters; welcome all.—I am glad to see thee well.—Welcome, good friends.—O my old friend! Why, thy face is valanced [framed by a beard] *since I saw thee last. Com'st thou to beard me* [corner me] *in Denmark?—What, my young lady and mistress!* [This is addressed to the boy who plays the female role.] *By'r Lady, your ladyship is nearer to heaven than when I saw you last by the altitude of a chopine* [by the height of a high-heeled shoe]. *Pray God your voice, like a piece of uncurrent gold, be not cracked within the ring* [that your voice hasn't cracked the way a gold coin could be cracked and made worthless]. *Masters, you are all welcome. . . . We'll have a speech straight* [right away]. *Come, give us a taste of your quality. Come, a passionate speech.*

This is a perfect speech for acting up a storm. Set up the scene: Your daughter is Hamlet. She is feeling angry and annoyed with Polonius, who has been meddling (as usual) and probing Hamlet for signs of madness. She is disappointed with her old school friends, who have just lied to her. And suddenly a troupe of actors enters the room. She perks up. Almost instantly she feels safe and happy. *You are welcome, masters; welcome all.* Have her deliver Hamlet's whole speech. Hamlet's love for theater and acting gleams from every sentence. And then, what a return to tragedy we feel when the players leave the room. This is the moment when Hamlet delivers his O, *what a rogue* soliloquy and excoriates himself for not having any of the passion within himself that he has just seen the Player King feel over "Hecuba."

> *What's Hecuba to him, or he to Hecuba,*
> *That he should weep for her? What would he do*
> *Had he the motive and the cue for passion*
> *That I have?*

A really wonderful acting exercise would be to act the speech above— *You are welcome masters, all*—and then follow it with the entire O, *what a rogue* soliloquy. Neither one has to be memorized. Just have a copy of each speech at hand, and let your daughter act her heart out.

3. Hamlet on Acting

The third thing I want to emphasize is a speech that Hamlet delivers to the players in the third act.

As you'll remember, in Act II, Scene 2, Hamlet asks the Player King to insert a speech into "The Murder of Gonzago" that is meant to enhance the possibility of catching Claudius. A few scenes later Shakespeare tells the players exactly how he wants to hear his speech played:

> *Speak the speech, I pray you, as I pronounced it to you, trippingly on*
> *the tongue;*

This is the most famous speech ever written about the art of acting, and you should read it to your children, then have them read it back to you. Here's the speech with a paraphrase so that your children understand every word of it.

Shakespeare's Lines	My *Paraphrase*
Speak the speech, I pray you, as I pronounced it to you, trippingly on the tongue; but if you mouth it, as many of your players do, I had as lief the town-crier spoke my lines.	Speak the speech, please, as I showed you, beautifully, so it trips off the tongue, but if you say it without expression, as many of your players do, I would just as soon have the town-crier speak what I wrote.
Nor do not saw the air too much with your hand, thus, but use all gently; for in the very torrent, tempest, and as I may say, whirlwind of your passion, you must acquire and beget a temperance that may give it smoothness.	And don't wave your hand around like this, but do everything gently; because in the excitement of your passion, you have to achieve moderation so that everything looks natural.
O, it offends me to the soul to hear a robustious, periwig-pated fellow tear a passion to tatters, to very rags, to split the ears of the groundlings, who for the most part are capable of nothing but inexplicable dumb shows and noise.	Oh, I'm deeply offended when I hear a noisy fellow who wears a wig on his head (*pate*) tear into a passionate speech so hard that there's almost nothing left of it when he's finished, or recite so loudly or badly that he hurts the ears of the lowest-paying, closest-to-the stage spectators, who don't understand anything but broadly acted entertainments like pantomime.

I would have such a fellow whipped for o'erdoing Termagant. It out-Herods Herod. Pray you avoid it.

I would have such an actor whipped for overacting roles like Termagant and Herod— known for the size and passion of their characters. Please avoid it.

Be not too tame, neither, but let your own discretion be your tutor. Suit the action to the word, the word to the action, with this special observance, that you o'erstep not the modesty of nature.

On the other hand, don't be too tame. Instead, let your own good judgment be your teacher. Make sure that your actions fit what you're saying—and that what you're saying fits the action, with one special note: Don't step beyond what is believable.

For anything so overdone is from the purpose of playing, whose end, both at the first and now, was and is to hold, as 'twere, the mirror up to nature,

Because anything overdone that way is opposite to the purpose of acting, which now and always is to hold, as it were, a mirror up to nature,

to show virtue her own feature, scorn her own image, and the very age and body of the time his form and pressure.

to show the character or quality we call Virtue just what she really looks like; to show that other character or quality named Scorn just what *she* looks like; and to show the times we live in—and even Time itself—their actual outline and shape.

Most theater professionals would agree that nothing better has ever been written about the profession of acting. If any of your children loves acting, have him learn every word of it. I learned it when I was about twelve, and my children learned it early as well. It will always, always be of value to anyone who loves the theater.

Reluctantly, we end our study of *Hamlet* at this point. Hundreds of books the size of this one have been written about *Hamlet* alone, and yet the nuances and meaning of the play have never been exhausted and never will be. It speaks to each new generation in a different way and casts its shadows differently with each century. Your children will always be wiser and better for knowing *Hamlet*. And with its vast intelligence, it serves as the perfect prelude to the final play we'll be studying together, *The Tempest*.

CHAPTER 40

Passage 25
A Summation

Our revels now are ended. These our actors,
As I foretold you, were all spirits, and
Are melted into air, into thin air;
And like the baseless fabric of this vision,
The cloud-capped towers, the gorgeous palaces,
The solemn temples, the great globe itself,
Yea, all which it inherit, shall dissolve;
And, like this insubstantial pageant faded,
Leave not a rack behind. We are such stuff
As dreams are made on, and our little life
Is rounded with a sleep.

(*The Tempest*, Act IV, Scene 1, lines 165–75)

*T*he *Tempest* is the last play wholly written by Shakespeare, and it is fair to think of it as his final, valedictory statement to his audience. It is also a mysterious play, mysterious in the manner of other great works of art by geniuses in their final maturity. The late novels of Henry James are mysterious in this way, as are the final string quartets of Beethoven and the final cutouts of Matisse. These works represent both a summing-up and a breakthrough: a new approach to presenting ideas that have become deeper and richer over a lifetime. Such works of art are often expressed in new forms and with new insights, building on the artistic complexity that has been growing within the artist over the years, yet with moments of simple clarity that make us pause with wonder. This doesn't mean that we have to like these later works more than their youthful counterparts, or that they're "better" or more artful. However, your children should gain an understanding of how late works like *The Tempest* contain sounds and images that somehow cross into new territory for the artist.

One of the comforts we can all share in our study of Shakespeare is the knowledge that as an artist Shakespeare completed the work that he was meant to do. He was not cut off in his prime like Mozart or Van Gogh, both of whom died in their thirties. Shakespeare finished *The Tempest* around 1611, at the age of forty-seven, and soon after that he retired to his hometown of Stratford, where he died in 1616. In his final years he collaborated on some minor works, but by the time he died, he had completed his life's work.

The Tempest is a spiritual play and an odd play. It draws on folklore, mythology, and magic, and it contains themes and situations from his earlier comedies. It also draws on reports of the discovery by European explorers of primitive, unsettled lands across the ocean that had filtered back to Elizabethan England. It is one of Shakespeare's four last plays, which include *Pericles, Cymbeline, The Winter's Tale,* and *The Tempest.* These four are similar enough in tone to warrant their own grouping in most modern editions, where they are usually called The Romances. The critic Barbara Mowat has emphasized the innovative nature of these works, in each of which Shakespeare combines tragedy, comedy, and romance, and she has suggested that they are best described as "dramatic romances."

I want your children to memorize the passage above because I believe it can be considered Shakespeare's personal statement of farewell to his art. This view may sound romantic on my part, and there are skeptics; but I'm joined by many scholars in believing that not only this speech but the play as a whole represents Shakespeare's valedictory to playgoers for all posterity.

Our revels now are ended.

The speech is spoken by a man named Prospero, who was once the Duke of Milan but was exiled twelve years ago, his title usurped by his ambitious brother. Prospero was cruelly set adrift on the ocean with his three-year-old daughter, Miranda; however, a wise old friend secretly smuggled supplies—as well as books on magic—aboard the rotting boat, and eventually Prospero and Miranda reached a remote island, which is where the play takes place.

By the time the play begins, Prospero has developed into a great wizard. Since arriving on the island, he has learned to control the elements, he has released a fairy sprite (now his servant) named Ariel from the prison of a witch named Sycorax, and he has enslaved the witch's son, a brutish monster named Caliban, whom he had once hoped to civilize.

When the play opens, Prospero has conjured up a storm around his island in order to wreck a ship carrying his villainous brother. Prospero's plan is to have his brother and his evil friends wash ashore on his island, where he can keep track of them and control them. He may have revenge

The Tempest at the Theatre Royal Haymarket, with Ralph Fiennes as Prospero and Tom Byam Shaw as Ariel

in mind—we're never quite sure; but as the play progresses, we see Prospero come to terms with his past and gain a spirit of forgiveness, regardless of the unforgivable nature of the injuries that were done to him. His change of heart results from a mysterious moral journey that comprises a series of incidents, including

- Ariel's desire to gain his freedom;
- the treatment that the lowly Caliban receives at Prospero's own hand;
- the philosophy espoused by the kind courtier who placed provisions on Prospero's raft those many years ago; and
- the benevolence Prospero feels when witnessing his daughter Miranda falling in love with one of the survivors.

Indeed, Prospero's spirit of forgiveness in the face of past injury seems to be the central theme of the play.

The Play-Within-the-Play

Like A *Midsummer Night's Dream* and *Hamlet*, *The Tempest* involves a play-within-a-play, only here it is more subtle. The outer play, or "real" events, concern Prospero as a sort of god—or playwright, if you will—who manipulates the lives of the shipwrecked visitors so that their stories become a kind of inner play-within-the-Prospero-play. Prospero's stage manager is Ariel, the fairy sprite he has released from prison who hopes that by doing Prospero's bidding this one last time he will gain his freedom for eternity.

The inner play is made up of three related stories that play out as Prospero manipulates the scenario from above: (1) the story of evil courtiers who plot to kill the current Duke of Milan and usurp the throne; (2) the parallel story of two clownish servants who join with the monster Caliban in a plan to kill Prospero himself; and (3) the story of the courtship of Miranda and Ferdinand, the prince of Naples. Explain to your children that one of the joys of the play is Miranda's innocence: When the play opens,

The Tempest at the American Repertory Theater,
with Vera Zorina as Ariel

the fifteen-year-old girl has never seen a fellow human being before except her father. She is amazed when she first sees Ferdinand, and she instantly falls in love with him. Then, near the end of the play, when she sees the other shipwrecked humans gathered together for the first time, she cries:

> *O brave new world,*
> *That has such people in it!*

Ironically, Miranda is standing on an island that will become the brave new world of the seventeenth century. European exploration will reach its height in the decades after this play is written. But Shakespeare seems to have an additional world in mind: He seems to be implying that human beings, not islands in the sea, will always be the "brave new world" that requires perpetual rediscovery if the human race is ever to grow in spirit.

The Masque

The specific circumstances of the speech we're memorizing have to do with the performance of a masque. A masque is an entertainment that was popular among nobility in the seventeenth century, where actors, dancers, and often nobles performed poetic scenes to the accompaniment of music, often wearing masks. About halfway through *The Tempest*, Prospero gives Miranda permission to marry Ferdinand, and in celebration he has Ariel and other spirits under his control perform a masque for the lovers. During the masque, something reminds Prospero of Caliban's treachery, and angrily he halts the festivities and makes the spirits vanish. Ferdinand looks frightened, and Prospero says to him:

PROSPERO
You do look, my son, in a moved sort [disturbed manner],
As if you were dismayed. Be cheerful sir.
Our revels now are ended. These our actors,
As I foretold you, were all spirits, and
Are melted into air, into thin air;

Indeed, the actors *were* all spirits and included the goddesses Iris, Ceres, and Juno. And when Prospero halted the revels, they *melted into thin air* like magic. As Hamlet said with regard to the Ghost, *There are more things in heaven and earth, Horatio / Than are dreamt of in your philosophy.*

Review the first three lines with your children one more time:

Our revels now are ended. These our actors,
As I foretold you, were all spirits, and
Are melted into air, into thin air;

And now add:

And like the baseless fabric of this vision [spectacle],
The cloud-capped towers, the gorgeous palaces,
The solemn temples, the great globe itself,

> *Yea, all which it inherit* [inhabit], *shall dissolve;*
> *And like this insubstantial pageant faded,*
> *Leave not a rack* [a wisp of a cloud] *behind.*

Here Prospero describes some of the scenery (*the baseless fabric*) used during the entertainment. It included depictions of *cloud-capped towers*, of *gorgeous palaces*, of *solemn temples*, and of *the great globe itself*. At the same time, Prospero is describing the towers, palaces, and temples of the real world, saying that they too, like the *baseless fabric* of the masque, will ultimately dissolve and disappear. Thus, here in the play is another theater metaphor, this one represented by the masque.

> *And like the baseless fabric of this vision,*
> *The cloud-capped towers,*
> *the gorgeous palaces,*
> *The solemn temples,*
> *the great globe itself,*
> *Yea, all which it inherit,*
> *shall dissolve;*

Once again Shakespeare is using the word *globe* in a double sense: first as the earth and second as the name of his theater, using the central metaphor of his career to remind us that we are actors on the stage of life.

And what will happen to the actors whom Ferdinand just saw? What will happen to the actors who filled the play and to the men and women who fill the Globe Theatre and indeed to *the great globe itself*, our universe? Just like the insubstantial pageant that Prospero has just presented, they will *dissolve* and *leave not a rack behind*.

The Meaning of Life

And now Shakespeare ends the speech with a kind of summation—a summation not only of the speech but of the meaning of the play, and of how Prospero and ultimately Shakespeare viewed our lives.

> We are such stuff
> As dreams are made on [of], and our little life
> Is rounded with a sleep.

Say it again, quietly, with your children, and feel the sense of finality and peace that is conveyed in this single ingenious sentence:

> We are such stuff
> As dreams are made on, and our little life
> Is rounded with a sleep.

The sense of finality that Shakespeare portrays here is neither angry nor discontented. It is not a shaking of the fist at the unfairness of having to leave this little life. Just the opposite—it is a farewell taken with understanding and a sense of fulfillment. Our lives are filled with trials and joys, frustrations and challenges, defeats and triumphs. And ultimately we fade, like dreams, rounded with a final, grateful sleep.

Shakespeare's ultimate statement on the meaning of life is not that of Jaques—cynical and sad—in *All the world's a stage*. It is that of Prospero, and it is filled with peace.

Epilogue

It is my hope that your children now have the tools to make Shakespeare a continuing part of their lives. Shakespeare should not be an occasional visitor. He should be a permanent houseguest, living in that spare room down the hall, ready to join you for a meal or an evening whenever you crave his company. Better yet, he should feel like a part of your family, the wise uncle who is always willing to give you the benefit of his considerable knowledge and artistry, the one who always knows right from wrong, on whom you can call at a moment's notice. Don't misunderstand: He is not complacent or easygoing. On the contrary, he is fierce in his beliefs and would defend them to the death. He can't be fooled, and his respect must be earned. But he is always wise, always tolerant, and he sees deeply, searingly, into the souls of us all.

The great Italian opera composer Gioachino Rossini admired Mozart above all the great musical artists who came before him. He recognized that Mozart was a genius of a kind that he, Rossini, as talented as he was, could never be. For Rossini, Mozart's gifts were from the gods above, of a different order from the gifts of men.

Toward the end of his life, Rossini said of Mozart: "He was the inspiration of my youth, the despair of my middle years and the consolation of my old age." I want Shakespeare to be all those things for your children.

First, I want your children to be inspired by Shakespeare for the many years to come when they believe that they can do anything as long as they work hard enough at it.

Second, I want them to recognize at some point in their maturity the genuine depth of Shakespeare's genius; and while I don't want them to despair over it, we all know that with maturity comes understanding of our own place in the universe. If we can't all be Shakespeares, it doesn't make us less in the world; the understanding makes us more.

Finally, I want Shakespeare to be your children's consolation in their old age. I want them to go on studying him and marveling at him and growing because of all he teaches us about art and about humanity. And perhaps, at the very end, he'll return to us again as sheer inspiration, just as he did when we were youngsters.

A Chronological List
of Shakespeare's Plays

Bear in mind that all these dates are approximate, as there is not enough historical evidence to date most of the plays with precision. However, this chronology will give you a good idea of the general order in which the major plays were written. Also, a few of the lesser plays were collaborations, but the details remain a subject of scholarly debate, so I don't list the names of the collaborators here, nor all the possible collaborations.

1589–90	*Henry VI, Part 1* (later revised or perhaps written after Part 3)
1590–91	*Henry VI, Part 2* *Henry VI, Part 3* *The Two Gentlemen of Verona*
1592–93	*Richard III* *The Comedy of Errors*
1593–94	*Titus Andronicus* *The Taming of the Shrew*
1594–95	*Love's Labour's Lost* *King John*
1595–96	*Richard II* *Romeo and Juliet* *A Midsummer Night's Dream*

1596–97 *The Merchant of Venice*
         Henry IV, Part 1

1597–98 *Henry IV, Part 2*
         The Merry Wives of Windsor

1598–99 *Much Ado About Nothing*

1599   *Henry V*
         Julius Caesar
         As You Like It

1599–1600 *Hamlet*

1601–2   *Twelfth Night*
         Troilus and Cressida

1602–3   *All's Well That Ends Well*

1604   *Measure for Measure*
         Othello

1605   *Timon of Athens*
         King Lear

1606   *Macbeth*
         Antony and Cleopatra

1607–8   *Pericles*

1608   *Coriolanus*

1609   *Cymbeline*

1610   *The Winter's Tale*

1611   *The Tempest*

1612–13 *Henry VIII*

1613   *The Two Noble Kinsmen*

Five Additional
Longer Passages

Here are five of my favorite long passages that your children may want to tackle as a culmination of their study. I don't want to overburden the text with them in light of their size, but I also don't want your children to miss them. There is a unique, almost Zen-like joy in rattling off long, meaty passages of Shakespeare, and if your children love studying Shakespeare as much as I hope they do, please look up these passages in your favorite edition of Shakespeare and memorize them with your children.

1. *Now is the winter of our discontent*
   Richard III, Act I, Scene 1, lines 1–31
2. *I do much wonder that one man,*
   Much Ado About Nothing, Act II, Scene 3, lines 8–35
3. *I left no ring with her. What means this lady?*
   Twelfth Night, Act II, Scene 2, lines 17–41
4. *My gentle Puck, come hither.*
   A Midsummer Night's Dream, Act II, Scene 1, lines 153–94
5. *The barge she sat in like a burnished throne*
   Antony and Cleopatra, Act II, Scene 2, lines 227–56

Fifty-five Additional Passages to Teach Your Children If They Want to Continue

Here is a list of fifty-five additional passages, in case your children want to push their Shakespeare studies even further. All are taken from the notebooks that I developed with my children, and one of the purposes of this book is to share them with you. The passages are listed in alphabetical order by title of play.

AS YOU LIKE IT:

Now my co-mates and brothers in exile,—Act II, Scene 1, lines 1–17

I remember when I was in love—Act II, Scene 4, lines 45–55

A fool, a fool, I met a fool i' th' forest—Act II, Scene 7, lines 12–35

The poor world is almost six thousand years old—Act IV, Scene 1, lines 100–13

Your brother and my sister no sooner met—Act V, Scene 2, lines 33–43

CYMBELINE:

The crickets sing and man's o'er-laboured sense—Act II, Scene 2, lines 14–54

HAMLET:

Oh that this too, too sullied flesh would melt—Act I, Scene 2, lines 133–64

Angels and ministers of grace, defend us!—Act I, Scene 4, lines 43–62

Speak the speech, I pray you—Act III, Scene 2, lines 1–26

O, my offense is rank—Act III, Scene 3, lines 40–76

Now might I do it pat, now he is a-praying—Act III, Scene 3, lines 79–101

There is a willow grows aslant the brook—Act IV, Scene 7, lines 190–208

HENRY IV, PART 1:

I know you all, and will awhile uphold—Act I, Scene 2, lines 202–24

Honour pricks me on—Act V, Scene 1, lines 131–42

HENRY IV, PART 2:

How many thousand of my poorest subjects—Act III, Scene 1, lines 4–31

HENRY V:

Now all the youth of England are on fire—Act II, Prologue

Nay sure he's not in hell—Act II, Scene 3, lines 9–26

Now entertain conjecture of a time—Act IV, Prologue

JULIUS CAESAR:

[H]e doth bestride the narrow world / Like a Colossus—Act I, Scene 2, lines 142–60

Friends, Romans, countrymen, lend me your ears—Act III, Scene 2, lines 82–117

KING LEAR:

O, reason not the need!—Act II, Scene 4, lines 305–28

Blow winds, and crack your cheeks—Act III, Scene 2, lines 1–11

Poor naked wretches, wheresoe'er you are—Act III, Scene 4, lines 32–41

How does my royal lord?—Act IV, Scene 7, lines 50–58

LOVE'S LABOUR'S LOST:

And I forsooth in love—Act III, Scene 1, lines 184–215

MACBETH:

Is this a dagger that I see before me—Act II, Scene 1, lines 44–77

That which hath made them drunk hath made me bold—Act II, Scene 2, lines 1–17

THE MERCHANT OF VENICE

I am a Jew. Hath not a Jew eyes?—Act III, Scene 1, lines 57–72

The quality of mercy is not strained—Act IV, Scene 1, lines 190–212

The moon shines bright—Act V, Scene 1, lines 1–21

How sweet the moonlight sleeps upon this bank—Act V, Scene 1, lines 62–73

A MIDSUMMER NIGHT'S DREAM:

Therefore, fair Hermia, question your desires—Act I, Scene 1, lines 69–80

How now, my love? Why is your cheek so pale?—Act I, Scene 1, lines 130–51

I swear to thee by Cupid's strongest bow—Act I, Scene 1, lines 172–81

How happy some o'er other some can be—Act I, Scene 1, lines 232–57

Either I mistake your shape and making quite—Act II, Scene 1, lines 33–60

These are the forgeries of jealousy—Act II, Scene 1, lines 84–120

His mother was a vot'ress of my order—Act II, Scene 1, lines 127–42

The lunatic, the lover and the poet—Act V, Scene 1, lines 7–18

Now, until the break of day—Act V, Scene 1, lines 418–39

If we shadows have offended—Act V, Scene 1, lines 440–55

MUCH ADO ABOUT NOTHING:

This can be no trick—Act II, Scene 3, lines 223–48

What fire is in mine ears?—Act III, Scene 1, lines 113–22

Lady Beatrice, you have wept all this while?—Act IV, Scene 1, lines 269–305

Dost thou not suspect my place?—Act IV, Scene 2, lines 76–89

RICHARD II:

For God's sake let us sit upon the ground—Act III, Scene 2, lines 160–82

ROMEO AND JULIET:

Two households both alike in dignity—Prologue to Act I

Even or odd, all days of the year—Act I, Scene 3, lines 18–53

O then I see Queen Mab hath been with you—Act I, Scene 4, lines 58–99

THE TAMING OF THE SHREW:

Good morrow, Kate, for that's your name, I hear—Act II, Scene 1, lines 190–202

I'll tell you, Sir Lucentio—Act III, Scene 2, lines 160–85

THE TEMPEST:

Be not afeard. The isle is full of noises—Act III, Scene 2, lines 148–56

You elves of hills—Act V, Scene 1, lines 42–66

TWELFTH NIGHT:

Tell him he shall not speak with me—Act I, Scene 5, lines 145–61

Now sir, what is your text?—Act I, Scene 5, lines 219–51

A List of Favorite Epigrams

Even so quickly may one catch the plague?

What great ones do the rest will prattle of.

Dost thou think because thou art virtuous there shall be no more cakes and ale?

Is it not strange that sheep's guts should hale souls out of men's bodies?

Speak low if you speak love.

There was never yet a philosopher / That could endure the toothache patiently.

All that glitters is not gold.

He jests at scars that never felt a wound.

Parting is such sweet sorrow.

A plague on both your houses.

Fair is foul and foul is fair.

Nothing in his life / Became him like the leaving of it.

Yet I do fear thy nature; / It is too full of the milk of human kindness.

Sleep . . . knits up the raveled sleeve of care.

Double, double, toil and trouble; / Fire burn and cauldron bubble.

Out, damned spot, out I say!

Something is rotten in the state of Denmark.

There are more things in heaven and earth, Horatio / Than are dreamt of in your philosophy.

All that lives must die, passing through nature to eternity.

Frailty thy name is woman.

The funeral baked meats / Did coldly furnish forth the marriage tables.

The play's the thing / Wherein I'll catch the conscience of the king.

As flies to wanton boys are we t'the gods, / They kill us for their sport.

Small cheer and great welcome makes a merry feast.

The better part of valor is discretion.

There is a special providence in the fall of a sparrow.

Use every man after his desert, and who shall 'scape whipping?

There is nothing good or bad but thinking makes it so.

How sharper than a serpent's tooth it is / To have a thankless child.

Some are born great, some achieve greatness, and some have greatness thrust upon 'em.

The man that hath no music in himself, / Nor is not moved with concord of sweet sounds, / Is fit for treasons, stratagems, and spoils.

What's past is prologue.

Misery acquaints a man with strange bedfellows.

That which we call a rose / By any other word would smell as sweet.

The purest treasure mortal times afford / Is spotless reputation.

Sample Quotation Pages

O, Romeo, Romeo,

                    Wherefore art thou Romeo?

Deny thy father and refuse thy name,

Or, if thou wilt not,

                    Be but sworn my love,

And I'll no longer be a Capulet.

Tomorrow
     and
          tomorrow
               and
                    tomorrow,
Creeps in this petty pace
               from day to day,

To the last syllable of recorded time;

And all our yesterdays
               have lighted fools

The way to dusty death.

               Out, out brief candle!

What is love?
            'Tis not hereafter.

Present mirth hath present laughter.

What's to come is still unsure.

In delay
            there lies no plenty,

Then come kiss me, sweet and twenty.

Youth's a stuff will no endure.

Our revels now are ended.

                      These our actors,

As I foretold you,

                      were all spirits, and

Are melted into air, into thin air;

                      . . . We are such stuff

As dreams are made on,

                      and our little life

Is rounded with a sleep.

Bibliography

BOOKS FOR CHILDREN

I have found the following children's literature particularly helpful in introducing and clarifying Shakespeare for children. Please note that this is a selection and not meant to be comprehensive.

Aliki. *William Shakespeare and the Globe.* New York: HarperCollins, 1999. This book for the very young tells the story of moving the Globe Theatre across the Thames.

Ganeri, Anita. *The Young Person's Guide to Shakespeare.* With performances on CD by the Royal Shakespeare Company. London: Pavilion Books, 1999. This book provides an intelligent overview of most of the plays, along with a brief life of Shakespeare and a description of his theater. It is beautifully illustrated, mainly with photographs, which makes it somewhat unique among children's books on Shakespeare. Highly recommended.

Greenhill, Wendy, and Paul Wignall. *Shakespeare Library* Series. Chicago: Heinemann Library, 1997. This series of brief, informative paperbacks approaches the study of Shakespeare by topic. They're all fun to read and very well illustrated. Greenhill was head of education at the Royal Shakespeare Company. The series includes:
Shakespeare: A Life
Shakespeare's Theatre

Shakespeare's Players
Julius Caesar
Macbeth
The Merchant of Venice
A Midsummer Night's Dream
Romeo and Juliet
Twelfth Night

Holdridge, Barbara, ed. *Under the Greenwood Tree: Shakespeare for Young People*. Illustrated by Robin and Pat DeWitt. Gilsum, N.H.: Stemmer House, 1986. This short book of passages from the plays and poems is beautifully illustrated.

Lamb, Charles and Mary. *Tales from Shakespeare*. New York: Puffin Books, 1994. Originally published in 1807, this book is the classic retelling of many of the stories for children. It has its nineteenth-century oddities, and there have been many retellings for children since 1807, but the Lambs' version has a strange way of staying with us.

Langley, Andrew. *Shakespeare's Theatre*. New York: Oxford University Press, 1999. This book tells the story of the original Globe Theatre and the construction of the new Globe in the 1990s.

Pollinger, Gina, ed. *Something Rich and Strange: A Treasury of Shakespeare's Verse*. Illustrated by Emma Chichester Clark. New York: Kingfisher, 1995. This book of passages from the plays and poems is nicely illustrated and attractive.

BOOKS FOR PARENTS, TEACHERS, AND ADVANCED STUDENTS

These books have all informed my understanding of Shakespeare in significant ways over the years, and they all make exciting reading.

Bate, Jonathan. *The Genius of Shakespeare*. New York: Oxford University Press, 1998. Bate is an outstanding modern authority on Shakespeare, and this wide-ranging book on everything from Shakespeare's life and times to his influence on subsequent generations is riveting.

Bloom, Harold. *Shakespeare: The Invention of the Human*. New York: River-head Books, 1998. Bloom is unique and exhilarating, a professor who has spent a lifetime thinking deeply about literature. This book (which has a separate chapter on each of the plays) takes the view that Shakespeare invented Western men and women by example. Bloom is Falstaffian in the breadth of his humanity and even in the way he writes.

Boyce, Charles. *Shakespeare A to Z: The Essential Reference to His Plays, His Poems, His Life and Times, and More*. New York: Dell, 1990. A good nuts-and-bolts encyclopedia of all things Shakespeare. I find that I use it all the time to answer questions about dates and characters. It also contains very good scene-by-scene synopses of all the plays.

Bradley, A. C. *Oxford Lectures on Poetry*. 1909; reprinted by Bloomington: Indiana University Press, 1961. Bradley based his immensely intelligent and intellectual view of Shakespeare's plays on character studies of Shakespeare's heroes and villains. This book contains a seminal essay on the character of Falstaff.

———. *Shakespearean Tragedy: Lectures on Hamlet, Othello, King Lear, and Macbeth*. 1904; reprinted by London: Penguin Books, 1991. Bradley was the great critic of the early twentieth century, and this is his most famous book. Justly so—it is magisterial and magnificent.

Brook, Peter. *The Empty Space*. Harmondsworth, U.K.: Penguin Books, 1968. The innovative British director discusses his theories of the theater.

Bryson, Bill. *Shakespeare: The World as Stage*. New York: HarperCollins, 2007. This is the best short biography of Shakespeare I've ever read. It doesn't analyze the plays; it's all biography and is immensely readable.

Crystal, David, and Ben Crystal. *The Shakespeare Miscellany*. New York: Overlook Press, 2005. This book is enormously fun. It contains hundreds of short observations about everything from boy actors to Arnold Schwarzenegger's Hamlet. I love every page of it.

———. *Shakespeare's Words: A Glossary and Language Companion*. London:

Penguin Books, 2002. This is the best general glossary out there. If you're stumped about a word, this is where to look.

Dobson, Michael, and Stanley Wells, eds. *The Oxford Companion to Shakespeare*. New York: Oxford University Press, 2001. This big, wonderful encyclopedia of Shakespeare is beautifully written and covers everything. Plot summaries, histories of the plays, biographies of actors—it's all here, with valuable illustrations.

Frye, Northrop. *Anatomy of Criticism*. Princeton, N.J.: Princeton University Press, 1957. This is the most famous book of literary criticism of the mid-twentieth century. It is not just about Shakespeare; it's about the rhythms of literature. It's a difficult book but indispensable to serious literary study.

———. *A Natural Perspective: The Development of Shakespearean Comedy and Romance*. New York: Columbia University Press, 1965. This book's observations about the nature of Shakespeare's comedies and dramatic romances are so intelligent and startling that over the years it has become my favorite book about Shakespeare. I reread it all the time.

———. *Northrop Frye on Shakespeare*. Edited by Robert Sandler. New Haven, Conn.: Yale University Press, 1986. These are Frye's lectures on Shakespeare to his classes at the University of Toronto. They are down to earth, very accessible, and filled with fresh insights on every page. I love this book.

Garber, Marjorie. *Shakespeare After All*. New York: Pantheon, 2004. An excellent study of each of the plays, always intelligent and always thoughtful. Garber is much admired among Shakespeareans, and rightly so.

Gibson, William. *Shakespeare's Game*. New York: Atheneum, 1978. This book is based on Gibson's lectures to a class at Harvard, and they are centered on how Shakespeare went about structuring his plots. Gibson is the author of several plays, including *The Miracle Worker* and a play about Shakespeare growing up in Stratford. These lectures, unique and interesting on every page, are full of insights that only a playwright would have.

Goddard, Harold C. *The Meaning of Shakespeare.* 2 vols. Chicago: University of Chicago Press, 1951. The title of this book makes it sound elementary, but in fact it is an excellent, sophisticated two-volume analysis of all the plays by a major scholar.

Granville-Barker, Harley. *Prefaces to Shakespeare.* 4 vols. Princeton, N.J.: Princeton University Press, 1946. For decades this book was considered the best handbook on the production of Shakespeare's plays in the theater. It is filled with good, practical advice.

Greenblatt, Stephen. *Will in the World: How Shakespeare Became Shakespeare.* New York: W.W. Norton, 2005. This book is the culmination of Greenblatt's many years as a great Shakespeare scholar at Harvard. It is an erudite and brilliant biography that draws heavily on Shakespeare's life and times to illuminate the plays.

Hall, Peter. *Shakespeare's Advice to the Players.* London: Oberon Books, 2003. Sir Peter Hall, founder of the Royal Shakespeare Company, is one of the greatest Shakespeare directors of the past hundred years. His book on how to speak Shakespeare is brilliantly practical. No one knows this area better.

Hodges, C. Walter. *Enter the Whole Army: A Pictorial Study of Shakespearean Staging, 1576–1616.* Cambridge, U.K.: Cambridge University Press, 1999. Hodges has drawn the greatest illustrations of Shakespeare's theaters I have ever seen. He has studied the plays in order to solve practical staging problems, and in the drawings in this terrific and unique book, he shows you his solutions.

Johnson, Samuel. *Selections from Johnson on Shakespeare.* Ed. Bertrand H. Bronson with Jean M. O'Meara. New Haven, Conn.: Yale University Press, 1986. The greatest literary critic of the eighteenth century, Doctor Johnson, produced his own edition of the complete works in 1765, and these are a selection of his notes on each of the plays. Quirky, riveting, and immensely intelligent.

Kott, Jan. *Shakespeare Our Contemporary.* New York: Anchor Books, 1966. This book, which was meant to shock us out of our complacency on the subject of Shakespeare, is a reevaluation of many things we thought we knew. It turned out to be groundbreaking.

Martineau, Jane, et al. *Shakespeare in Art*. London: Merrell, 2003. This is the best book about Shakespeare-inspired prints and paintings that I know. Based on a 2003 exhibit at Dulwich College in London, it is beautiful and profusely illustrated.

McLeish, Kenneth, and Stephen Unwin. *A Pocket Guide to Shakespeare's Plays*. London: Faber and Faber, 1998. This short, simple book contains plots of the plays, character sketches, and mini-essays. It's perfect for a quick overview or for taking to the theater.

Mowat, Barbara. *The Dramaturgy of Shakespeare's Romances*. Athens: University of Georgia Press, 1976. Mowat was head of research for many years at the Folger Shakespeare Library, and no one knows more about this subject. This is a wonderful book by one of our greatest Shakespeareans.

———. "The Founders and the Bard." *Yale Review* 97, no. 4 (October 2009): 1–18. This riveting essay is one of my favorite short pieces on Shakespeare: It addresses what the Founding Fathers knew about Shakespeare and discusses Shakespeare's influence on Jefferson and Adams in particular.

———. " 'What's in a Name?' Tragicomedy, Romance, or Late Comedy." In Richard Dutton and Jean E. Howard, eds., *A Companion to Shakespeare's Works*, vol. 4: *The Poems, Problem Comedies, and Late Plays*. Oxford: Blackwell, 2003. This essay contains Mowat's enlightening views on the "dramatic romances."

Paster, Gail Kern. *Humoring the Body: Emotions and the Shakespearean Stage*. Chicago: University of Chicago Press, 2004. Paster was the director of the Folger Shakespeare Library, and this scholarly, fascinating book is about sixteenth-century concepts of the body represented by the four humors.

Priestley, J. B. *The Art of the Dramatist and Other Writings on Theatre*. London: Oberon Books, 2005. Priestley wrote one of my favorite novels of all time (*The Good Companions*) as well as several memorable plays (including *An Inspector Calls* and *When We Are Married*). He was one of those companionable literary figures who knew something about everything, and his essays on the theater are enjoyable and full of insights.

Quiller-Couch, Sir Arthur. *Shakespeare's Workmanship,* 2nd ed. Cambridge, U.K.: Cambridge University Press, 1937. Like Gibson's book, this one offers a practical viewpoint on how Shakespeare worked. Quiller-Couch, with his intelligence and wit, influenced a whole generation.

Reade, Simon. *Dear Mr. Shakespeare: Letters to a Jobbing Playwright*. London: Oberon Books, 2009. This hilarious and terrific book is a series of letters from theaters to Shakespeare as though he were living today and offering up his plays for performance. It's full of insights on all the plays. Reade was literary manager of the Royal Shakespeare Company and knows his Shakespeare backward and forward.

Schoenbaum, Samuel. *Shakespeare's Lives*. New York: Oxford University Press, 1993. A classic book on Shakespeare's legacy and influence on subsequent generations.

———. *William Shakespeare: A Documentary Life*. New York: Oxford University Press, 1975. This is the definitive documentary biography of Shakespeare, a big book with all the evidence.

Shakespeare, William. *The New Folger Library Shakespeare*. Edited by Barbara A. Mowat and Paul Werstine. New York: Simon and Schuster, 1992 to present. This is the edition I refer to in this book. It's always reliable, smart, scholarly, and easy to use.

———. *The Norton Facsimile: The First Folio of Shakespeare*. Prepared by Charlton Hinman, 2nd ed. New York: W.W. Norton, 1996. This is a facsimile not only of the First Folio but of the perfect First Folio, using pages from different versions around the world. It's thrilling to hold and turn the pages of the miracle that Heminges and Condell wrought.

Shapiro, James. *Contested Will: Who Wrote Shakespeare?* New York: Simon and Schuster, 2010. Another Shapiro classic, it discusses the history of the authorship question. However you feel about the issue, it's fascinating reading and beautifully conceived and written.

————. *1599: A Year in the Life of William Shakespeare*. London: Faber and Faber, 2005. This hugely popular book looks at Shakespeare from the viewpoint of a single year, 1599, when he wrote *Henry V, Julius Caesar*, and *As You Like It* and started *Hamlet*. It is consistently brilliant and wonderful to read.

Shaw, George Bernard. *Shaw on Shakespeare*. Edited by Edwin Wilson. New York: E.P. Dutton, 1961. This book is a selection of reviews and other commentaries on Shakespeare written by the second greatest playwright in the English language. As you can imagine, it's always interesting.

Sher, Antony. *Year of the King: An Actor's Diary and Sketchbook*. New York: Limelight, 1987. A memoir of Sher's year tackling the role of Richard III for the Royal Shakespeare Company. One of the best theatrical memoirs ever written and full of insights about Shakespeare.

Spurgeon, Caroline. *Shakespeare's Imagery and What It Tells Us*, 5th ed. Cambridge, U.K.: Cambridge University Press, 1966. This is the classic work about Shakespeare's use of imagery. Spurgeon's knowledge of the plays is comprehensive, and the book is tremendously interesting.

Traversi, D. A. *An Approach to Shakespeare*. 2 vols. New York: Anchor Books, 1969. This two-volume set contains an essay on each of the plays and gives a solid overview of the basics.

Trewin, J. C. *The Pocket Companion to Shakespeare's Plays*. Revised by Stanley Wells. London: Mitchell Beazley, 2006. This compact companion is designed to fit in a pocket or purse, to be taken to the theater for easy reference. It's filled with interesting facts about each play.

Van Doren, Mark. *Shakespeare*. 1939; reprinted by New York: New York Review Books Classics, 2005. Van Doren was intensely intelligent and totally original in his thinking. A true intellectual, he brought new insights to every one of the plays. This book, like those of Northrop Frye, is indispensable, and I have drawn on it heavily throughout my career.

Vaughan, Virginia Mason, and Alden T. Vaughan, eds. *Shakespeare in American Life.* Washington, D.C.: Folger Shakespeare Library, 2007. This catalog from an exhibit at the Folger Shakespeare Library in 2007 is filled with exciting stories and illustrations about Shakespeare's afterlife in America.

Wells, Stanley. "Shakespeare and Revision." Hilda Hulme Memorial Lecture, University of London, December 3, 1987. Stanley Wells has been perhaps the most influential Shakespearean commentator of the past fifty years yet wears his mantle lightly. In this little-known but terrific lecture, he demonstrates his love of Shakespeare with fresh insight after insight.

———. *Shakespeare: A Life in Drama.* New York: W.W. Norton, 1995. This book is accessible and easy to read, yet deeply informed and extremely thoughtful. This may well be the best single source for an intelligent overview of Shakespeare's life and work. Don't miss it.

———. *Shakespeare for All Time.* London: Macmillan, 2002. Wells discusses Shakespeare's afterlife in the world's literature and on the world's stages. Like all of his books, it's fascinating reading.

Williams, Owen, and Caryn Lazzuri, eds. *Foliomania!: Stories Behind Shakespeare's Most Important Book.* Washington, D.C.: Folger Shakespeare Library, 2011. The Folger Shakespeare Library mounted one of its best exhibits ever in 2011, about Shakespeare's folios, and this is the catalog. It is filled with interesting anecdotes and reads like a series of detective stories—loads of fun.

Wills, Garry. *Verdi's Shakespeare: Men of the Theater.* New York: Viking Penguin, 2011. Wills discusses, in addition to the topic suggested by the title, the role of boy actors in Elizabethan England, particularly the leading boy actor John Rice. As always, Wills is illuminating and erudite.

FILMS

Movies are a wonderful way to bring Shakespeare's texts to life for your children, and I recommend all of the following films for additional study and entertainment. Hundreds of Shakespeare movies are available—this is a selective listing guided solely by what I've been able to see over the years.

Kenneth Branagh's Adaptations

All the work of this highly gifted actor and director is inspiring. He single-handedly rescued the whole practice of putting Shakespeare on film in the late twentieth century, and we owe him a huge debt of gratitude.

Much Ado About Nothing (1993). Directed by Kenneth Branagh, starring Kenneth Branagh, Emma Thompson, Denzel Washington, and Richard Clifford, rated PG-13. I'm putting this one first—out of alphabetical order—because I think it's the best Shakespeare movie of all time. If your children don't love Shakespeare after watching it, you can have the price of this book back. (Not really.)

As You Like It (2006). Directed by Kenneth Branagh, starring Bryce Dallas Howard, Kevin Kline, and Richard Clifford, rated PG. Set in Japan, this film is colorful and fun and conveys the essence of the play very well.

Hamlet (1996). Directed by Kenneth Branagh, starring Kenneth Branagh, Derek Jacobi, and Kate Winslet, rated PG-13. Pretty much full text, this one's an excellent way to introduce your children to the play. Branagh makes a great Hamlet, and Derek Jacobi and Kate Winslet are breathtaking as Claudius and Ophelia.

Henry V (1989). Directed by Kenneth Branagh, starring Kenneth Branagh and Derek Jacobi, rated PG-13. Branagh's revisionist view should be contrasted with Olivier's classic view, below. It makes for a stirring movie.

Love's Labour's Lost (2000). Directed by Kenneth Branagh, starring Alessandro Nivola, Alicia Silverstone, and Richard Clifford, rated PG. This rather unique take on the play contains little of Shakespeare's text but instead adds some vintage songs from the 1930s and 1940s. Still, it conveys the essence of a complex play very well.

Laurence Olivier's Adaptations

Hamlet (1948). Directed by Laurence Olivier, starring Laurence Olivier and Jean Simmons, not rated. This film takes a Freudian view of the play, but nothing Olivier ever did was less than brilliant.

Henry V (1944). Directed by Laurence Olivier, starring Laurence Olivier, Robert Newton, and Leslie Banks, not rated. One of the greatest movies ever made from Shakespeare. Olivier used it to rally England at its time of crisis in World War II, and it also contains a prettified but enjoyable view of Elizabethan stage conditions. It is excellent in every way.

Richard III (1955). Directed by Laurence Olivier, starring Laurence Olivier and Cedric Hardwicke, not rated. Olivier as the humpbacked, crooked-nosed Richard is fascinating to watch and loads of fun.

Other Notable Adaptations (in alphabetical order)

Chimes at Midnight (1965). Directed by Orson Welles, starring Orson Welles, Jeanne Moreau, and John Gielgud, not rated. This unique film is not just one play; rather, it compiles text from five different Shakespearean plays, to make a film entirely about Falstaff. Though it's in black and white and was made on a tiny budget, Welles embodies Falstaff better than anyone I have ever seen. It's a difficult film, but if you love Shakespeare and Falstaff, it's indispensable.

Hamlet (1964). Directed by John Gielgud, starring Richard Burton, not rated. Burton's *Hamlet* was a landmark for an entire generation of theater lovers. I can think of no performance that is more inspiring or touching. Because the concept of the production was a rehearsal, it is not colorful and the DVD feels a bit drab. But Burton's performance is electrifying. For me, it kicked off a lifetime of Shakespeare study.

The Merchant of Venice (2004). Directed by Michael Radford, starring Al Pacino, Jeremy Irons, and Joseph Fiennes, rated R. Pacino is always brilliant, and never more so than in this intelligent, disturbing movie.

A Midsummer Night's Dream (1999). Directed by Michael Hoffman, starring Kevin Kline, Michelle Pfeiffer, and Rupert Everett, rated PG-13. I'm not much of a fan of "popular" Shakespeare, but this enjoyable film captures the spirit of the play and makes it accessible.

Ran (1985). Directed by Akira Kurosawa, in Japanese with English subtitles, rated R. This story of a Japanese warlord and his three sons is a powerful, devastating adaptation of *King Lear*. For many buffs, this and Kurosawa's adaptation of *Macbeth* (*Throne of Blood*, 1957) are the height of Shakespeare on film.

Romeo and Juliet (1968). Directed by Franco Zeffirelli, starring Leonard Whiting and Olivia Hussey, not rated. Zeffirelli is a great director, and his productions of opera around the world are legendary. This one made everyone sit up and take notice when it first came out, and it is indispensable for anyone who loves movies and Shakespeare.

Romeo + Juliet (1996). Directed by Baz Luhrmann, starring Leonardo DiCaprio, Clare Danes, and John Leguizamo, rated PG-13. This film is set in modern Italy but has dialogue by Shakespeare. It uses guns instead of swords. It's violent but hip, and some kids will love it.

The Taming of the Shrew (1967). Directed by Franco Zeffirelli, starring Richard Burton, Elizabeth Taylor, and Michael York, not rated. This film is everything a Shakespeare movie should be: faithful to the spirit of the play, beautiful to look at, and with two big stars who are worthy of their parts. Burton is still at his peak, and Taylor is glamorous and wild. The whole thing is rip-roaring fun, and your kids will love it.

Twelfth Night (1998). Directed by Kenneth Branagh, starring Frances Barber and Richard Briers, no rating. This is the only great video of the whole play, and it's stunning. Frances Barber is transporting. Don't miss it.

Films of Stage Productions

The Folger Theatre has put its 2008 production of *Macbeth* on DVD, and it's thrilling. Directed by Aaron Posner and the magician Teller, it stars Ian Merrill Peakes and Kate Eastwood Norris. It's available through the theater's website.

Much Ado About Nothing (1973). Video of the Broadway production directed by A. J. Antoon, starring Sam Waterston and Kathleen Widdoes, not rated. Waterston's portrayal of Benedick is miraculously good. He's hilarious, and Kathleen Widdoes is every bit his romantic equal. This play brings out the best in actors and directors because it's such a surefire comedy, and this rendition is terrific. Because it's a film of a stage production, it contains much more of the original text than do most Shakespeare films, and so it's particularly recommended. I absolutely love this production.

The New Globe Theatre in London is starting to put its productions on DVD, and many of them are wonderful. My guess is that this project will continue to grow. They're available through the theater's website.

Films and Miniseries About Shakespeare or Acting Shakespeare

Acting Shakespeare (1982). Directed by Kirk Browning, conceived by and starring Ian McKellan, not rated. In this one-man show, McKellan performs some of Shakespeare's greatest passages and recounts personal anecdotes about life in the theater. McKellan, of course, is a miracle in himself. Highly recommended.

Discovering Hamlet (1988). Directed by Mark Olshaker, narrated by Patrick Stewart, not rated. This behind-the-scenes documentary follows Derek Jacobi and Kenneth Branagh through rehearsals of a memorable production. It's filled with enormously interesting backstage insights.

In Search of Shakespeare (2003). Written and hosted by Michael Wood, not rated. This biographical series is never less than fascinating.

Playing Shakespeare (1984). Not rated. This documentary series shows excerpts from master classes with John Barton of the Royal Shakespeare Company in the early 1980s. It is especially fascinating to see some of the greatest Shakespearean actors of our time when they were younger, including Judi Dench, Ben Kingsley, Ian McKellan, and Patrick Stewart. For real Shakespeare lovers this is indispensable.

Shakespeare in Love (1998). Directed by John Madden, starring Gwyneth Paltrow and Joseph Fiennes, rated R. This witty, creative, and all-around wonderful movie depicts Shakespeare as he was emerging as a young playwright. It won the Academy Award for Best Picture.

Will Shakespeare (1978). Written by John Mortimer, starring Tim Curry and Ian McShane, not rated. This A&E miniseries covers the early years of Shakespeare's life; it's tame but fun.

AUDIO RECORDINGS

The Ages of Man (1939). John Gielgud performed this one-man show around the world on and off for decades. Consisting of readings of a selection of passages and poems, it is a landmark of twentieth-century Shakespeare and remains vital to this day.

As You Like It (1962). This Shakespeare Recording Society production stars Vanessa Redgrave, Keith Mitchell, and Stanley Holloway.

BBC Radio Collection's Shakespeare (2001). This set contains fine performances of Shakespeare's plays by many of our greatest actors.

BBC Radio Presents *William Shakespeare's All the World's a Stage* (1995). An anthology of Shakespearean speeches performed by the world's leading actors, it features Laurence Olivier, Richard Burton, and Vanessa Redgrave, among others.

Classic FM *Favourite Shakespeare* (1998). *Classic FM* magazine polled its readers to discover their favorite Shakespeare scene, speech, or sonnet; this collection contains performances by Derek Jacobi, Richard Griffiths, and others.

The Complete Arkangel Shakespeare (1998). This series recorded all thirty-eight plays, fully dramatized and performed by members of the Royal Shakespeare Company and others. The performances are of consistently high quality.

Much Ado About Nothing (1963). A Shakespeare Recording Society production, starring Rex Harrison and Rachel Roberts. This is one of the best recordings of a Shakespeare play ever made, thanks to Harrison's Benedick, one of the most beautiful and hilarious comic performances of all time.

Acknowledgments

My thanks to Barbara Mowat, former Director of Research at the Folger Shakespeare Library, co-editor of the Folger editions of the plays, and Executive Editor of *Shakespeare Quarterly*, who read this book in manuscript and offered me her advice. Her suggestions shine through, while any errors in the book remain mine. My thanks also to Robert Young, Director of Education at the Folger, who took time from running the best Shakespeare education department in the country to read this book and give me his excellent thoughts; to Rosey Strub, my friend and manager who helped so enormously on the illustrations for this book; to Eric Simonoff, the best literary agent in the business, for his careful guidance; to Jonathan Lomma, the best theatrical agent in *his* business, for wisely suggesting Eric; and to my scrupulous editorial assistant, Rebecca Phillips.

At Crown Publishers, my thanks go to Sean Desmond, my editor, for all the care he took with this book, as well as his never-ending encouragement and problem-solving; to Molly Stern, Crown's publisher, for choosing the book; and to the wonderful team that Molly and Sean chose to guide this book through its creation, design, and publication, including Annsley Rosner, Jay Sones, Elizabeth Rendfleisch, Jennifer Ann Daddio, Catherine Cullen, Danielle Crabtree, Cindy Berman, and Stephanie Knapp.

At the Folger Shakespeare Library there are many friends to thank for their encouragement and advice, including Janet Griffin, the Director of Public Programs, who has helped me on so many occasions; and Steve

Ennis, Michael Whitmore, Gail Paster, Lou Cohen, and Jim Shapiro. My thanks also to Christopher Griffin for sharing with me his vast knowledge of the theater.

My thanks also to Richard Clifford and Derek Jacobi for taking the time to record the excerpts for this book. Friends go out of their way for each other, but this was above and beyond the call of duty. Equal thanks to John Lithgow for his kindness in writing such a fine introduction. This was generosity indeed. And to Frances Barber for so kindly stepping into the breach, my thanks as well.

Enormous thanks to my brother, Gene, for his encouragement and support—there was never a better brother or a finer human being; to my sister-in-law Carol; to Jim Davidson, fine friend and fellow writer whose own wonderful books are always my greatest encouragement; to Simon Reade, writer, producer, and former literary manager of the Royal Shakespeare Company, who first suggested that I write this book and who set me an example with his own joyous book *Dear Mr. Shakespeare*; to Marty and Lenore Schneiderman, best of friends and lifelines to the world beyond Shakespeare; to Harry and Kathie Teter—we follow their example with love and gratitude; and to Kenny Stilwell and Charles "Papa" Williams for keeping music in our lives.

Finally, of course, for their forbearance and patience, my ultimate thanks go to my wife, Adrienne, with whom I've shared all manner of Shakespeare over the years, and my children, Olivia and Jack, for putting up with me but enjoying Shakespeare.

PHOTO CREDITS

Page 9. Geraint Lewis
Page 10. Photofest
Page 20. Shutterstock
Page 24. Public domain
Page 25. Public domain
Page 29. Scott Suchman
Page 33. Geraint Lewis
Page 42. Public domain
Page 46. Geraint Lewis
Page 68. Joan Marcus
Page 77. Geraint Lewis
Page 92. Geraint Lewis
Page 94. Geraint Lewis
Page 97. Geraint Lewis
Page 102. Geraint Lewis
Page 103. T. Charles Erickson
Page 106. Geraint Lewis
Page 115. Shutterstock
Page 122. Public domain
Page 128. Photofest
Page 133. Public domain
Page 134. Public domain
Page 135. Public domain
Page 136. Public domain
Page 138. Shutterstock
Page 150. Public domain